Praise for *The Messenger Within*

"I absolutely love this candid, no-nonsense and completely responsible approach to self-empowerment. A heart-based purpose filled life is being offered to all those that dare to allow themselves to truly prosper and radiantly glow."

—Gudni Gunnarsson, Author of *Presence is Power*

"Dhebi DeWitz reveals her best from her many decades of research and practice in the fields of self-empowerment and energy healing. Her book is an excellent combination of science, consciousness, and transformation—powered with love."

—Darryl Gurney, Shadow Energetics (*Canada*)

"I couldn't put it down! Although schooled in traditional medicine, I've utilized many forms of complementary medicine as well. This ground breaking system gives wonderful new tools for personal transformation. A must read!!"

—P.S. Rowland M.S., L.P.N., Author of *Lest We Forget Life's Passion* and
   Cut Both Ways (USA)

"This book is a valuable addition to the field of energy medicine and personal transformation and should be read by any practitioner interested in the energy healing arts. It describes a comprehensive, yet well-presented system for self-discovery—so methodical, yet flexible at the same time. The process of narrowing down the wealth of sources was elegantly simple and would give anyone a direct place to start. It's like having your own conversation with someone gently leading you through 'de-fragging' your brain."

—Dr. Karen Shue, Neuropsychologist, Author of the upcoming book,
   The Way of the Brain (Canada)

"*The Messenger Within* offers a unique opportunity for people of all walks to transform their lives. In a crowd of books that promise transformation, abundance, and the answer to creating the life you want, Dhebi's clear approach places the responsibility for conceiving and shaping the life you want in your hands—no middle man/woman. *The Messenger Within* has the added bonus of providing the reader with an elegant system for self-discovery and a way to resolve obstacles without years of costly therapy! Become the source of your own answers, explore the connection between you and your inner guidance system—and use this Wisdom to BE the person you always knew you were!"

—Gabrielle Leslie, MA, CADC II, Counselor, Intuitive, Consultant (*USA*)

"A priceless resource by a gifted healer. I love how the reader can hone into the source of the problem that has been hidden in the vast subconscious mind and transform it to pure presence. The reader is guided so clearly with this knowledge and these processes through their own 'inside landscape' and can feel totally confident carrying out the process of transformation. At once the reader is not just the reader any more, but becomes the empowered person they have always wanted to be. Thank you, dear Dhebi, for the gifts of your wisdom and experience. This L.E.E.P. System is a valuable addition to the clinical practice in the field of energy medicine and personal transformation."

—Aleksandra Prijic, Psychotherapist and Neurofeedback Facilitator
  (Palma de Mallorca, Spain)

"Dhebi DeWitz engages readers with her clear, conversational style as she delves deep into the inner world of intuition, emotions, and energy. Her L.E.E.P. System provides practical, simple techniques for accessing "Inner Wisdom Communication." While readers gain greater understanding of energy psychology, they will also experience moments of self-discovery, forgiveness, and revelation."

—Gloria Thomas, Wizard Workforce Development *(USA)*

"I love Dhebi's vast experience. The L.E.E.P. System has been beneficial to me and my patients. It is life changing to be able to empower your life in such a positive direction. Thank you for this gift."

—Tami Tanninen, LMHC, Licensed Mental Health Counselor *(USA)*

"Welcome to the most elegant system to resolve the pain of life and open the path of the heart. This book goes directly to the source of the problem and is brimming with time-tested processes anyone can use to create a better life."

—Bruce Hinson, CADCIII, NCACII *(USA)*

"Dhebi is a perfect blend of head and heart who creates a space for exploration that is nurturing and safe. I appreciate the evident amount of research and knowledge shared in *The Messenger Within*. It's a beautiful synthesis we can all learn from!"

—Sandra Wallin, MA, Founder of Chiron's Way Counselling
  (Vancouver BC, Canada)

"An important work that can awaken anyone's truth in the heart and soul of their very being. This book shows the blueprint for changing patterns in the human condition. It opens an avenue of hope and joy to individuals. Part of the value of this work is in its clear explanations, easy to read charts, and step-by-step instructions of how to manifest anything. It is carefully written and backed with the science of how manifestation actually takes place."

—Michelle Jensen, Psychologist, Family Counseling *(USA)*

"*The Messenger Within* is not only a book but a guide that helps us unfold, step by step, the blockages in our subconscious, bringing us the possibility of finding our real needs and desires in a simple and easy way. Dhebi, as a gifted healer, masters the techniques that help utilize love energy and gives us a road map to follow that leads us back home, to unity, where only perfect health and abundance is possible. Thank you, Dhebi, for sharing your wisdom and experience and putting it all together in a great book. It will help many people in their transformation process."

—Cristina Beascoechea, Personal Life Coach *(Illes Baleares, Spain)*

"A fantastic resource with effective processes individuals can use to change and empower their life. A most elegant system for self-discovery. With this knowledge and these processes, you truly have a system for resolving obstacles that have held you back until now."

—Lori-Ann Speed, Transformational Clairvoyant Facilitator and Healer, Composer, Recording and Performing Artist *(British Columbia, Canada)*

"I believe the people who read this book will experience massive positive shifts in their life. Dhebi DeWitz guides you on a journey to the deep and darker side of our souls and encourages one to look, learn, reclaim, accept, and love the wholeness of our being. The exercises are easy, yet have profound results, and will be of benefit no matter what stage you are at in your personal awakening."

—Kelly Chamchuk, Advanced Soul Coach and Mentor *(British Columbia, Canada)*

"These processes are powerful! The spirit soars with pleasure and your body-mind-spirit is invigorated with renewed energy with this book, *The Messenger Within*. What a tool for living large and learning!"

—Anine Grumbles, Certified Master Practitioner of Hypnotherapy, Neuro-Linguistic Programming and Wellness Coach *(USA)*

"Excellent book! Takes energy healing, personal growth, and effectiveness to a whole new level. I love Dhebi's presentation and discussion of the process of healing. I am not only excited to learn and practice L.E.E.P.s for myself, but I also look forward to offering this solution to life's obstacles to my clients. I would highly recommend this book to others."

—Liane Fitzpatrick, Certified Relationship Coach *(Canada)*

"I didn't want to put it down! Dhebi's beautiful book guides the questing voyager into deep valleys, high mountains, and unknown lands as well as deep waters of the subconscious mind and always brings you back safe and sound. Thank you for this beautiful trip into wonderlands of the subconscious mind. A must read for everyone who wishes to become whole and heart-centered."

—Sandra Lehnis, Personal Empowerment Coach, and Artist
(*Mallorca, Spain*)

"Excellent book! I love how Dhebi combines talking about the metaphysical, scientific, and very practical processes with such playfulness and ease. I would recommend this book to anyone who has an interest in energy healing, personal growth, and effectiveness. A brilliant source of combined information, whether someone is completely new to or has an abundance of knowledge and experience with these topics."

—Claudia Tressel, Facilitator for Emotional and Spiritual Health
(*British Columbia, Canada*)

"Dhebi is a highly intuitive, committed, and passionate human being. Her purpose is simple and clear. Her soul longs to help others in living as beautiful a life as she is blessed with. She walks her talk. I am blessed to have her in my life as a trusted friend, mentor, and collaborative partner in shifting human consciousness. She shares her great wisdom and tools in this book, which I highly recommend people to read."

—Rita Soman, MA, CADC III, MA, Founder of Addictions & Family
Counseling and Belief Mantra (*Portland, Oregon, USA*)

"Most of the books I have read go directly to my head and stay there, having no effect on the rest of me. *The Messenger Within* is different. It is one of those books that enters through the depths of my being and without even knowing how, changes the cells of my body, creating new options for me. I now feel I can take hold of my own life, expanding my horizons."

—Engracia Villar, Gestalt Therapist, Family Constellation Practitioner, Sacred
Feminine Workshops (*Mallorca, Spain*)

"Dhebi has developed an elegant and efficient process for self-healing and transformation. The techniques presented are user friendly and easy to follow. Her genuine desire to help people with their personal growth and self-empowerment shines through in her writing. As an energy medicine practitioner for the past 15 years, I am excited that she has composed a process easily accessible to all. If you are ready to break through your blocks holding you back from living the life of your dreams, then I can highly recommend this book."

—Tess Thompson, energy medicine practitioner and owner of
Bio-Energetics Wellness Center (*Washington, USA*)

THE
MESSENGER
WITHIN

Unlocking the Secrets to
Greater Freedom and a Better Life

DHEBI DeWITZ

CONSCIOUS
EVOLUTION
PRESS

Published by Conscious Evolution Press
Ashland, Oregon

Copyright ©2016 Dhebi DeWitz
The Heart and Soul Academy for self-empowerment and conscious evolution
www.theHeartAndSoulAcademy.org

Disclaimer
This book is sold with the understanding that the author and publisher are not engaged in
rendering medical, psychological, legal or financial advice nor meant to treat, diagnose or
cure any disease. Every effort has been made to make this book as complete and accurate as
possible. However, there may be mistakes, both typographical and in content. Therefore, this
book should be used only as a general guide and not as the ultimate source of the information
contained herein. We offer no representations, warranties or guarantees verbally or in writing
regarding your results. The author and publisher shall not be liable or responsible to any
person or entity with respect to any loss or damage caused, or alleged to have been caused,
directly or indirectly, by the information contained in this book.

Design and composition by Sheila Parr
Cover design by Sheila Parr
Cover image © nednapa/Shutterstock
Permission was given by Brain Gym to use the Hook-up posture illustration.
Brain Gym is a registered trademark of the Brain Gym International.

Library of Congress Cataloging-in-Publication data is available upon request.

Print ISBN: 978-0-9970940-0-8
eBook ISBN: 978-0-9970940-1-5

Printed in the United States of America on acid-free paper
First Edition

Requests for permission to make copies of any part of this work can be made to
The Heart and Soul Academy
dhebi@theheartandsoulacademy.org

For ordering information or special discounts for bulk purchases, please contact
dhebi@theheartandsoulacademy.org

Contents

Acknowledgments

Dear friend, I dedicate this book to you, the reader. If it wasn't for individuals like yourself who have asked me to write a book and share what I have to share, then this book would never have been written.

Special thanks goes to my very dear friend Darryl Gurney for all our shared work, brainstorming, and the good humor we've shared throughout the years. Thank you for believing in me and for your encouragement and support. I treasure our friendship.

A warmhearted thank you to Tracy Teel for being my editor. Your editing skills have made a huge contribution to this book, and I truly appreciate you. Thank you for your guidance, insights, and commitment to this book. You are a real joy to work with.

Thank you Yolanda Barton for being an 'Author's Best Friend' and for navigating the world of publishing with such ease and grace. Your guidance and vast knowledge has made a world of difference for me, and I have appreciated every moment.

Thank you Jill Cheeks for your dedicated coaching and for keeping my forward momentum with frequent emails and phone calls. And thanks to John Eggen of Mission Marketing Mentors for your wonderful writing program. It was just what I needed.

Thank you Sheila Parr for your beautiful book cover artwork and interior design. You have amazing skills and talent and are wonderful to work with.

Thank you to all those who gave me valuable feedback and peer reviews on the manuscript: Bruce Hinson, Dr. Karen Shue, Michelle Jensen, Pamela Rowland, Sandra Lehnis, Claudia Tressel, Gloria Thomas, Aleksandra Prijic,

Anine Grumbles, Tami Tanninen, Lori-Ann Speed, Cristina Beascoechea, Kelly Chamchuk, Liane Fitzpatrick, Sandra Wallin, Gabrielle Leslie, Rita Soman, Tess Thompson, Engracia Villar, and Jeff Jensen. Thank you for believing in me and my work. I deeply appreciate the helpful insights, valued feedback, and encouragement you have given me that helped shape this book.

Thank you Peter González for the analogy about 'telling the waiter what you don't want,' which is included in Chapter 6.

Thank you to everyone who helped me to pick and develop the title for this book, especially Cynthia Salbato. Your suggestion was truly appreciated.

Thank you Cindy Abrahams, mentor, coach, and healer of healers, for all the training.

Thank you, Spirit, for the love and inspiration you give me and the wisdom you share with me. Your guidance enables me to do what I do. Thank you for helping me make a positive difference in the world.

I would also like to acknowledge those who I will always have a deep love, appreciation, and respect for and who have shaped my life the most: my family and my soul friends. Those who have passed: my mom Layne DeWitz, and my grandparents Ray and Shirley Munns. And those living who bless my life, my beautiful children: Danika Walter and Steven Jensen, and all my grandchildren. My soul friends: Darryl Gurney, Sandra Lehnis, Lori-Ann Speed, and many more than I will list. And my Beloved, Garry Raymond, who is my hero and lovingly holds my heart with his. Without all of you, I wouldn't be who I am today.

My Life's Calling

My journey began early in childhood. Ever since I was a little girl, as early as six years old, I wanted to know what the mystery of magic and life held. Do you remember the old TV show 'I Dream of Jeannie?' Well, I wanted to become a genie when I grew up, and I have been enchanted with the subject of magic my whole life.

At the age of eleven, I learned how to access higher states of consciousness when my mom started me in a practice of Transcendental Meditation (TM). I was hooked! Soon after, I read the *Autobiography of a Yogi*, and by age twelve she and I had joined Paramahansa Yogananda's *Self-Realization Fellowship*. My early desire to be a genie when I grew up stemmed from a much deeper desire that I couldn't yet define—the mysteries of consciousness itself. I was inspired to read and explore anything I could get my hands on that had to do with:

- Enlightenment
- Expanded states of consciousness
- Mysteries of the mind
- Magic
- Healing and how we create our reality

My explorations into the mysteries of life led me to Tibetan practices, shamanic training, hypnotherapy, numerous spiritual initiations, Huna teachings, apprenticeships, a variety of healing practices, the study of alchemy, academic lectures, reading books galore, and delving into all manner of Internet sites. These studies, plus tapping into other dimensions through hours of meditation, have made for a priceless journey.

Many interesting teachers have crossed my path throughout the years, and I truly stand on the backs of giants. I have gleaned knowledge from several sources, including the participants of my workshops while teaching around the world. Therefore, much of my life's work has involved synthesizing hard-earned knowledge combined with the warm generosity of friends, colleagues, and others, who have thoughtfully shared their wisdom with the world, into a system I could personally use for transformation, self-empowerment, and conscious evolution. I believe this is what I was born to do—it is my life's calling. It integrates everything I know, believe in, and love.

In 2011, while visiting Sedona, Arizona, I was given quite a push to write this book when Uqualla, a Havasu Medicine Man, said it was time to speak my voice—to step more fully into my power and my life's work. By this time, I had already spent several years traveling and teaching thousands of students worldwide. He said that I was a being who sees out from my heart; a ceremonial sentinel; a beautiful medicine woman without a tribe; a medicine being of the star nations, of the four winds of this world, and of the human journey. He told me to go forth and teach—teach what I have to offer in *a bigger way* and awaken the hearts of others. What Uqualla said stirred something within me, compelling me to coalesce my life's journey and experiences into writing a book about my passions of expanding conscious awareness. The purpose of this book is to help create shifts that empower and align us with our essential nature, so as to become masters of our own energy and life experiences.

Introduction

"The destiny of man is in his own soul."
~ Herodotus

In today's world, too many individuals are disillusioned, stressed out, overcome with worry, living with illness, or fearing the future. We need a way to re-pattern our lives to enable us to create the life we want to live.

I know it is possible to live a magical, self-empowered life filled with adventure, love, and freedom. It is possible to move beyond the self-imposed limitations we live with and the emotional traumas or heartaches we've endured, and yet still acknowledge and honor the inner strengths our struggles have given us. It is possible to glimpse enlightenment, here and now, to envision the potential of all things, and to know that magic really does exist in our everyday lives.

But how is this possible? How can such a shift occur when every moment of every day we find ourselves confronting obstacles or encountering events that are totally unexpected? What if we experience a loss we couldn't have foreseen and weren't prepared for? How is this possible when our lives seem to be falling apart, and there appears to be nothing we can do to stop it except watch while it crumbles down around us? What do we do when we find ourselves standing face-to-face with the gap? The gap between where we thought we'd be and where we actually are. Between our expectations of what we planned would happen and what has actually happened. Between the life we had envisioned and the life we are living.

The Messenger Within is an exploration into the nature of consciousness and how it forms our life's experiences, how we access our inner wisdom to discover the messages life is sending us, and how we connect with the mysterious force that appears to lie beyond ourselves. It's about the discoveries I've made along the way to unlock our hidden power within. To transform those things that are not working and to empower us to live from our authentic self; to align us with who we are at our depth and who we are becoming, and ultimately to evolve our consciousness, so we can live a soul-filled life, healed of our illusion from separation in the world. This book contains answers to an age-old inquiry of life: *How do I make the necessary changes in order to live with greater freedom and to create a better life?*

For over 25 years, I have witnessed these life-enhancing energetic processes (which, together, have become known as the L.E.E.P.s™ System) having a profound, positive effect in thousands of individuals, vastly improving the quality of their lives. These Life-Enhancing Energetic Processes (L.E.E.P.s) have allowed virtually everyone who has used them to experience greater inner peace, health, wellness, and also increased their sense of personal power in the world. As you journey through the pages of this book, you will discover how this system can allow you the freedom to navigate the path that is right for you.

L.E.E.P. processes can best be summarized as a specific way to bring about a deeply powerful, personal transformation. Scientific research informs us that consciousness is a field of energy that conveys information, and that these fields of information give order to our physical world. Even the new science research of biology is studying how fields of energies and information direct and shape our lives. Harmful information and distorted energy patterns create interferences within us that wreak havoc in our lives. Within the pages of this book you will find:

- Step-by-step instructions to utilize information and life-enhancing energetic processes to shift from restriction and limitation to empowering patterns in any area of your life.

- A detailed description of a time-tested health and wellness system (L.E.E.P.s) that can easily be integrated into your healing practice to increase efficiency and effectiveness.

- Discover the message from your inner wisdom to understand the struggles or obstacles that block you from your goals, health, wealth, and happiness.

- Learn how to identify what the top priority is for unraveling the source of the issue.

- Go beyond transforming detrimental beliefs and emotional wounds to explore other *vital* elements that contribute to or hold you back in life (such as unmet human needs, the impact of your ancestral lineage and past lives, disowned selves, or lifestyle influences).

- Receive revolutionary, transformative energetic processes that support your personal success easily and effortlessly, enabling you to provide greater service to others.

The end of most chapters will include materials that are available for download for easy reference or learning support. Not only are these Life-Enhancing Energetic Processes (L.E.E.P.s) powerful, they are also practical, spiritual, and results oriented, so you can actively participate in creating the life you want.

Starting at the Beginning

The first step in solving any problem is recognizing there is one. We have become so accustomed to the struggles in everyday life that we are conditioned to believe it's the way life is supposed to be. This book begins with taking a look at problems we find in our lives, then moves into how we can find the messages and solutions within our own being. The following chapters describe a step-by-step procedure that transforms the problems we can resolve and shifts us into empowerment and alignment with who we are and who we are becoming. Then, the reader is given a results-oriented formula for putting it all together, so by the very end, you'll receive resources for increasing knowledge, mastering skills, and deepening the art of working with life-enhancing information and energetic processes.

I believe that when one person is empowered we all win. Ask yourself this: Does your life resemble what you want it to? Are you living your dreams, aspirations, and empowerment? It is my hope that the techniques you learn within this book will help you, your friends, and the individuals you work with to live a better life. The techniques are designed to help you explore ways to use the unseen forces around and within you to learn basic skills in the transformational processes for self-empowerment and conscious evolution. In this way, we not only heal ourselves, but we also heal our world. This book offers you everything I have learned about harnessing your own inner wisdom to guide you through whatever you are facing on your journey through life.

With love and blessings,

Dhebi
Ashland, Oregon
2016

"How we see and hold the full range of our experiences in our minds and in our hearts makes an enormous difference in the quality of this journey we are on and what it means to us. It can influence where we go, what happens, what we learn, and how we feel along the way."
~ Jon Kabat-Zinn

CHAPTER 1

We All Have Our Struggles

"Consciously or not, we are all on a quest for answers, trying to learn the lessons of life. We grapple with fear and guilt. We search for meaning, love, and power. We try to understand fear, loss, and time. We seek to discover who we are and how we can become truly happy."
~ *Elisabeth Kubler-Ross*

- When you find yourself feeling disempowered, what do you do?
- When it seems that someone has taken you down a notch, undermined you, or betrayed you, how do you handle it?
- How do you move out of the rut when the attitudes of those around you continuously erode your peace of mind, leaving you feeling drained?
- Have you ever behaved in ways that were out of integrity with your personal values and wished you could handle it better?
- Have you ever wished the universe would give you a sign or deliver a message that would help you resolve a problem in life, so you could finally move forward?

I know I have! I've been there—we all have. In my own journey to overcome health-challenges, heartbreak, and the trials of everyday living that adversely affect humanity, I've learned that we each hold our own unique key to our healing. My deepest heartaches had to do with the things life handed to me that I had not expected or anticipated. I know what it's like to feel your heart sink while watching a loved one die and knowing there is nothing you can do to prevent it. I know what it's like to be in the midst of building your dream home only to discover the contractor had not only damaged property he refused to pay for, but also neglected to follow the blueprints, then doubled the charges of his estimates and walked off the job, leaving behind an unwanted legal battle. The events seem horribly unfair, and the sense of betrayal runs deep. I know what it's like to have a broken heart and all your hopes and dreams shattered with the loss of a lengthy marriage to a person you loved. I know what it feels like to have the earth fall out from under you when you hear that your beautiful child is diagnosed with an aggressive cancer. You wonder where you'll find the strength and courage to see it through to the end.

I know what it's like to experience senseless acts of violence, having my head hit with a wooden baseball bat, and experiencing a complete visual blackout while still being conscious of the pain. And, I know what it's like to have a health condition that leaves a person uncertain of what's in store for his or her future. Our fears and sufferings can take on a life of their own, leaving us on unsteady ground.

Common Frustrations

You've probably found yourself asking, *"Why me?"* on more than one occasion, not just with big things but *even with everyday life*. It seems as though our outer world experiences touch off our inner world frustrations, leaving us disappointed, disillusioned, feeling defeated, and wondering if we have the energy to keep going. These are just some of the frustrations I am sure you've felt:

- Happiness that eludes you, even though you strive for it.
- A meaningless, unfulfilling work life seemingly without purpose.
- Relationships that appear to lack the level of romance or nurturing you had dreamed of.
- Health and vitality missing from your physical well-being.
- Finances not stretching as far as you had hoped.
- Addictions undermining your self-worth and personal freedom.

Life throws us incredible problems, challenges, and struggles that can leave us stuck if we don't find resolutions or a way to move forward.

The Bane of Powerlessness

Not only does our own life leave us unfulfilled at times, but our world also faces problems that leave us feeling disempowered. We observe racial hatred that disconnects us from our humanity, religious dogma that separates us from one another, political parties with hidden agendas that divide our nation, corporations profiting without regard for integrity or individuals, and wealth that classifies us and averts us from sustainable living. The media leaves us feeling inadequate, and commercial advertising convinces us that something is missing from our life. We see levels of unemployment, homelessness, poor living conditions, and poverty that we wouldn't wish on anyone.

We have organizations with power but who are not connected to their heart. Government officials who look the other way as businesses poison our food, our air, our bodies, and our water, and somehow justify it to meet their bottom line, and countries at war with each other, perpetrating violence that the human spirit was never meant to endure. It goes against all common sense and our sense of right and wrong.

The Disconnect

Sadly, in many ways, we've lost touch with what is real. As we struggle to live a purpose-filled life, a meaningful life, we are slowly disconnected from the heart of who we are. We search for what we believe we lack. Men are expected to prove their masculinity over and over again—to work hard, be accomplished, be good fathers, to control their emotions, compete to win, and "be a man." Women are to be beautiful, accommodating, have flawless bodies, be perfect mothers, and possess the balanced grace of both angel and sex symbol. All too often, individuals are focused on the pursuit of the American Dream, competing for the next big toy or golden ring, rather than learning how to be happy or how to make a positive difference in the world.

Are you aware that we have the technology, the knowledge, all the resources, and more than enough money to make this planet an absolute living paradise? Ever wonder what's preventing us from doing this? Where is our heart, our wisdom, our consciousness? We live in a world that has so much to offer, but we can't access the offerings as a result of life-long, ingrained patterns stored in the subconscious—patterns which have a significant impact upon our actions and behaviors. Studies in neuroscience reveal that as much as 95–99 percent of our brain's activity is devoted to functions below our normal levels of awareness—in the subconscious.

We often develop negative thought patterns from our experiences in life because we suffer from improper training, which eventually drains us of our precious life-force energy. It is vital to our health and well-being that we replace the negative patterns within us with life-enhancing ones in order to reclaim our self-empowerment and make a more positive contribution to the world we live in.

The World Imbalance

We live in a society and culture that values instant gratification and throw-away goods instead of respectful, sustainable living. Our landfills are filling up with all of our throw-a-ways—the very things we 'just had to have' not all that long ago, all for the sake of convenience beyond consciousness. Who decided it was okay to buy plastic water bottles to drink out of once then throw away? Where's the consciousness in that? Have you ever asked yourself why we engage in such wastefulness?

In a world where violence is a form of entertainment, and action-packed thrillers aim to top one adrenaline rush after another, our spirit is numbed, our life stripped of joy, and the path before us becomes dimmed.

Moreover, moral issues, misguided ethics, corruption, abuse of power, dishonesty, family decline, and poor leadership become the norm, increasing and confounding the world's problems, which greatly impact our lives. To behave in these ways is out of alignment with our spirit, which knows better. In our Deepest Selves, we know better.

A Failure to Listen

When we ignore our inner voice, we find ourselves sinking into greater and greater unrest, stress, anxiety, and separation with our soul and are left wondering, *"What do we do now?"* These pivotal moments of unrest beckon to us to slow down and pay attention to what we are doing. We must ask ourselves who we are at our core. Where do we go from here? How do we make a change for the better?

The Era of Self-Help

I love this era of unlocking the hidden potential within us—it speaks to my soul as I am sure it does to yours, but unfortunately it has also created a lot of unforeseen problems. The personal growth expansion of the last 30 years has given us knowledge as we've explored our inner psyche. It has touched the depths of our souls and inspired us, yet it hasn't necessarily empowered us to live better lives. If it had, we wouldn't be struggling more than ever with these problems:

- Financial decline
- A dwindling middle class
- Sky-high mortgages and homeowner-debt
- Increased health and weight issues
- War and continued violence
- Relationship and family disturbances
- Rising unemployment and homelessness

The list grows worse every year with no improvement in sight. We have more and more people filled with wishful thinking, absolutely sure that if they just program another positive belief into their mind, life will magically become more abundant without them having to participate or take any responsibility in the co-creative process.

The gap between the "haves" and "have-nots" has grown tremendously over the last 25 years. Where is the evidence of self-empowerment in that?

Changing from Within

During my life-long search into the nature of consciousness, facing my own challenges, and helping others to do the same, I have become skilled in the art of transformation. We were intended to be whole, healthy, happy, and thriving. I have found that the belief change movement of the last 20 years is only the tip of the iceberg of what we can do for ourselves. Anything you 'struggle' with, that you have to 'work hard' to overcome, or have to put 'a lot of effort' into, is holding you back from synchronicity and flow. Once we recognize and acknowledge that there are unresolved conflicts within us, we can set about finding ways to heal them. However, until we know how to negotiate the rooted subconscious dynamic and energetic patterns, we are not really in charge of our own life experiences.

Getting to the Heart of the Matter

One of the most frustrating challenges people or therapists can have is being unable to get the desired results they are seeking. The most effective way to move through whatever has been holding you back or pushing your buttons is by unraveling the problem at its source where it is being stored within you. As it often turns out, the problems, challenges, and issues we face in life are caused by energetic disturbances—waveforms with an intensity and duration that cause distortions—that interrupt the natural flow of life-force in our energy fields.

Research shows how our bodies function and how our lives unfold depends on the quality of the information and energy we bring into ourselves. It influences the networks and energy fields that make up who we are. This information and energy can be beneficial and supportive, or quite trouble-some, and create energetic interference patterns which cause the problems, challenges, or issues we face.

Unraveling Interference Patterns

Interference patterns consist of well-defined detrimental energies that move in pulse-like waves and influence us in a powerful way. They are created by:

- Repressed, denied, or unresolved emotions that can distort and close off the natural life-force energy of the body.
- Limiting, judgmental, and disharmonious beliefs that don't support who we are or are becoming.

This damaging vibration, combined with the energy generated by intense emotions, is carried into the energetic networks of our body-mind-spirit, creating an obstruction in its proper functioning. This subconscious stress not only creates a blockage within the physical body by sending out a continuous interfering resonance that wreaks havoc with our health, but it also disrupts our peace of mind, slowing down our personal growth.

Interference patterns are like parasites that can be picked up through our life experiences. They can remain lodged in our body-mind energy field, potentially causing significant physical and emotional distress. These energies, with their specific vibrational patterns, rob us of our joy and our vitality. They prevent us from seeking applicable resources, therefore, hindering us from fulfilling our deeper potential in every aspect of our life.

Finding Their Hiding Places

It is possible to find these interference patterns using energy testing, also known as muscle testing, or bio-kinesiology. Energy testing allows us to set up a reliable feedback system for communicating with our subconscious mind, as well as our higher wisdom. Our subconscious knows where the interference pattern or blockage is that causes the problem. It has a message for us—a message explaining the root of the problem. Overcoming obstacles or challenges is much easier when you discover the message within your specific interference patterns. A problem that has meaning and carries a message is much easier to resolve than one that appears pointless—or worse—one that is misinterpreted and leads to destructive thoughts or the belief that you are being punished by the Almighty. The message could be any one of a number of things or a combination, such as:

- Limiting or detrimental beliefs stored in the subconscious
- Emotional wounds or trauma
- Unmet essential human needs
- Ancestral lineage or past-life influences
- Disowned selves or shadow personalities
- Lifestyle influences
- Other energetic disturbances

Resolution Requires Three Crucial Elements

1. Locate the source of the energetic influence that is being stored within you in order to interpret its message.

2. Discover the message and learn the lesson that the problem contains, so you won't have to repeat it.

3. Shift the energy with a Life-Enhancing Energetic Process (L.E.E.P.) in order to resolve the interference pattern and free yourself to let go and move forward.

Learning to Communicate with Your Inner Wisdom

All individuals have the resources they need within themselves to make changes in their life experiences. Our inner wisdom knows how to guide us to the highest priority for resolving the challenges in our lives. Being able to easily communicate with our subconscious mind and higher wisdom through energy testing allows us to find the path of least resistance to make the change. This can be easy and effortless when we have a system in place that we can rely upon.

In the next 13 chapters, you will learn an effective system to discover what's holding you back, so you can resolve the detrimental patterns held within your personal energy field that makes up who you are. As self-aware beings, we are able to determine our own path and transcend that which does not serve our souls. When we gain a deeper understanding about ourselves and heal our illusions of separation in the world, our souls rejoice as we establish more harmonious patterns for our personal well-being.

Maintaining problems requires a certain amount of energy. When the problem is solved it frees up the energy. We have to close the gap between the problem and the solution, so we can live a better life. Our psychological, emotional, and physical systems need to stay in harmony. When we bring about a life-enhancing shift within, rather than trying to force our will to create change, we are able to make improvements and still maintain harmony. When you learn how to access your inner wisdom, and use a transformational, life-enhancing system to help free yourself from personal bonds, you can change your experiences and navigate anything life throws your way. The decisions you make will help you gain greater access to your essential nature.

It takes courage to stand and face your problems, to heal the past, and to step into greater self-empowerment because every time you do you are expanding into the uncharted territory of your soul. When, at last, you face whatever it is that has been holding you back, fear loses its power, and the restrictive energy dissipates. So ... are you ready to take a journey into your soul? A journey into healing and wisdom?

You will gain wisdom every time you receive a message and learn a lesson. You will rise to a higher level of consciousness each time you resolve something that has been holding you back. When you reclaim your vital life-force energy, it will no longer be channeled into keeping an internal problem alive. How do you find the message and resolve that particular interference pattern? Why does this system work so effectively? This is what you will learn, and this is what soul growth is all about.

"Your vision will become clear only when you can look into your own heart . . .
Who looks outside, dreams. Who looks inside, awakens."
~ Carl G. Jung

CHAPTER 2

Origins of L.E.E.P.s™

"Up to a point a man's life is shaped by environment, heredity, and
movements and changes in the world about him. Then there comes a
time when it lies within his grasp to shape the clay of his life into
the sort of thing he wishes to be."
~ Louis L'Amour

Knowing "how to create" or manifest a new experience in your life easily and effortlessly is one of the greatest secrets of all time. My love and fascination with science, energy healing, and the mystical, combined with my knowledge, experience, and training, gave me insights and inspiration to synthesize processes for making real life changes. I wanted to overcome my struggles and find a better way to live. I also enjoy helping others lead healthier, happier lives and assisting them to access their own healing abilities and self-empowerment within. This led to developing powerful, practical, spiritual, and results-oriented processes for resolving interference patterns—processes that work with a person's inner wisdom, while honoring his or her power and ability to make the necessary changes.

Key Principles

- Maintaining or re-establishing health enables life-force energy to flow freely throughout the body.
- Life-enhancing information and loving heart energy has the power and ability to heal, directly influence, and improve the quality of your life experiences.

- Your higher wisdom, working in concert with your subconscious, can provide messages about what isn't working, guide you in resolving the blockages, and help you discover what to work on first.

- The more you work with your inner wisdom, the more it will guide you.

- The more you work with your subconscious, the more it can support rather than block you.

The L.E.E.P. System—Life-Enhancing Energetic Processes—integrates specific information with heart coherent energy and is combined in a way to support personal transformation, self-empowerment, and conscious evolution. These processes are based upon the understanding that everything in the universe is an interconnected network of information and energy. This includes our body as well as our experiences.

Your Heart—The Ultimate Power Source

Heart coherency is *the vital key* and ultimate *power source* for your transformation, or for co-creating with the universe. This is where the magic really begins to happen. It goes beyond the idea that 'thoughts create your reality.' Here's why: the electrical currents in the brain are going in all sorts of different directions, which means that often the brain's magnetic fields cancel each other out. Imagine throwing a handful of pebbles into a pond; they each create their own little ripples and collide with one another, each interfering with the other and creating patterns of chaos. This is the effect of the brain's electrical pulses firing in every direction, colliding with other electrical pulses, that make a person wonder, *"How can I create my own reality if brainwaves are canceling each other out?"* We have to become synchronized, or coherent, not just in our brains, but also throughout our bodies in order to accomplish more. The greater coherency of your brain's functions means there is less internal electromagnetic chaos. And, the less chaos, the more you are able to access your conscious awareness. This also results in greater access to your intelligence, wisdom, creativity, and self-empowerment.

The reason heart coherency is more powerful than the brain's thought process is that our heart's electrical field is more than sixty times greater than the electrical field generated by the brain.

Electrical Fields Come from the Heart

I learned from Leonard Laskow, MD, author of *Healing with Love,* and creator of Holoenergetic Healing, that the heart creates electrical fields in three very important ways:

1. As blood is being pumped through the body, electrons are rubbed off. The stream of moving electrons creates an electrical current. Since more blood is pumped through the heart than the brain, the heart, in turn, creates more electrical current.

2. The actual pumping of the heart creates a very strong energy field, in contrast to the brain, which has no such pumping mechanism of its own.

3. There is a select group of pacemaker cells in our heart that stimulates each beat and also creates an electrical pulse.

Heart coherency is more powerful than thought processes alone because the energy field generated by the heart is *more than* five-thousand times greater in strength than the energy field generated by the brain. In addition, the heart has been found to have rhythmic beating patterns that can either be coherent or incoherent. These patterns are closely linked to our emotions and how we feel.

Understanding Heart Rhythms

Feelings of anger, frustration, irritation, and stress create disordered patterns, known as incoherent rhythms, whereas feelings of love, compassion, enthusiasm, appreciation, and joy create smooth and ordered, coherent rhythms. Incoherent patterns affect our personal energetic field, interfering with and preventing us from achieving our goals, while coherent patterns synchronize the brain's rhythm. If we liken heart coherency to light, it would be like the difference between diffused light and magnified light. Diffused light has very little power on its own, but when light is focused through a magnifying glass, it concentrates the energy immensely, enough to set fire to paper. When focused even further, such as light from a laser, it can cut through steel.

The body's nervous system, organs, and gland systems all come into harmony with the heart's coherency, and this leads to increased heart-brain synchronization, which fully supports us in attaining our goals. This unified consciousness within our body-mind energy system communicates our intentions with the universal field through a greater, more harmonized, synchronized connection. Because the heart's magnetic field is not impeded by the body's tissues, and thus easily transmitted outside the body, we can see how a life-enhancing intention aligned with coherent heart focus, resonating with the universal field of all possibilities, is *vital* for creating the reality we want to experience. Its power to shift our perception of reality is *beyond anything* previously known.

Thoughts + Emotion = Manifestation

In general, while thought processes do have some feeling attached to them, they are not energetically vibrating at a higher frequency and can be quite neutral. For example, when we think of the weather, these thought processes are usually not vibrating with much emotion. The power increases when coupled with emotion. Think of emotion as energy in motion. The more strongly you feel the emotion (coupled with a thought), either for the good or the bad, the more powerful the vibration you send out.

Heart coherent energy combined with beneficial, life-enhancing information is the real key to living the life of our dreams. Rollin McCraty, PhD and Director of Research at the Institute of HeartMath, states that, "a coherent electromagnetic field is the inner glue of every system. When a system is coherent, it means that virtually no energy is being wasted, and therefore its power is at maximum." This energy-information communication creates a more harmonious and cooperative internal working environment, functioning with greater efficiency, having the power to be flexible and adapt, yet remain stable.

You Get What You Give

When you have this kind of power at your command, working with the Law of Attraction becomes possible. You experience, for yourself, the truth that whatever you are vibrating in your energetic field—whether good, bad, neutral, or indifferent—that is what you will attract. Your energy can either expand to embrace a beautiful life or withdraw for protection against a harsh environment. It starts within you. You vibrate these things based upon "what" and "how" you are feeling—and this is the "information" and "energy" you are sending out.

Heart-Brain Communication

Our heart energy profoundly influences brain functions and our body's major organs, which ultimately determines the quality of our lives. I learned from Joseph Sundram, Ed.M., who contributed to the founding of the Institute of HeartMath, in his talk on Heart Intelligence at the International Conference on Science and Consciousness that our heart communicates with our brain and body in four ways:

- Neurologically—through the transmission of nerve impulses
- Biophysically—through pulse waves
- Biochemically—via hormones and neurotransmitters
- Energetically—through electromagnetic field interactions

Communication along these conduits significantly affects our brain's activity. Research from the Institute of HeartMath shows that the messages the heart sends the brain affects our behavior and what we notice in the environment around us, thus influencing how our lives unfold.

What is truly fascinating is that researchers have discovered that with all the automatic downstream information flowing from the brain to the heart, spinal column, and organs, there is a huge volume of information going back upstream by way of the vagus nerve. In fact, the heart sends *more* information to the brain than the brain sends to the heart. With this two-way communication system of information coming downstream and going upstream, the heart and brain are hard-wired together, most importantly via the vagus nerve—where 80–90 percent of nerve fibers are dedicated to communication.

It turns out that whatever is happening in the heart, every second, is being sent up to the brain, which in turn sends information and messages down to the body, creating an interactive loop.

It was also determined that the heart has approximately forty-thousand brain neurons and is saturated with sensory neurites—the same type of neurons that *feel*. This means that your heart has sensory neurons that *feel* and *brain neural circuits* that transmit and receive information and energetic signals. This plays a bigger role in heart-intelligence and our level of consciousness than previously understood.

The Heart-Brain Connection

Did you know that you have brain cells distributed throughout your body? Not only do you have an estimated 86-100 billion neuron cells in your brain, but there are also:

- Approximately 1 billion in your spinal column (transmitting information)
- Approximately 40,000 around your heart (contributing to conscious thought and emotions, functioning in much the same way as parts of the brain)
- Approximately 100 million neurons in your gut that help you feel your inner world

The actual numbers will vary, changing all the time, and are dependent upon our personal learning history. Why is this important? It means that the most advanced and comprehensive way of programming, or re-patterning our subconscious mind and healing our emotional wounds, comes from heart coherent methods of transformation that affect the brain cells distributed throughout the whole body—*no matter where they reside*. This is precisely what L.E.E.P.s do—they entrain the brain cells that are spread throughout our entire body with life-enhancing information that gets carried on the current of heart energy.

Another way the heart is hard-wired to the brain is through the amygdala (a center deep within the brain), which is tuned to the signals coming out of the heart.

- The amygdala is a nodal point that directly routes incoming sensory information in all forms to the higher centers of reasoning in the frontal cortex.

- The amygdala can either send messages on to other parts of the brain— for intelligence—or it can shut down the information right there, so we never consciously receive it.

What becomes a thought rising to consciousness, and what remains a hidden thought pattern buried at a deeper level in the body, is determined by the emotionally-driven subconscious.

Intelligence Is Affected by Emotions

While your brain can influence the heart, and preside over different functions and process different kinds of information, the heart is the loudest voice in heart-brain communication. This is why it is important to look at how your intelligence is affected by your emotions and how heart-energy impacts the outcome of your daily life. Failure to effectively deal with repressed and denied emotions creates an unending cycle of brain signal breakdown that cannot integrate valuable information that could serve you. It prevents you from being able to use your emotions as feedback for change and growth opportunities that lead to developing your higher mental powers. The solution is to resolve your interference patterns, so the amygdala does not shut down the information that rises up to your higher reasoning and higher levels of conscious awareness.

Rollin McCraty states that, "We tend to think [of] our information input system as being entirely in the brain, but we are now discovering that the heart receives information first and then relays it on to the brain. Studies have shown that the heart responds faster than the brain to outside stimulation."

Heart energy has far greater impact overall and is, therefore, a more efficient means for shifting your subconsciously-held programs than the standard mental belief change techniques that don't use heart-energy and don't influence the brain cells spread throughout the body. When we are in a heart coherent state, we are more intelligent. We influence the neural cells stored throughout our entire body, rather than in just the brain alone. We literally change what signals are sent to the cortex and have higher levels of brain function available for use. Our conscious awareness increases; we experience increased synchronicities in our life and an increased sense of harmony. But, it all starts with the heart.

Cell Receptors Receive Energy

Science now recognizes energy as a vital, living, flowing force that is the foundation of our well-being. Recent research has confirmed the validity of energy for making changes within our body by reporting that the cell's membranes have receptor sites or receptor "antennas" on them that vibrate like tuning forks and read vibrational energy fields. Dr. Bruce Lipton, cell biologist and author of *Biology of Belief*, says that because these receptors can read energy fields, the notion that only physical molecules can impact cell physiology has become outmoded. Invisible forces, such as those of thought, sound, and energy, have been shown to have a profound, influential, and positive effect on our biological behavior, our physiology, and our health.

Dr. Lipton says that the receptor sites on our cells receive information in the form of vibration, or energy, as well as chemical signals, and that the energy signals are, in fact, more than 100 times faster and more efficient than chemicals. In an important study conducted at Oxford University, biophysicist C.F.W. McClare discovered that the speed of electromagnetic energy signaling is 186,000 miles (299,338 kilometers) per second—whereas the speed of the chemical signal is considerably less than half an inch (1 centimeter) per second. This translates to energy signals being *more efficient* and *infinitely faster* than physical chemical signaling.

The L.E.E.P. System (Life-Enhancing Energetic Processes) Overview

Knowing "how to create" or manifest a new experience into your life, easily and effortlessly, is one of the greatest secrets of all time. Here is how it is done, using the *7 Areas of Influence chart* on the following page:

WHAT'S HOLDING YOU BACK?

Discover the Message with Energy Testing

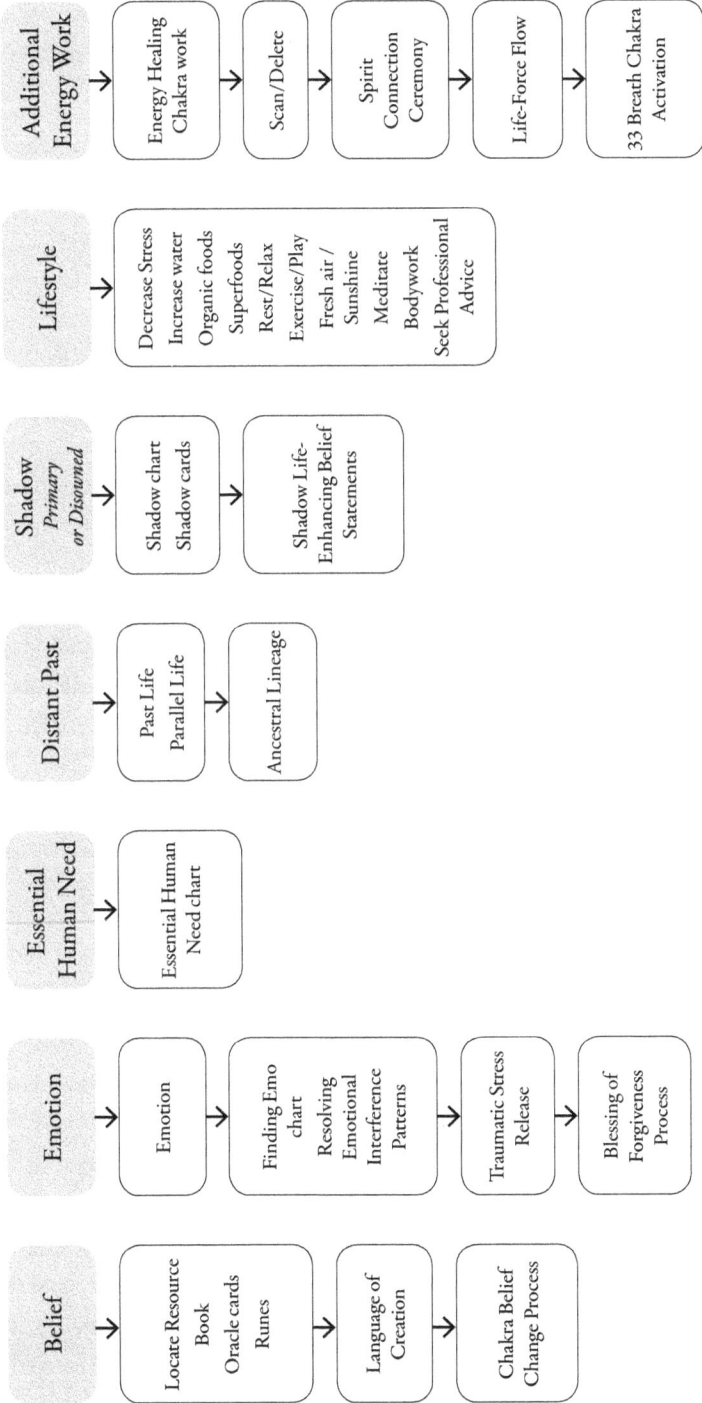

Belief

→ Locate Resource
Book
Oracle cards
Runes

→ Language of
Creation

→ Chakra Belief
Change Process

Emotion

→ Emotion

→ Finding Emo
chart
Resolving
Emotional
Interference
Patterns

→ Traumatic Stress
Release

→ Blessing of
Forgiveness
Process

Essential
Human Need

→ Essential Human
Need chart

Distant Past

→ Past Life
Parallel Life

→ Ancestral Lineage

Shadow
*Primary
or Disowned*

→ Shadow chart
Shadow cards

→ Shadow Life-
Enhancing Belief
Statements

Lifestyle

→ Decrease Stress
Increase water
Organic foods
Superfoods
Rest/Relax
Exercise/Play
Fresh air /
Sunshine
Meditate
Bodywork
Seek Professional
Advice

Additional
Energy Work

→ Energy Healing
Chakra work

→ Scan/Delete

→ Spirit
Connection
Ceremony

→ Life-Force Flow

→ 33 Breath Chakra
Activation

- Define what's holding you back: the challenge—problem—issue
- Discover the message in one of the 7 areas of influence with energy testing
- Access higher wisdom and create change while being guided by the priority process
- Combine life-enhancing information with a heart-energy process for transformation
- Verify that change has been made where appropriate
- Experience the results

The L.E.E.P. System is a holistic approach rooted in the premises that the body-mind energy system is a living matrix, a complex energy system that serves as the blueprint for your life's experiences. It's a body-wide information network that is ever changing, dynamic, and infinitely flexible. It is at the level of energy and information within our subconscious, and within the luminous field that surrounds us and makes up who we are, identifying where we need to correct distortions in order to return to a state of health and wellness. A valuable piece missing from many self-help techniques is the failure to check-in with higher wisdom. Many people overlook the possibility that the problem may be a covert messenger bringing awareness and an important life-lesson. Many challenges in life are:

- Disguised conscious or subconscious strategies for meeting important needs in life
- Undeveloped or inadequate coping skills to handle difficult situations
- Insufficient learning or inability to use the learning already acquired

A beneficial feature of this system is that through energy testing (a.k.a. muscle testing or bio-kinesiology) your inner wisdom helps you choose the highest priority for change and the right process to get the job done effectively.

The transformational processes shared in the L.E.E.P. System are the result of a unique system of healing that works in concert with the subconscious mind and higher wisdom to directly engage your own self-healing, empowerment, and wellness capabilities. It doesn't decide what you should change, but it gives valuable insights as to how the problem came into your life, so that you can choose a better option. Simply put, it helps you get to where you want to be. In a way, the L.E.E.P. processes can be compared to traversing stepping-stones into a new way of perceiving. Every time you learn the message behind an interference pattern in your life, it shifts the constricting energy pattern. You then reach a more expanded level of consciousness, which opens you to further possibilities of enlightenment.

Beneath all the outdated beliefs, hurt emotions, unmet needs, and past constrictions that make up every person is a divine being who deserves all the goodness that life has to offer. Let's heal what needs to be healed so that together we can bring about a revolutionary shift for our world.

"We must make the choices that enable us to fulfill
the deepest capacities of our real selves."
~ *Thomas Merton*

See Appendix II for instructions on how to download the 7 Areas of Influence chart at: www.theHeartAndSoulAcademy.org/resource-page/

CHAPTER 3

The Messenger Within

"I am not afraid of storms for I am learning how to sail my ship."
~ Louisa May Alcott, Little Women

Our body is a complex, energetic system that is in continuous motion, and energy testing is a valuable skill that allows us to set up a fairly reliable feedback system for communicating with our subconscious mind as well as our higher wisdom. Over the years, energy testing (a.k.a. muscle testing) has proven to be an exceptional, useful process for obtaining current information about the body's changing needs. The term "energy testing" was coined by Donna Eden, author of *Energy Medicine*, (which I prefer to use rather than the more common terms of muscle-testing or bio-kinesiology). This emphasizes that the objective of the bio-feedback test is *not* to determine the strength of the muscles, but, rather, how the body's energetic signals are flowing through them.

It is crucial to understand that the ideas, thoughts, and emotions contemplated in the mind significantly affect the internal electrical signals flowing through the body. These signals show what is strengthening us or supporting us; or if there is internal conflict, it shows what is weakening or restricting us. It is the strength of the electrical signal that determines the response of the muscles. And it can be a convenient YES/NO feedback system as well.

We use energy testing to discover which energies are beneficial for our purpose and those that are not. It offers invaluable feedback that makes use of our inner wisdom, giving us the ability to discover what we need for our own transformation.

The History of Energy Testing

Doctors have been using energy testing since the 1940s to evaluate muscle strength and to assess the extent of an injury. Today, we know that it has many more applications than doctors first believed. Dr. George Goodheart, DC, the founder of Applied Kinesiology, brought energy testing to the United States in 1964 and further developed it. It has been found to be a useful and effective way to communicate with our subconscious since the subconscious mind controls the autonomic nervous system and is responsible for our automatic and neurological functions, which includes our muscle activity. For example, when we reach for an object, our body moves because the subconscious mind directs a complex set of electrical signals to a specific set of muscles at just the right time to perform the task. Additionally, since energy testing corresponds with electrical activity in the central nervous system, the information gathered reflects brain activity as well as the electrical impulses traveling through the muscles.

Energy testing allows us to:

- Assess the state of our energy system
- Identify imbalances, interference patterns, and blockages
- Access our higher wisdom for guidance
- Tailor transformational procedures to suit our own personal needs
- Test and verify for our conscious mind that changes have been made in our subconscious mind and energy field

If we don't learn how to communicate with our subconscious mind and access our inner wisdom properly, we will become frustrated with the struggles in life and won't go very far.

There are various ways to do energy self-testing. Once you have this skill, it becomes a fairly dependable and useful feedback system for your body, your energies, your life experiences, and your environment. Most everyone I've taught wanted to learn how to do energy testing for themselves in case they didn't have someone to work with. I've included a description of how to practice it for yourself, but there will be times, such as when you are stressed, when it will be more effective to work with someone else.

Objectives for Energy Testing

The basic purpose for using this tool is:

- To discover whether energy signals in the body-mind energy system are blocked or flowing
- To discover subconsciously held truths (such as being a good or bad person, loved or unloved, worthy or unworthy, etc.)
- To develop a useful YES/NO feedback system
- To communicate with your higher self and be guided by your inner wisdom

This will allow you to discover what is encoded or carried within your subconscious mind—supporting, limiting, or defeating you—then you can decide whether or not to change your internal thought patterns. Your higher wisdom can benefit and guide you in your journey.

First Things First

Before inquiring into your subconscious mind, you'll want to set up a procedure, like the one that follows, for accessing your inner wisdom with energy testing. By doing this, you will be better able to trust the responses you receive. Many individuals who practice forms of bio-kinesiology—or energy testing—and work with others do not always receive accurate results. When this happens, they do not necessarily know how to correct what they are doing to obtain the outcome they want. Unfortunately, when working with their client instead of admitting that they don't know what to do, they will usually end up saying, "*You just can't be muscle tested.*" This can be very frustrating and disempowering for both the practitioner and the client.

I would like to assure you that most everyone can be energy tested and can learn to do it for themselves. If you can hold a focused thought for a few seconds, then you can do energy testing. The only times this will not be true is if you are dehydrated, too tired, overly stressed out, or are under the influence of a mind-altering substance (such as alcohol or medication) because these things weaken the electrical signals flowing through the muscles.

Helpful Tips

- **Keep your body relaxed.** Take a relaxing breath, and let it out slowly.

- **Let your mind be calm, curious, and open to exploration.** Stress can interfere and inhibit the test. The more curious and open you can be, the better the feedback. Being curious about what comes up helps you to discover the programs and interference patterns in your subconscious and energy field that have been limiting, restricting, and hindering you all this time—and that's a good thing. Stay curious rather than judging what is about to be discovered. Let go of the belief or idea that it is good, bad, or scary—staying curious is much more helpful.

- **Make 'statements-of-fact' rather than asking questions.** Your subconscious mind doesn't reason things out, so it doesn't always know what you are truly after when asked a question. Although it does want to please you, it is, after all, programmed. Therefore, when you want to discover what is in your subconscious mind, make your inquiry a statement-of-fact, so your subconscious can more easily provide a clear YES/NO response.

- **Speak your 'statement-of-fact' with feeling, meaning, and conviction.** The reason for this is that it will create more of an emotional connection with the words you are speaking. Then, as you say them, your emotionally-driven subconscious mind will both identify with them and confirm that they are part of the programs stored within you, signaling YES with an agreed upon bio-electrical signal. Or, if your subconscious mind does not identify with them, then it is not part of your subconscious mind's programs, and it will send a different bio-electrical signal for a NO response. These electrical signal responses are ones you pre-programmed and have agreed to use.

- **Focus your eyes gently downward when performing the energy test.** During Neuro-Linguistic Programming, also known as NLP, researchers found that when your eyes shift upward when recalling events and talking about certain topics, you are most likely processing visual data. When your eyes are level or to the sides, you are most likely recalling or processing auditory data you have stored. And, when your eyes are focused downward, you are more kinesthetically connected to, and processing information from, a feeling perspective.

This feeling sense is key to something as subtle as thoughts being processed through your body-mind energy field.

The thoughts held within our subconscious mind, and the electrical signals flowing through our bodies, are subtle things—it is a kinesthetic thing, a feeling perspective. Having our eyes focused downward during the energy test helps to keep us more connected to the information moving through the most elusive part of ourselves, information we are processing through our central nervous system. Individuals who find themselves shifting their eyes "up" during the energy test are actually disconnecting from the feelings associated with the thought processes and the statements they make and will receive a less accurate or dependable response. Therefore, you want to keep your eyes focused downward when performing the energy test itself.

Let's take a look at how this works. Here are three options for energy self-testing—pick the one that works best for you.

Using the Pendulum

You can buy or make your own pendulum. In a pinch, you can even use a damp tea bag that is attached to its string. You can hang a ring on a string and energy test with that as well. It doesn't matter what material you use—wood, crystal, metal, or tea bag. It's simply a tool to give you feedback with the micro-muscular movements conveyed from your subconscious mind through your body. Keep in mind, there's not some mysterious outside force moving your pendulum—it is the subtle electrical signals moving throughout your body that create the movements in your muscles that communicate with you. You are not trying to consciously move the pendulum—you are letting your subconscious mind give you bio-feedback.

By swinging your pendulum forward and backward you teach your subconscious mind to signal you for a YES answer. It will be much like nodding your head YES. Next, show your subconscious mind a NO answer by swinging your pendulum side-to-side, as if shaking your head NO. Your subconscious mind understands and remembers. You don't need to ask it to show you a YES or NO—just show it the responses that will best communicate with you. You have just set up a binary YES/NO communication system with your subconscious mind by using a pendulum.

The Sway Test

This is probably one of the easiest and most accurate energy tests for anyone to use. Begin by standing with your feet shoulder-width apart.

When you make a statement that your subconscious mind agrees with and identifies as its inner truth, your body tends to want to sway forward, as if going toward the statement. This would be a YES signal.

When you make a statement that your subconscious mind does not agree with or does not identify as a truth or part of its programming, then your body will rock backward, as if pulling away from your statement. This would be a NO signal.

Finger Lever Variation

Place the thumb of your left hand under the left side of your collar bone and the three outside fingers just under the right side of your collar bone and arch your hand slightly. Extend your index finger out away from your body—this is your "finger lever." Place the index finger of your right hand just below the fingernail of your extended finger. Keep your chin level and your eyes focused downward.

When you make a statement that your subconscious mind agrees with and identifies as its inner truth, your extended finger will remain strong when you apply a little pressure to that finger. This is your YES signal.

When you make a statement that your subconscious mind does not agree with, does not identify as a truth or part of its programming, then your extended finger will weaken when you apply a little pressure to your finger because electrical signals fluctuate and falter. This is your NO signal.

Training Wheels for Your Intuition

There are many different ways to energy self-test. These are only a few variations you can use to get started. Test them and find out what works best for you—you may already have a method that provides accurate feedback. Think of energy testing as training wheels for 'tuning in' to your subconscious mind or higher wisdom to give you feedback. Your intuition is flowing though you all the time, bubbling up into your conscious awareness, and sometimes you just 'know' what the answer is. The more experience you have with energy testing, the better you get with 'tuning in' and finding out what has been below your level of conscious awareness. There will be times, as you become more and more familiar with listening to your intuition, when you discover that you already know the answers within.

Practice: Accessing Inner Wisdom

It's time to set up a reliable feedback system. It will be STEP 1 in most of the processes and looks something like this:

Women	Men
"I am a woman."	"I am a man."
"I am a man."	"I am a woman."
Show me a YES.	Show me a YES.
Show me a NO.	Show me a NO.

The Energy Test:

- If you are a woman, say, *"I am a woman."*
- If you are a man, then start with, *"I am a man."*

Say it with feeling, with meaning, and with conviction.

If using a pendulum: Watch for it to swing forward and backward as soon as you've made your statement. You are not consciously intending to move the pendulum—the movement will come from micro-muscular movements generated by your subconscious mind. You are simply remaining curious to see what happens.

If using the sway test: Your body will naturally want to move forward.

If using the finger lever variation: Gently apply a little pressure to your extended finger just after you have said your statement. It should stay strong.

Now, energy test just the opposite.

- For women, say, *"I am a man,"* with feeling and conviction.
- For men, say, *"I am a woman,"* with feeling and meaning.

If using a pendulum: Watch for it to swing side-to-side. When you say something that is not a truth for you, with lots of feeling and conviction, your subconscious mind will be in conflict over the statement—it is not true for what is contained within and, therefore, does not identify with the statement and will signal a NO answer.

If using the sway test: Your body will naturally want to rock backward.

If using the finger lever variation: Gently apply a little pressure to your extended finger. It should feel weaker.

Next, say, *"Show me a YES."*

If using a pendulum: Watch for it to swing forward and backward signaling a YES.

If using the sway test: Your body will naturally want to move forward.

If using the finger lever variation: Gently apply a little pressure to your extended finger. It should stay strong.

Then say, *"Show me a NO."*

Your subconscious should signal you a NO. If these tests are accurate, then you have just set up your binary feedback communication system for accessing inner wisdom.

Tips for Improving Feedback Accuracy

If you are not getting clear or accurate feedback, relax. A couple of things may be going on.

1. Get a glass of water and take a few sips. When you are dehydrated, the electrical signals necessary to create the micro-muscular movements may not be quite strong enough. A few sips up to a full glass of water will help increase the electrical conductivity within your body. Retest and see if you receive better results.

2. When you are in an over-energized state-of-being, it will be difficult to get a clear, accurate signal. Why? Because you are not relaxed and at ease within, so this creates a chaotic electrical environment. Possible reasons for being overly energized could include:

   ○ Being stressed

   ○ Feeling rushed

   ○ Running behind schedule

○ Being put on the spot

○ Feeling panicky

Or maybe you've consumed too much sugar, caffeine, or something else that creates jittery feelings inside. All these things can cause over-energization of electrical signals and internal chaos, which makes it difficult to get accurate feedback. Getting your internal system calm and relaxed before energy testing will greatly support your success.

Calming an Over-Energized State of Being

One thing you can do is place the palm of your hand on your forehead. You can do this for thirty seconds or up to a minute or more. This gesture helps to process stress and soothes the fight-flight response of our autonomic nervous system because it sends increased blood flow to the prefrontal cortex, which is involved with reasoning, focus, insight, impulse control, and empathy.

Another thing you could do is what is called a 7-Breath Activation, which activates your heart-energy, moves it through higher consciousness, and brings that energy into your power center.

• For 7 breathes as you inhale, visualize beautiful heart energy flowing out from the back of your heart and up over the top of your head through expanded consciousness.

• Then, as you exhale, imagine the shimmering heart energy flowing down the front of your body and into your second chakra, a center of power.

This calming and centering exercise quickly helps bring your body-mind energy field into greater coherency.

After trying one or both of these calming techniques, re-try your energy tests to see if you get better results. These practices help to calm down the over-stimulated electrical signals and de-stresses you.

A Caveat to Take to Heart

There is a huge difference between energy testing to discover if there is a subconscious interference pattern contributing to a health problem (and further to unravel that interference pattern) versus diagnosing a health problem. Please don't use energy testing for health diagnosis, such as inquiring if you have cancer, diabetes, heart problems, etc. If you have any concerns, questions, or uneasiness about your health, see a professional. When it comes to our health, we are much more emotionally involved, and therefore, it is difficult for us to stay curious and neutral. If we fear or suspect we may have some life-threatening disease and attempt to energy test this, our emotionally driven subconscious mind detects our fear and will pull away from the thought pattern. It will go into withdrawal mode and shut down or give off chaotic energy signals. When this happens, our subconscious mind cannot provide accurate results. Remember, you need to stay relaxed and curious when energy testing subconsciously held truths. Attempting to inquire about a health diagnosis of any real concern conjures up electrical signals going haywire on the inside. The same thing holds true for highly stressful or panicky situations, which cause your electrical system to become over-energized and block you from receiving a clear signal until the body's energy system calms down and becomes coherent. Please leave the health diagnoses to the professionals.

Energy testing subconsciously held truths and re-patterning your energy field to support you, rather than using it for health detective work, is the most effective use of this tool—you can't go wrong with making life-enhancing changes for yourself. As we use these skills more and more, we become increasingly more accurate. Energy testing may not be a perfect system when we are stressed and electrical signals are chaotic, but the benefits of immediate feedback and verification for self-improvement far outweigh its drawbacks. Outside of medical situations, energy testing helps individuals become better problem solvers, leads to gathering more complete information, and helps us improve our decision making process.

Trust + Practice = Improvement

It's natural to question the answers we get when energy testing ourselves; however, we simply need to trust. Trust your higher wisdom, where the answers are coming from, and practice this skill. Thousands of physicians, practitioners, and individuals around the world use energy testing on a daily basis to help themselves or others. Your ability will improve with practice and experience. As much as possible, maintain a neutral or curious attitude while energy testing. Say things with feeling, meaning, and conviction. Trust the process and practice. This will ensure a more reliable response from your inner wisdom. If you are uncertain or unable to achieve a neutral or curious state of being for yourself, then practice with someone until your confidence and accuracy increases.

Self-Discovery Using the L.E.E.P. System

This is your opportunity to discover if a problem you have contains a subconscious message or interference pattern in any of the 7 important areas of influence as designated by the chart below. These include:

- **Beliefs:** limiting, detrimental, or those that don't support your life experience
- **Emotions:** unresolved emotional wounds that distort and close off the natural life-force energy of the body
- **Essential Human Needs:** ones that are unrecognized or not being met
- **Distant Past:** ancestral lineage or past-life influences
- **Shadow:** a disowned part of yourself that is wreaking havoc
- **Lifestyle Choices:** actions or decisions at the root of the problem
- **Other Energetic Disturbance:** something impacting you here and now

WHAT'S HOLDING YOU BACK?
Discover the Message with Energy Testing

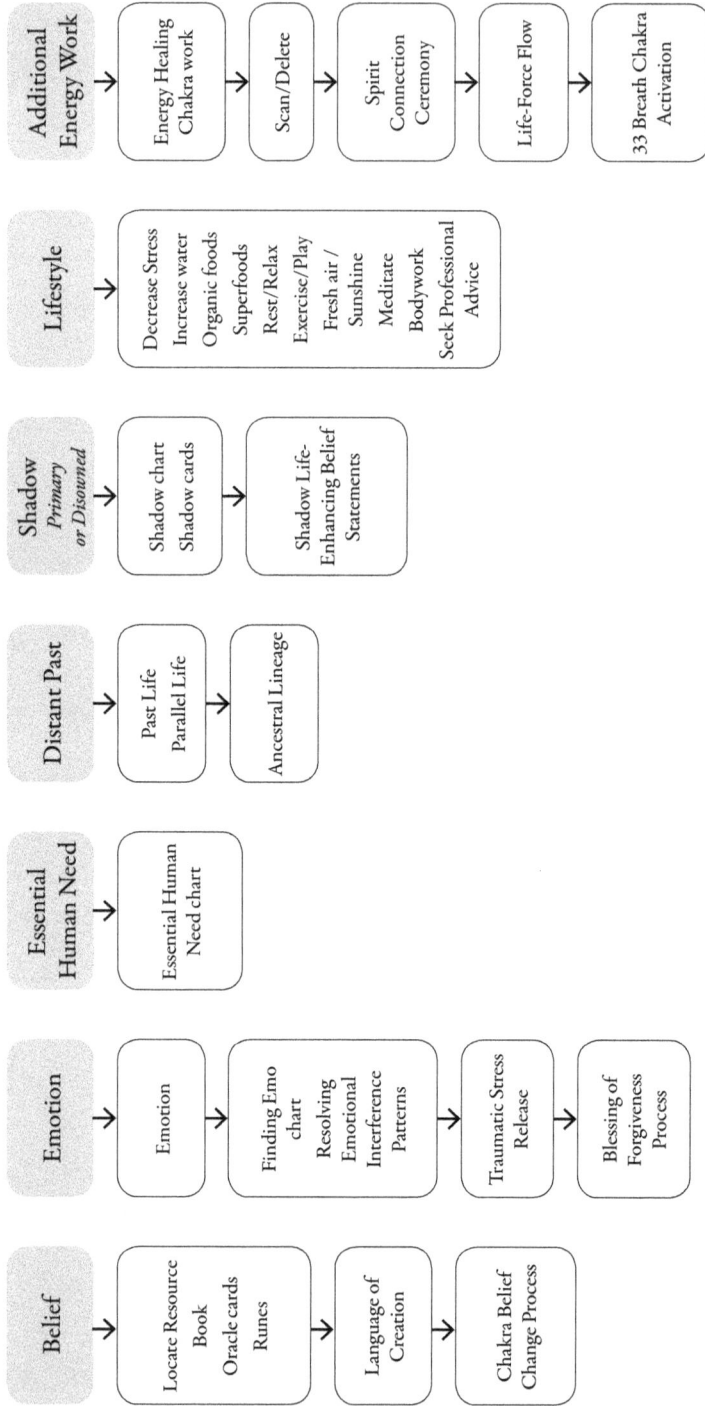

Belief
→
- Locate Resource
  - Book
  - Oracle cards
  - Runes
→
- Language of Creation
→
- Chakra Belief Change Process

Emotion
→
- Emotion
→
- Finding Emo chart
- Resolving Emotional Interference Patterns
→
- Traumatic Stress Release
→
- Blessing of Forgiveness Process

Essential Human Need
→
- Essential Human Need chart

Distant Past
→
- Past Life
- Parallel Life
→
- Ancestral Lineage

Shadow
Primary or Disowned
→
- Shadow chart
- Shadow cards
→
- Shadow Life-Enhancing Belief Statements

Lifestyle
→
- Decrease Stress
- Increase water
- Organic foods
- Superfoods
- Rest/Relax
- Exercise/Play
- Fresh air / Sunshine
- Meditate
- Bodywork
- Seek Professional Advice

Additional Energy Work
→
- Energy Healing
- Chakra work
→
- Scan/Delete
→
- Spirit Connection Ceremony
→
- Life-Force Flow
→
- 33 Breath Chakra Activation

Practice: Briefly describe a problem you are experiencing in your life.

Energy Test: *"Does this (name of problem) have a message for me?"*

- If the response is YES, then energy test: *"I can find the message behind this problem in one of the 7 areas of influence."*
- If the response is YES, then energy test each of the following areas until you come to a YES:
  - *"The highest priority message is in Beliefs."*
  - *"The highest priority message is in Emotions."*
  - *"The highest priority message is in Essential Human Needs."*
  - *"The highest priority message is in the Distant Past."*
  - *"The highest priority message is in a Shadow."*
  - *"The highest priority message is in a Lifestyle Choice."*
  - *"The highest priority message is in Other Energetic Influences."*

Once you receive a YES response, you have found your highest priority, and this will hold a clue as to what message is behind the problem.

Rest assured that you have all the resources inside you to make the changes that are needed in life. With the guidance of your inner wisdom, it is simply a matter of finding the beliefs, emotions, disowned parts of yourself, or energetic disturbances that are at the root of the problems, challenges, and obstacles you face, so you can free up their energies in the most appropriate and useful ways. How to do this will be revealed in the upcoming chapters.

> *"The most important thing in communication is hearing what isn't being said. The art of reading between the lines is a life-long quest of the wise."*
> ~ *Shannon L. Alder*

See Appendix II for instructions on how to download Access Inner Wisdom at: www.theHeartAndSoulAcademy.org/resource-page/

CHAPTER 4

Energy: The Link Between You and Everything

"The visible world is the invisible organization of energy."
~ Physicist Heinz R. Pagels

Your energy field is a vital, living, flowing force that establishes an invisible, yet luminous blueprint for your life. It creates the foundation for your health, your well-being, and your life's experiences. It makes up who you are, for we are all beings of condensed, solidified light and energy. Your body is composed of energy centers and pathways that flow and interact with your cells, nerves, and organs. They even influence your moods, emotions, and thoughts.

Our universe is made up of countless bands of electromagnetic frequencies and energies; some are beneficial, and some are detrimental to the various systems of our bodies. The human body functions on an incalculable number of tiny pulses of electrical currents—frequencies that travel from cell-to-cell within the brain, heart, and nervous system, which depend on these minute electrical signals. We are susceptible to the influences of the more powerful natural and man-made electrostatic energy fields that permeate every area of our planet.

All stressful, disruptive, and incoherent energy fields wreak havoc within us. They imbalance our body's chemistry and electrical functions. Other disharmonious frequencies that invade our body come from things like computers, cell phones, hair dryers, television sets, microwaves, and the electrical wiring in our walls. All these things modulate the energy field transmission of our cells and impact not only our state of health, but also our level of conscious awareness.

Taking Control for Transformation

Problems start to show up in our health or in our life's experiences as a way of sending us a message that we are low on energy, have blockages within our energy fields, or have developed interference patterns that we need to uncover. When we can shift and direct these energies, we influence our experience of reality.

Channeling energy is one of the most ancient forms of transformation and healing on the planet, a skill that has been handed down through the centuries. Focusing energy plays a vital role in the transformation processes used in the L.E.E.P. System.

Vital Life-Force Energy Has a Rich History

Our ancient ancestors knew about the energies of the body and how to work with them. Throughout history, life-force energy has had many names associated with it. For example, "Vril" is a word alleged to have its origin in the ancient language of Atlantis, a lost continent believed to have been wiped out thousands of years ago. Tradition says that the Atlantean root *vri*, meaning life, is the source of the word Vril and expresses the idea of the vital principle of life-force energy. This original Atlantean root word is believed to have influenced similar terms we use today, such as vitality, vigor, and virility.

Most of our ancient ancestors and mystery schools of wisdom, if not all of them, taught about the existence of the wonderful source of vital life-force energy found in all forms of matter. From the ancient Persian mysteries term *glama*, to Hindu's term *prana*, and the Chinese term *chi*, we find references to energy healing.

Anglo-Saxon: *wer* = man, vitality
Atlantean: *vril* = life
Aztec: *tona* = vital energy
Babylonian: *vahu* = breath of life
Chinese: *Chi* or *qi* = vital life-force
Egyptian: *shem* = life-force
German: *orgon* = life-force energy

Gothic: *wair* = man, vigor
Greek: *pneuma* = luminescent life-force
Hindu: *prana* = life-force, vital air
Irish: *vear* = vigor, vitality, man
Islamic: *baraka* = life-force energy
Japanese: *Ki* = life-force
Jewish Kabbalists: *nephesh* = the force, energy flow, life breath
Lakota: *woniya waken* = holy air
Latin: *vir* or *vita* = vital life-force energies
Persian: *glama* = vital energy
Polynesian: *mana* = vital life-force energy
Quechua: *huaca* = source of everything, life-force power
Russian: *bio-plasma* = vital life-force energy
Sanskrit: *vira* = vital energy, breath, hero
Tibetan Buddhism: *tung* = natural energy, energy flow

Health is life-force energy flowing freely through the thousands of channels in our body, and illness or disease is caused by obstacles to this flow. When we overcome the obstacles and restore the flow of life-force energy, it then produces a "healing response," which restores health. When nature fails to do this spontaneously, learning to channel energy—these days, it is also known as energy medicine—is a necessary component in the treatment of a health condition.

Interestingly, in the early years of China, you paid for energy medicine to keep you healthy. They recognized that energetic interference patterns occurred in the energy field before symptoms of illness or disease appeared and corrected these disruptions before they manifested into bigger health issues, such as heart problems, cancer, diabetes, or other life-threatening diseases. It was the job of the "village doctor" to keep you healthy. If you did get sick, more intensive treatments were offered, but they were usually free. There is an old Chinese saying: "You pay the doctor when you are healthy; you do not pay the doctor when you are ill."

We Are Living Antennas

Science now recognizes energy as a vital, information-filled, living-essence that is the foundation of our lives, not just our health, but also for our life's experiences.

The code that makes up who we "are" surrounds us in our energy field. How that energy field becomes informed, and how we interact with it, determines how the world and our environment are reflected back to us—it determines our experience of reality. As the information and energy of the Field becomes increasingly dense, it becomes the center of us, known as our physical body.

Our body is like an antenna that picks up and interprets the vibrations all around us. Paramahansa Yogananda, in the early half of the 20th century, explained that our spinal column and brain function like a human antenna and are transmitters and receivers of frequencies. What science knows today is that every cell of our body is a transmitter and receiver of frequencies, and that our heart is the strongest transmitter and receiver. Every cell emits a different vibration, and, at the sub-atomic level, the human body is made up of different types of vibrating energy. When a person radiates a coherent frequency that is focused, we now know that *it does affect physical matter*. It passes through the ether, through the environment that surrounds us, and, because it is not matter or bound by physical laws, can instantaneously infuse everything.

All matter vibrates like an antenna moving back and forth in resonance with the energetic fields of nature and the environment surrounding it. There are an infinite number of potential combinations of these frequencies, and everything you see and experience around you is a matrix of these combinations. Since energetic fields exist, and we can communicate, interact, and influence them at any time with our thoughts, emotions, and participation, we truly have more empowerment than we have previously been aware of or given ourselves credit for.

21st Century Knowledge

What the science of this century is beginning to understand (that spiritual teachers have known for centuries) is that *the space between things* is anything but empty. It is full of a living, vibrating essence. This intelligent Field of infinite energy has many names:

- Zero Point Energy Field
- Quantum Field
- Source Field, as coined by David Wilcock
- Nature's Mind, courtesy of Edgar Mitchel, the Apollo astronaut

- "The Matrix," named in 1944 by Maax Plank. As the father of quantum physics, he asserted that this matrix underlies everything that we see and everything around us, including our body. It is what was determined to be a conscious and intelligent mind—the matrix of all matter.

In ways that we are only beginning to understand scientifically, but which our ancient ancestors, indigenous cultures, and mystery schools around the world have known about for centuries, this Field exists as energy with infinite potential, and we have the opportunity to influence it. This is done most efficiently through the human heart. Thinking alone is an inefficient process (as described before). Thoughts are important—they make a great guidance system—but they are not, in and of themselves, enough. Emotions—energy in motion—coupled with a thought have a far greater impact on the world around us.

The Potential for Change

Keep in mind that all matter is comprised of energy or fields of energy. When you change the field that the atoms are in, you change how they express themselves. We are made of those atoms, as is our world. Einstein taught us that matter and energy are essentially interchangeable, and their transformations are forever continuous. All matter is made of oscillating, vibrating, swirling bits of energy of different sizes and speeds. Whether human, animal, tree, stardust, or the environment around us, all form is comprised of energy at the quantum level. All these forms are evolving subsystems that have the ability to receive, transmit, and convert different kinds of information and energy vibrations. They can assemble to be beneficial or detrimental to the receiver, depending on their form and structure. Disharmonious vibrations create distortions in the fields that surround us and can persist for many years, creating havoc in the various areas of our lives until they are resolved.

Energy Centers and Energy Fields

We have three main types of subtle life-force energies that flow through us. That's not to say there aren't other kinds—just that there are three main types for the purpose of our discussion. Two of these energies are the result of the polarity that is formed from the two poles of our body, and they are always in a constant energetic relationship with each other.

1. Higher consciousness descends down the spine from the crown chakra like a beam of light or like continuous flashes of lightning.
2. Earth energy ascends up the spine from our feet and the base of our spine in a spiraling motion.

These two flows contribute to the spin of the chakras—energetic processing centers of the body that have a spinning motion to them. Then, the third flow is the direct result of the life-force energy as it moves through the body, flowing from the heart to the head and to the abdomen and back to the heart, similar to the movement of the infinity symbol.

- Physically, it is associated with the flow of blood through your body.
- Spiritually, it is associated with the soul infusing your being.

Energy Flow Can Become Blocked

There are many reasons why these three energies can become blocked within us over time.

- Trauma, abuse, bodily shock
- Emotionally painful experiences, abandonment, grief, loss, and betrayal
- Feelings of unworthiness, inadequacy, or lack of love

When our energy flows become blocked, it creates feelings of separation from the world. The blockages also separate us from our happiness, one another, and from our ability to accomplish the lives of our dreams.

Energetic Processing Centers of the Body

As you see in the illustration below, the chakras are powerful focal points of energy in your body that are associated with different types and different levels of consciousness flowing through our body-mind energy field. When we are living in harmony, understanding, compassion, and love, the energies flow through our body, opening and activating the chakras, increasing our life-force and consciousness. When we experience disharmony, challenges, stress, emotional hurt, and difficulties in our lives, the life-force energy closes and constricts our energy flows.

Problems (both internal and external) occur when our chakras get clogged with darkened, energetic debris; they get stuck in a habitual mode or become distorted with habitual stress, adrenaline, caffeine, or sugar. When this happens, it affects our overall consciousness as well as several other levels—physical, emotional, and mental. Toxins, stress, and electromagnetic chaos also impact our health and how the energy of our body-mind energy field functions. This blocked energy will have a message for us that will let us know what needs to change in order to bring peace, synchronicity, and flow back into our life.

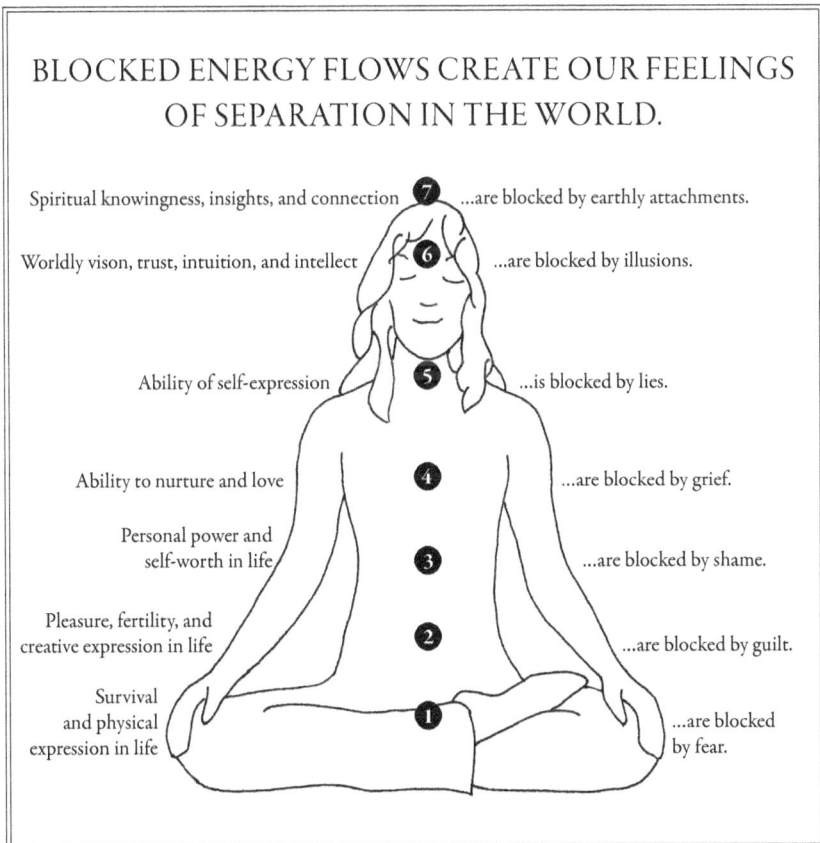

BLOCKED ENERGY FLOWS CREATE OUR FEELINGS OF SEPARATION IN THE WORLD.

Spiritual knowingness, insights, and connection **7** ...are blocked by earthly attachments.

Worldly vison, trust, intuition, and intellect **6** ...are blocked by illusions.

Ability of self-expression **5** ...is blocked by lies.

Ability to nurture and love **4** ...are blocked by grief.

Personal power and self-worth in life **3** ...are blocked by shame.

Pleasure, fertility, and creative expression in life **2** ...are blocked by guilt.

Survival and physical expression in life **1** ...are blocked by fear.

The Wisdom of the Chakras

Earth Chakra Super Root	Did you know that there are chakras outside your body? This chakra sits approximately 12–18 inches below the bottoms of your feet. It aligns and connects the body and soul to the powerful energies within the magnetic core of our planet. It is the grounding point of our entire extended chakra system and our relationship to the planet and universe. This chakra is believed to hold the keys to our past lives, karmic patterns, and DNA origins. Sometimes referred to as the earth star chakra, it is responsible for us feeling deeply connected to our own energies as well as the earth.
Feet & Hand Chakras	The foot chakras relate to our ability to connect with and receive the earth's energy. They help us stay grounded and allow the earth's energy to flow through our body. The foot chakra is actually a split energy center with each half located in the arch of the feet. When your feet are next to each other, the chakra halves combine to make a complete energy center. However, they are always linked together whether they are beside each other or not. The hand chakras, located in the palms, are associated with creating what you want in life and receiving information from the universe. They can open and shut at will or when the body gives or receives healing energy. They work together with the heart chakra, enhancing healing and creative artistic flow for those who work with their hands. The chakras remain active in your energy field and your etheric body, even when you are missing an arm or a leg.
1st Chakra Root Chakra	The root chakra physically influences our bones, spinal column, joints, cell production, and immune system as well as our ability to feel safe, secure, and protected in the world. It represents our physical expression in life and informs us of external control and expectations from family and our bloodline.
2nd Chakra Sacral Chakra	The sacral chakra physically influences our reproductive organs, hips, kidneys, bladder, blood, and lymphatic system as well as our fertility and the expression of our sensuality and pleasure. This chakra impacts our relationships and is influenced by peer pressure. It is the center of our creativity, new ideas, and financial security in life. It is a center of power for us, also known as the Dan Tien. It represents the Seat of Our Emotions.
3rd Chakra Solar Plexus	The solar plexus chakra physically influences our digestive system, weight, lower back, stomach, liver, adrenal glands, pancreas, autonomic nervous system, and addictions as well as our intuition and gut feelings. It represents our personal power and informs us when our own individuality is being undermined and reflects our self-worth issues.

4th Chakra Heart Chakra	The heart chakra physically influences our heart, blood and circulatory system, upper back, lungs, breasts, and skin as well as the expression of our needs balanced with respecting the needs of others in relationships. It represents our ability to nurture and to give and receive love. It also represents our freedom and passions for living life and is the Seat of Our Soul and access to deeper consciousness.
Thymus Chakra High Heart	The thymus chakra, also known as the High Heart, influences our immune system and governs forgiveness and the release of fear. It is considered to be the bridge between our emotions and intellect. It is the chakra of selfless spiritual love, empathy, truth, joy, and compassion. The spoken word resonates here; therefore, it has within it the ability to influence the patterning of our DNA.
5th Chakra Throat Chakra	The throat chakra physically influences our neck, mouth, voice, hearing, arms, thyroid, and metabolism as well as our expression of laughter, tears, thoughts, anxiety, intentions, and ideas. It represents our ability for self-expression, finding our voice, and guiding our vocation in life.
Alta Major	Located at the indent at the base of the back of our head, it monitors oxygen content in the blood, controls respiration, and supports restful sleep. It stimulates creativity and productivity and supports balance and coordination. When fully developed and activated, this chakra forms the communication center between the vital energies of your 3rd eye and crown chakras. It brings intuition into greater conscious awareness.
6th Chakra Third Eye Chakra	The third eye chakra physically influences our brain, vision, eyesight, sinuses, sense of taste, and pituitary gland as well as the ability to see the overall big picture or the details of the next necessary step for us to take. It represents our worldly vision and trust and helps provide insight with a balanced mix of intuition and intellect. It is the seat of our knowledge and psychic vision.
7th Chakra Crown Chakra	The crown chakra physically influences our pineal gland and brain and offers spiritual insights, knowingness, and growing awareness of our potential and unique place in the world. It represents our connection with spirit—living transmitters and receivers—human antennas unified and interconnected with the universe.
Soul Star 8th Chakra	The soul star chakra is another external chakra that sits anywhere from 6–18 inches above the top of the head. This is where spiritual energy and Divine love enters into your body. Divine love, light, and energy filters down into your crown chakra for distribution throughout your body. This chakra is associated with our expanded consciousness, spiritual wisdom, and ascension.

The circulation of energy via our chakras not only nourishes us physically, but it also nourishes our expanding consciousness. Although there are many more chakras in our body-mind energy field, this brief description of the seven major chakras (plus a few others) will help you understand their value and make use of them to create changes within your lives. Our chakras have been greatly overlooked or misunderstood as to their value in personal empowerment. I believe the main reason for this is that most people don't know what to do with the information and how to put it to use. The L.E.E.P. System allows us to take the information, knowledge, and wisdom of the ancients, and the great thinkers, researchers, and scientists, and transform it into ways that individuals can not only access, but benefit from as well. There are ways we can embody the knowledge of our time, as well as the wisdom of the ancients, and apply it in our lives and use it to accelerate our personal growth. It helps us to further step into our self-empowerment and allows us to expand our conscious evolution.

A Network of Information and Energy

Peter Fraser, author of *Decoding the Human Body-Field*, and an independent researcher in bioenergetics and body information systems, explains that the "human body field" (as he calls it) is a network of information and energy that serves as a master control system for the physical body and coordinates all our physiological functions. In other words, if the cells, organs, and systems of our physical body lack the proper information and energy, they cannot do their jobs correctly. Over time, without the right information, the body's energies become distorted by being exposed to too much stress, including over-exposure to electromagnetic fields, environmental toxins, pathogens, poor diet, and such. This results in the processes of our body breaking down, eventually creating symptoms of disease. Today, many leading-edge scientists and researchers believe information and energy underlie everything in the universe and are the fundamental building blocks of our reality.

The Light in DNA Energy

Under a microscope, you would be able to see that the energy deep within our cells gives off light, and that our emotions are also chemical in nature and affect the amount of light in the cells. In turn, the amount of photonic light stored in our DNA plays a significant role in health, consciousness, and our life's experiences. Dr. Fritz Albert Popp, a German physicist known for his research of bio-photons, noticed that DNA absorbs photons of light, which are little packages of energy. The entire code and blueprint to build your body is stored in your DNA. When he opened up a DNA molecule, a thousand photons burst out of it (they can count those photons with a photomultiplier machine that measures ultraviolet light, photon by photon).

He also observed that when the light in your DNA (the energy) is reduced, you get sick. Negative emotions and disease scrambles the healthy information and energy signals flowing through your body, creating interference patterns. When you are sick, it is because your cellular light has been reduced. As it turns out, psychological factors (which will be discussed in the next few chapters) play a huge role in how much light is able to move through the cell that is stored in your DNA.

The body does not know how to return to health if it doesn't have the right information. To support healing, we need to restore healthy life-enhancing information and get healing life-force energy flowing through our body. Whenever we make changes within the energy field, we alter the DNA, which in turn modifies our physical body. Science has also discovered that DNA molecules are hungry for photons—they will actually capture photons of light and draw the life-force energy into them. Your DNA uses this photon light to send out signals for health and wellness. The amount of light being stored in your DNA is the real basis for your level of health and consciousness. So, how do we get the light into our DNA? It is not as simple as sitting in the sun. Your DNA naturally absorbs photons when it unfolds, and it does this in the presence of love energy and the intention of conscious awareness.

How Energy Heals the Body

Leonard Laskow, MD, and Dr. Glen Rein, PhD, discovered that the DNA molecule begins with an intention to unwind when loving energy was sent to it, and that it began to heal itself when given an intention with specific directions to return to health. This means that in the presence of intention and loving energy, you are truly able to restructure and heal DNA molecules.

Let's take a look at three easy, powerful practices we can use to create flow in our energy fields that make up who we are, then we'll learn how to work with channeling energy to make changes in the interference patterns we carry within us. As Wilhelm Reich, psychoanalyst and theorist, said, "Once we open up to the flow of energy within our body, we open up to the flow of energy in the universe."

Life-Force Flow

The Life-Force Flow practice is a multi-purpose meditation. While possessing many of the benefits of meditation, it also stimulates and rejuvenates your whole being, helping to bring balance and health to your body and endocrine system. This practice develops:

- Concentration
- Body Integration
- Awareness of universal life-force
- Awareness of your "energy body" and its interrelation with your physical body

Meditation helps to balance and increase the universal life-force flowing through your body via its main energy centers and pathways, known as chakras and meridians. This energy is a very powerful healing force for both your body and your mind.

Overview:

This practice may be done lying down or sitting with your spine straight. If you find yourself falling asleep, you may wish to do this sitting up.

This breathing meditation involves circulating energy up from your earth chakra (located 18 inches below your feet), flowing it up your spinal column with your focused intention, and out the top of your head to your soul star chakra (located approximately 6–18 inches above your head), then flowing like a shower down around the outside of your body, back to your earth chakra with your focused intention. This movement of energy nourishes your chakras and meridians with luminescent life-force and is coordinated with your breathing. Even though you are concentrating on moving the energy along each portion of its route, you will want to keep the flow of energy moving smoothly without stopping.

Practice:

1. **On your inhalation:** with intention, envision nurturing, life-force energy slowly rising up from your earth chakra, moving up your legs, up the base of your spine, flowing gently up your spinal column, nourishing each of your chakras along its path from the small of your back, past the middle of your back, moving upwards between your shoulder blades, flowing up your neck, your head, and out through the top of your head to your bright, shining soul star.

2. **Then, without pausing, on your exhalation:** envision and intend the life-force energy infused with expanded consciousness flowing downward like a waterfall, showering over your scalp and head, down your face and the back of your head, down around your body, over your chest, back, abdomen, and down your legs, infusing your entire being with luminous life-force energy until it reaches your earth chakra once again. In essence, allow this energy to wash over you and experience it to the best of your abilities.

3. **When you get to the end of your exhalation,** repeat this same cycle without pausing to keep the flow of energy moving smoothly—circulating this energy as one gracefully flowing stream. Continue for as long as you have time to do this. 20–30 minutes is a good goal to work toward. It won't take long for you to consciously coordinate your breathing with your envisioning, and you'll be flowing life-force energy easily throughout your body-mind energy field.

33-Breath Chakra Activation

Within all of us is an incredible energy that can be accessed and circulated for wonderful results. The 33-Breath Chakra Activation focuses on 11 specific chakras that play a vital role in our health, well-being, and spiritual development. The ancients were well aware of the connection between breath, life-force energy, and consciousness, and how to open the chakras properly and effectively. Once activated and energized, your chakras are better able to support you by nourishing you physically, nurturing your expanding consciousness, promoting your healing abilities, increasing stamina and psychic development, heightening self-awareness, reducing stress, and slowing down the aging process.

Overview:

This practice may be done sitting in a comfortable position or lying down. If you find yourself falling asleep, you may wish to do this sitting up.

This practice encourages deep breathing to oxygenate your body while you activate and energize your chakras. By envisioning your breath moving in and out of a specific area of your body, you strengthen and energize that location. Open your heart to feelings of love to the best of your ability—this will enhance the effects of this chakra activation and help you to more easily experience the shift taking place. The energy fields that surround and inter-penetrate your body register your intention and attention.

Practice:

1. Take a moment and recall a time when you felt deep, nurturing love and *feel* that love now.

2. Next, when you are ready, begin by envisioning your earth chakra, located approximately 18 inches below your feet, and imagine breathing into it.

   - *Breathe into it for 3 full, deep breaths.*
   - *With the first breath, your intent is to Activate it.*
   - *With your second breath, your intent is to Energize it.*
   - *With your third breath, your intent is to Nurture it.*

3. Repeat this 3-breath process while moving up to each of the following chakras (as described previously in this chapter):

   - 1st chakra—root
   - 2nd chakra—sacral
   - 3rd chakra—solar plexus
   - 4th chakra—heart
   - Thymus chakra—high heart
   - 5th chakra—throat
   - Alta Major
   - 6th chakra—third eye
   - 7th chakra—crown
   - 8th chakra—soul star

Light Infusion Breathing

As discussed earlier, the amount of light stored in our DNA plays a significant role in our health, consciousness, and life experiences. It naturally absorbs photons of light, drawing the life-force energy into it when it unfolds, and fully activates in the presence of love energy and the intention of conscious awareness.

This practice may be done lying down or sitting in a comfortable position.

Practice:

1. Remember a time when you felt deep, nurturing love and *feel* that love now.

2. As you breathe in, imagine breathing in photons of love and light. Then, as you exhale, imagine the light infusing your cells, the space between them, and your entire being with luminous life-force energy. It automatically goes wherever the body needs it. Inhale, imagining breathing in photons of light, and exhale, allowing them to infuse your body wherever necessary, healing what needs to be healed, restoring health and rejuvenating your body, mind, and spirit, and infusing your spirit with higher consciousness.

3. Continue this breathing and envisioning process for at least five minutes or longer.

See Appendix II for instructions about how to download the Chakra and Energy Practices at: www.theHeartAndSoulAcademy.org/resource-page/

*"The best methods are those which help the life energy
to resume its inner work of healing."*
~ Paramahansa Yogananda

CHAPTER 5

Channeling Life-Force Energy
for Health and Wellness

"In every culture and in every medical tradition before ours,
healing was accomplished by moving energy."
~ Albert Szent-Gyorgyi, Nobel Laureate in Medicine (1937)

Now that you know how to consciously channel energy through your body, how do you use it to make energetic changes within the body-mind energy field? While everyone naturally has life-force energy moving through them, an energetic attunement to healing energy is recommended, though not necessary. An attunement is an initiation that *supports* and *amplifies* the amount of energy moving through a person. It does this by gently opening the energy channel pathways to allow greater amounts of universal life-force energies to flow through the energy field, the chakras, and the body. This, in turn, amplifies the vibratory rate of the physical and etheric bodies, which loosens up and sloughs off the dense, lower vibrational patterns and constrictions within the body-mind energy field that can no longer resonate with the finer vibrations of the attunement. As the old accumulated energetic debris is cleansed from the system, a person's overall energetic vibrations rise to a higher level than before. A guided Violet-Golden Light Attunement is included here for your support.

Violet-Golden Light Attunement

This energetic ceremony attunes you to the violet light of transformation and the golden light of expanded consciousness that will enhance and support your ability to channel life-force energies.

Violet light, in many circles, is the primary energy frequency of transformation and transmutation, which converts chaos to greater peace and harmony. It is utilized to support a return to wholeness and is referred to as a scientific ray, an energy signature that facilitates the transmutation and manifestation of matter.

Golden light possesses the properties of higher cosmic consciousness, which brings an awakening of awareness. The light acts to lighten the body, opening doors of perception, and is highly energizing and restorative. This energy of expansion is associated with understanding, abundance, and higher wisdom.

Overview:

The guided ceremony used here has been handed down from ancient teachings borrowed from the East as well as those from the Native Americans. It creates an image of connecting with the earth and the sun. These energies symbolically represent the fusion of matter with Spirit.

If you have a more personal connection to what represents the energetic power of transformation, expanded consciousness, compassion, and love, then substitute your image where appropriate. You may guide yourself through this attunement procedure here, or you may enjoy listening to the guided attunement on the Heart and Soul Academy website (see Appendix II for details).

Practice:

Sit comfortably. Take a deep breath in, then slowly let your breath out. Relax. Take another deep breath and hold it. Allow the tension to flow away as you exhale completely—just let it go. Do this again. Take another deep breath and allow yourself to relax even more as you exhale. Relax your shoulders. With every breath you take, allow yourself to relax even more. When you are ready, imagine a beam of light extending down from the bottom of your feet, through the ground, through the earth, and all the way down to the very center of the earth where it instinctively goes to a special grounding spot just for you. Use your intention to connect with the center of the earth. Imagine a return beam of light, the violet light of transformation, coming up from the center of the earth, through the rocks, through the ground, where it moves to gently meet the bottoms of your feet. Allow this energy to move up through your legs, your spinal column, your heart, and release this beautiful, iridescent violet light of transformation into the very center of your heart. It's okay if you can't visualize the violet light—just pretend that you can. It is your intention that makes this happen.

Next, imagine a beam of light extending up from the top of your head, up to your soul star that sits 6–18 inches above your head. Your soul star shines like the sun. Imagine a return beam of energy, the golden light of expanded consciousness, coming down from your soul star. It gently kisses the top of your head before coming in and flowing down through your head and neck. Move it downward into the very center of your heart, where it meets the violet light of transformation. Together, they mingle and shimmer. Swirl these beautiful healing energies of transformation and expanded consciousness in your heart. With every breath, you automatically draw in more and more of these healing energies to form a small ball of beautiful, violet-golden light.

Imagine these shimmering energies of light expanding to fill your heart, then your chest, and all your internal organs. Allow them to expand until they fill your entire body. Concentrate on the sense of fullness as violet-golden light fills every cell of your body and flows into every space in between, filling each molecule of your being. It goes to wherever it is most needed—soothing, nurturing, nourishing, and rejuvenating. Allow this violet-golden light to expand and grow further until it can no longer be contained within your physical body. Imagine it radiating beyond your physical being and surrounding the space around you, filling your entire field. Allow the energy to flow through you and notice that the same amount of energy—and more—is automatically flowing into you.

Your energy can never be depleted as the supply is unlimited. It is always available; you simply need to call it forth. Any time you intend it to flow, it nurtures and rejuvenates you, filling you with peace. Allow it to flow and then bask in its nurturing and healing light as your body, mind, and spirit radiate with violet-golden luminescence.

Bring your awareness back to the present moment. You are now attuned to the energies of the violet light of transformation and the golden light of expanded consciousness with a more open flow and access to healing energies. You may channel these transformational energies for yourself or others at any time.

Release Interference Patterns by Channeling Energy

Channeling energy allows us to direct it easily and effectively, enabling us to change the configuration of the interference pattern at its source of origin. Remember, Dr. Bruce Lipton asserted that energy signals are at least 100 times faster and more efficient than chemical signals. If we were to use the analogy of energy likened unto light, channeling energy allows us to focus it into a beam like a laser, which is many times more powerful than the diffused energy of a light bulb.

Dr. Candace Pert, neuroscientist and major advocate of alternative medicine, stated in her book, *Molecules of Emotion, the Science Behind Mind-Body Medicine*, that invisible forces—meaning energy—attract molecules to one another, so that they adhere together as an identifiable substance. These invisible forces of attraction can overcome a disruptive or unhealthy pattern if enough healthy energy is applied. She states that molecules respond to energy and chemical cues by vibrating. They wiggle, shimmy, and even hum as they bend and change from one shape to another, often moving back and forth between two or three pattern configurations until the old pattern can no longer retain its shape. It is then released. Simply put, when the disruptive interference pattern is released with channeled life-force energy, healing can take place.

Your Cells Have Antennas

There are receptors that are like little antennas hovering in the membranes of your cells. They move and vibrate, waiting to pick up messages carried by other vibrating signals. When a message of health, wholeness, and healing energy is transported to the cells, organs, and body systems, it becomes a very beneficial experience.

Scientists have discovered microtubules, which are found in the billions of neural cells throughout our central nervous system and spinal cord. They are natural, miniature resonators—little resonating chambers that have actual physical dimensions. They amplify the internal frequencies of energy, light, and sound, and carry that communication and information to other cells.

When microtubules resonate with a distinct vibration, others nearby are also stimulated to resonate at that frequency. This is very similar to a tuning fork—the resonating microtubules serve to amplify both acoustic and electromagnetic vibrations. Think of them as bundles of glass fiber optic cables that carry information in the form of light pulses through the spine. When we channel life-force healing energy frequencies to an area within our body, the microtubules help to return the cells and body back to a healing resonance. It boosts our immune system, reminding our cells of health, and supports our healing capabilities.

Our Ever-Changing Biology

The good news is that every time we channel vibrant life-force energy, it is accompanied by an appropriate change in our biology—our body—and this is accompanied by a change in the energetic field that surrounds us.

Energy flows where you put your attention and is a conduit for your intention. It is something you allow, not something you do. The energy flows through you, not from you, always maintaining a sense of fullness. There is no limit to the supply. It nourishes and nurtures you, filling you with peace, even as you channel it somewhere else. Starting the flow of energy is simply a matter of intending to do so.

Channeling Through Multi-Dimensional Grounding

When we are grounded and fully in our body, we can bring more energy into our system and experience higher states of consciousness. We can only access and process a limited amount of our expanded consciousness flowing through us if we are not an open conduit. When we connect to the vastness of our spirit, our energy flows evenly; we initiate a higher level of spiritual presence and are in sync with our energy.

There are many ways to ground. In the past, we were taught to ground into the planet, which is good, but we were guided to do so as a way to send dense, heavy, mucky energy into the earth for it to be transformed and returned to us. Now that Mother Earth is undergoing climate and environmental changes, it is time that we learn how to ground into the vastness of our own spirit. We can easily do this with a simple, effective Sacred Heart Alignment adapted from Sri Yukteswar's Unity Breath that was taught to Paramahansa Yogananda, founder of the Self-Realization Fellowship. It allows us to create flow and heart coherent energy in any given moment.

Sacred Heart Alignment

Overview:

The purpose of this practice is to create a loving flow of energy between the earth and the expanded consciousness centered within your heart. It can easily be done anywhere and at any time.

Practice:

Close your eyes.

Connect with Earth: Envision the beauty of Mother Earth and feel the love and joy you have for nature. Feel this love in your heart and imagine sending a beam of love from your heart down deep into the earth. Notice that Mother Earth sends a return beam of nurturing love energy back to you. Breathe this energy up through your feet, draw it up your spinal column, and release it into the very center of your heart. Feel the flow of energy between you, the earth, and your heart.

Align with Spirit: Envision the expanse of the heavens and the depths of space. Feel the awe, wonder, and love you have for the stars and all of creation. Imagine sending a beam of love from your heart up to your soul star and the heavens above. Immediately, your soul star sends a return beam of warm, golden energy to you. Breathe this expanded consciousness down through the top of your head and release this radiant energy into the very center of your heart. Feel the flow of energy between your soul star and your heart.

Center within Heart: Feel both energies flowing into your heart simultaneously—nourishing earth energy flowing up your spine and expanded consciousness traveling down through your head—and swirl these shimmering energies into the center of your heart.

These energies symbolically represent the fusion of spirit with matter—the divine feminine and masculine joined in pure love within you. Remember a time when you felt deep, nurturing love and feel that love now, then continue breathing as if through the center of your heart.

Let yourself *feel* your connection with your expanded consciousness and with the earth. This is a tremendous source of strength because there is a great deal of power within your body when Spirit is fully integrated. Open your eyes whenever you are ready.

With this Sacred Heart Alignment, you are grounding into the vastness of your expanded consciousness and connecting with Mother Earth and the nurturing energy she has to offer. Allow your spirit to support and strengthen you as you continue breathing through your heart. You are grounding yourself across multiple dimensions of your growing awareness. This happens because your heart is the space where, as your skills develop, you become more consciously aware of your connection with other dimensions and realities.

Use this Sacred Heart Alignment to reconnect and ground yourself as often as you like, and especially when channeling energy. We'll learn how to put channeling energy to good use for making changes within your body-mind energy field in the following chapters. Though, for now, here is a little experiment I encourage you to try that will give you a little taste of what channeling energy can do.

The Energy Taste Test

- Slice a lemon or orange in half or open a bottle of wine and pour two glasses.

- Leave half of the lemon or orange (or one of the glasses of wine) in the kitchen or some place that is at least 20 feet away from where you are.

- Move to another room with the other half of the lemon or orange (or glass of wine) and hold it in your hands, sending life-force healing energies to it. Conjure up all those really good feelings of love and joy and send them into the fruit or wine. Do this for five minutes, then set it down.

- *First,* taste the lemon, orange, or wine that you *did not* send love to. *Then,* taste the one you sent the loving, healing energies to. Notice the difference? Notice how the "unenergized" fruit or wine tastes less sweet and less full bodied than the energized fruit or wine? The orange may have become juicier, the lemon less sour; red wine becomes smoother, and white wine will sometimes deepen in color.

The reason for tasting the energized portion second is that it raises your vibrations—even those of your taste buds. Once those are raised, it will be more difficult to taste the unenergized portion because you've already changed the vibration in your taste buds.

In a very short time, the vibrations of the fruit or wine have changed. You couldn't *see* anything change, and yet it did. Healing energies and love vibrations change the physical properties because you were consciously altering the flow of energy and enhancing it. Thus, it becomes possible to change our lives, our environment, and our world.

* Impaired taste is caused by a wide variety of things, and not everyone has the same number of taste buds. For this reason, there are times when it may be more difficult to taste the difference between energized and unenergized foods and beverages.

*"There is a force in the universe, which, if we permit it,
will flow through us and provide miraculous results."*
~ Gandhi

*See Appendix II for instructions on how to listen to the Violet and Golden Light
Attunement at:* www.theHeartAndSoulAcademy.org/resource-page/

CHAPTER 6

Unlocking Your Belief Potential

"Your imagination is your preview of life's coming attractions."
~ Albert Einstein

- Imagine unleashing a power within and creating a life that reflects the very best you.
- Imagine transforming your detrimental, limiting beliefs into empowering ones that support who you are and who you are becoming.
- Imagine being able to get in touch with your inner strengths.

The main benefits derived from learning how to program beliefs into your subconscious include:

1. The power to set a new direction in your life.
2. The ability to re-pattern a belief that doesn't serve you or one that's been holding you back.

Belief Interference Patterns

The greatest hindrance to achieving success in any area of our life lies hidden in our mind. Our subconsciously held beliefs have a far more powerful effect in our lives than most of us realize. At least 70 percent, if not more, of our self-talk is negative talk. Any time we place a negative thought in our subconscious mind it is like dropping a poison tablet into a vessel of water from which we must drink. This poison creates what I call Belief Interference Patterns—a set of vibrational patterns in our life's blueprint that interfere with our joy, freedom, and essential nature. These patterns are detrimental, self-limiting beliefs that exert a powerful influence upon us. They are the primary reason we separate ourselves from what we want and are blocked from enjoying life.

From the moment of conception to our present day, beliefs have formed and created energetic patterns for our behaviors and our personality, influencing how we respond to life's circumstances. In our early years, we didn't get to choose what we believed or didn't—it was handed to us as truth from parents, teachers, and leaders in our society. Whether they were helpful and supportive or disharmonious and harmful, the subconscious mind does everything in its power to bring forth what is programmed. Fortunately, we can change these patterns by replacing them with healthy, positive, and supportive ones—we just have to know how to communicate with our subconscious mind.

One of the secrets to creating a magical life—one where you are healthy, empowered, living joyously and abundantly, and raising your conscious awareness—is to *know* 'what you want' and how to communicate that desire with the unseen forces of the universe in order to manifest it in your life. Otherwise, it is just a wish. One of the other great secrets is *being able* to change any sabotaging beliefs you hold at the subconscious level. You must do this; otherwise, they will continue to torment you.

What Do You Want?

Do you know that your first and foremost mission (as an infinite spiritual being having this temporary human experience) is to live from a place that brings meaning and purpose to your life? Think of all the wonderful ways you want to enjoy your life and the exciting adventures you want to experience. Your life needs to not only fulfill the needs of your body, but also the wants and needs of your mind and spirit in order to fully engage and live life to its fullest potential. Sounds easy, doesn't it? To know what you want and what you want to be, have, do, and experience in your life.

But, what if like many individuals, you are having trouble knowing what it is you want? What if you feel stuck and uncertain about what you want to create in your life? Many times, in my travels, I have come across individuals who have lost touch with their hopes, dreams, and desires. I look into their eyes and see emptiness or sadness. They would fall silent when I asked them what they wanted to create, and many said they didn't really know anymore. They wanted a more fulfilling life but couldn't tell me what that was for it is rarely explored at a deeper level. My heart aches when I hear of someone who has lost touch with his or her soul. I feel a deep sadness in my heart when I realize their spirit isn't shining, and that they have lost contact with their inner life-force and passion for living to the fullest. If I were to ask you that same question, *"What do you want?"* could you give a definitive answer in this moment? If you don't already know, you may want to gain some clarity and perspective before you continue.

The Value of Putting Pen to Paper

Becoming clear on what you do and don't want from life is one of the most important steps you can take in terms of finding your true self. I recommend getting a blank journal or spiral notebook and using it to create a "Goals and Desires Journal" or a "Heart and Soul Journal." This is much like a "Bucket List," though the focus is on writing down your dreams and passions as well as what you'd like to be, do, or have in this experience of life. What would be the very best expression of you?

Do you find yourself asking, *"How do I find out what I want?"* Relax. That's easy. Begin by making a list and taking inventory of all the things in your life that you don't want or identify as problems. List any circumstances, situations, conditions, or unhappiness that you could do without. If you don't like what you see in your life, you need to know that you can create a different reality with a new choice.

Then, make a list that would be the positive-opposite for every item you wrote down on your "Don't Want" list. This way you will know what belongs in your life and what doesn't.

Exercise: Your List of "Wants"

Don't Want List	Positive-Opposite Want
* to be stressed out and frustrated all the time.	* to be calm, confident, filled with peace.
* to live in a noisy apartment, stressful neighborhood, or cramped house.	* to live in a nurturing home in a nice neighborhood.
* to live alone.	* to be in a loving, nurturing, supportive relationship, community, or environment.
* to feel helpless, powerless, worthless, or sad.	* to feel empowered, optimistic, worthy, self-assured, happy.
* to struggle to make money.	* to make money easily and naturally with meaningful work.

The things you desire to manifest in your life start out as spiritual impulses of love that want you to grow and connect with an expression of your creative self. Keep your journal close and add to your list every time you think of something new. This keeps your mission dynamic and alive. If you don't already know what you want, here are some questions to contemplate to help you get started:

- What do you want to create for your life?
- If you could do anything, what would you do?
- If you could be anything, what would you like to be?
- If you could have anything, what would you like to have?
- What would make your life worth living?
- What would bring meaning and passion to your life?
- What do you long for?
- Where do you want to live?
- What would you most like to learn?
- What would you like to develop within yourself?
- If you want to travel, where do you want to go, and what do you want to see?
- When someone asks, "What do you do for a living?" what would you like to be able to say?
- How would you like to make a positive difference in the world?

The first part of the magic formula for living the life of your dreams is to *know what you want*. The second part is to *unify your consciousness* around that.

Aware and Unaware

We have two major aspects to our consciousness: the part we are aware of—our conscious mind—and a far greater aspect that we are unaware of—the incredible depths of our mysterious subconscious (below our normal level of awareness). We have a tendency to identify our "self" with the consciously aware aspect of our mind and forget about our subconscious. After all, it is outside the realm of our normal level of awareness. So, let's ponder that.

Our subconscious is a substantial reservoir of information. To give you an idea of the vast amounts of storage it has, Lynn McTaggart, a researcher and author on the New Physics and Consciousness, revealed in her book, *The Field,* that according to distinguished neuroscientist Karl Pribram, the brain processes information in wave-frequency patterns, holding unimaginable quantities of data—more than 280 quintillion (280,000,000,000,000,000,000) bits of information in its database. This constitutes the amount of gathered information and memory that the average adult accumulates over a lifetime. That's mind-boggling!

Comparing Bits of Memory

Large laptop computer hard drive contains 500 GB	4,000,000,000,000,000 bits
The human brain contains	280,000,000,000,000,000,000 bits

We have 70 times more bits of memory in our brain than a large laptop computer!

Studies in neuroscience indicate that 95–99 percent of everything that we think, feel, or do originates in our subconscious mind first. This is where the influence originates from, directions are issued, and power is initiated. It is where we create our experience of reality—outside our conscious level of awareness.

Our subconscious moves through this storehouse, pulling up memories as though they are happening in this moment because it doesn't operate on a timeline of past or future—it reactivates the pathways, thereby perceiving as if it were in-the-now. The brain processes the subconscious mind's interpretations then influences the conscious mind to make unconscious choices and take action based on what's stored there, creating events and circumstances in our outer world.

As it turns out, our conscious and subconscious minds communicate with different languages. The one thing that prevents us from achieving personal empowerment and effectively creating the reality that we want stems from *not knowing how to communicate with* our subconscious mind.

You Have Two Minds and One Brain

Conscious Mind	Subconscious Mind
Reflective: Has ability to make conscious decisions. Self-awareness. Alert. Observant. Mindful.	**Reflexive:** Conditioned by beliefs and past experiences. Survival and pleasure oriented.
Thinks Abstractly: Has ability, or capacity, to think about abstract ideas: peace, love, justice, etc.	**Thinks Literally and Specifically:** Is sensory based: what it can see, feel, hear, touch, taste, and smell.
Power of Choice: Motivational. Creative. Rational mind. Has ability to dream in new ways, form new ideas, make new choices. Positive thinking. Wishes. Desires.	**No Power of Choice:** Habitual. Conditioned. Controls operations of the body. Has persistent or ingrained behaviors. Likes the familiar and doesn't like to change.
Decision Maker: Able to meet challenges and opportunities. Has goal setting ability and likes to judge results. Is open to trying new things. Takes action.	**Is Programmable:** Has ability to accept a new set of associations or learn a new course of direction. Can be taught new habits.
Transitional: Moves from one state of mind to another. Past and Future: looks for new ways to do things based upon past experiences and future goals.	**Timeless:** Everything is in present time, not restricted to a particular time or date. More fluid in its nature.
Limited Processing Capacity: The prefrontal cortex can process and manage an average of 40 nerve pulses per second. Working-memory, which is the idea of holding info (like a phone number) while doing something else (like dialing).	**Expanded Processing Capacity:** The rest of the brain processes and manages an average of 40 million nerve pulses per second. Stores your past experiences, values, ideas, beliefs, attitudes, information, trauma, and frustrations.

Comparing 40 nerve pulses of the conscious mind to 40 million nerve pulses of the subconscious, there is a million to 1 ratio between the speed of the conscious mind and the subconscious. In other words, the subconscious mind processes information a million times faster. That difference alone should be enough to convince you that learning to access, communicate with, and use the power of your subconscious for unlocking your potential and living the life of your dreams is a critical skill to develop.

We do not know exactly how the brain processes information. Almost all of this neural data processing goes on outside the level of awareness—at the subconscious level of the mind. Our conscious mind can have all these wonderful plans for a future filled with adventure, happiness, love, and prosperity. Yet, while we are focusing our thoughts on these visions of happiness, guess who is directing the outcome? Your subconscious mind—exactly the way it was programmed.

I'll share an example with you. Imagine the conscious mind like a handcar on a railroad, the railroad of life. You're looking down the track toward the goal—your hands on the lever, pumping your arms up and down real hard to get there. That is like your conscious mind at work. Compare the subconscious mind to a locomotive engine coupled to the handcar. The locomotive is a million times stronger, but which way is the engine pointed? Is it pointed in the same direction as your goal, or is it pushing you in the opposite direction, defeating your best efforts? How this energy is directed makes a huge difference in the success, or lack thereof, when attempting to accomplish a goal.

The odds are clearly stacked against your conscious mind achieving its goal without the cooperation of your subconscious, primarily because ingrained subconscious conditioning takes over the moment your conscious mind is not paying attention. Willpower won't get you there either. It may get you a little further, but when it comes up against any oppositional programs in the powerhouse of your subconscious, a frustrating battle will take place within. Willpower turns into won't-power. Just ask anyone who has tried to lose weight or stop an addiction.

It's not that your subconscious is intentionally keeping you from being happy or achieving your goals. It is simply running old patterns on autopilot out of ignorance. However, the good news is that you are soon going to learn how to communicate with your subconscious. When both your conscious and subconscious agree in 'unified consciousness,' you will become more successful in accomplishing your goals and creating the reality you want. Your conscious mind will become the pilot setting the direction, and your redirected subconscious mind will be the autopilot working in the background to help you go where you want to go.

You Can't Fix Problems

As Albert Einstein said, "Problems cannot be solved with the same mind-set that created them." If we continue to focus on the problem in an attempt to resolve it, our mind continues to use the same neural pathways that created the problem in the first place. When we focus on the outcome and experience that we would like to have instead, our higher-consciousness and creative process use different neural pathways. Therefore, each time life-enhancing beliefs and thought patterns are programmed into us, they help take us to a higher perspective of mind by focusing on something of greater value than the problem, challenge, or issue itself. We are then transported out of the old mind-set into an expanded one that supports us in creating and living a better outcome.

Willpower and the Infamous Affirmation Fizzle

Some ways of communicating with our subconscious mind are less effective than others. Many individuals are led to believe that saying affirmations over and over again is a way to communicate with, or harness the power of, the subconscious. Unfortunately, this is an inefficient method—at best, it only works about 20 percent of the time. Do you know the main reason affirmations and willpower don't work effectively? It is because they are too abstract. There is simply not enough understanding for the subconscious mind to comprehend. It won't matter *how passionately* or how *diligently* they are repeated if your subconscious doesn't understand what you are talking about.

- *"I am rich beyond my wildest dreams."* 'Rich' is something your conscious mind understands, and it means something different to everyone. What does it mean to you? What are your 'wildest' dreams? Be specific and descriptive.

- *"Every day, and in every way, I am getting better and better."* Better? Better than what? In every way? What way is that? What does it mean to you?

- *"I am healthy, wealthy, and wise."* What is healthy to you? What does it mean? What is wealthy to you? Wise in what way?

Another reason affirmations don't always work is because you are speaking to the conscious mind rather than the subconscious, and there are not enough life-enhancing, positive beliefs in the subconscious to support what a person is affirming. It is like preaching to the choir. In other words, you are already speaking to the part of your mind—your conscious mind—that is in agreement with you *and wants* to make the changes. On the other hand, if the subconscious has more detrimental beliefs stored in its programming than positive beliefs (because the remaining 80 percent has won), it creates an internal battle, and you will often end up becoming easily discouraged.

And many affirmations fail us simply because they are stated in a negative way.

- *"There are no obstacles too great for me."* This is placed in the negative. The subconscious mind can't picture "no obstacles," so it sidesteps the 'no' and registers, *"There are obstacles too great for me."* (The better phrase would have been, *"I push all obstacles aside,"* which is an image the subconscious can understand.)

Our conscious mind easily comprehends these abstract ideas and what they mean to us.

Over 20 years ago, I bought a home-study course for programming affirmations into my subconscious mind. Repetition was their key method, and it boiled down to this: If I said my affirmation 1,000 times a day, consistently for 40 days, my subconscious mind would be programmed. Well, it didn't work. And, I've since discovered why. Like many people, I wasn't actually communicating with my subconscious mind. I was trying to coerce it with a language it didn't understand. The sensory-based subconscious is geared more toward understanding literal and specific concepts, so unless you get more detailed and capture its attention, it doesn't matter *how passionately* or how *many times* an affirmation is repeated, your subconscious mind just tunes you out and waits until there is something it can understand. And, all the while, your subconscious will fill in the gaps with bits and pieces of programs that are already running.

Abstract concepts are just jumbled language to your subconscious. You may know what you mean consciously, but abstraction can take on different meanings to different people at different times, such as, peace, justice, or love. Let's take love as an example: how I convey the meaning of love is different when I speak of the love I have for my significant other versus my love for my child or dog. My love of a magnificent view in nature is different than my love of a good dark chocolate.

Belief System Battle

In addition to a language barrier, I discovered that saying daily affirmations over and over without first learning how to speak the language of the subconscious mind often invokes the 'Belief System Battle,' causing a rebellion inside your head. The Belief System Battle is a strange phenomenon but familiar once understood. Whenever we begin to reshape our lives, and we haven't yet enlisted the support of our subconscious mind, we set up the possibility of creating conflict between our conscious and subconscious minds. Putting ideas into our conscious mind that differ from our subconscious belief systems can cause quite a clash, and our subconscious beliefs will fight for their very survival.

Some of the physical ways that our old belief systems protect themselves when we attempt to make changes include: unexplained headaches, uncharacteristic physical ailments, mood swings, gloominess, melancholy, or tiredness that causes you to fall asleep at inappropriate or inconvenient times. All of these defense mechanisms are designed to take your conscious mind away, to distract your energy, diverting it into something else that needs your attention in the moment. Have you ever experienced something like this? You put your mind to accomplishing something, then all of a sudden, you have other commitments or tasks that come up that *just have to get done first*. Or, suddenly you develop relationship or financial problems, creating the potential to become angry. We need to be aware that these sudden flare-ups could very well be the result of an energetic disturbance pattern present in the subconscious mind that MUST defend its programmed beliefs.

Recognizing Conflict

What is the best way to deal with this rebellion? First, recognize that this battle between the conscious and subconscious mind is part of the process—there is a difference of opinion going on internally. Now that you are aware that there is an internal conflict, you can take action to resolve it. Proper communication will enable you to reclaim your empowerment at the subconscious level by aligning with the thought-patterns and the beliefs that you desire to have in your life. Once your subconscious has a new set of programmed beliefs, it is now obliged to defend them. Your goal is to make your subconscious your best friend.

Since the subconscious mind thinks literally, rather than abstractly, and most affirmations are stated in an abstract way that your conscious mind understands, the BEST use for affirmations is AFTER you have rewritten your subconscious thought patterns and enlisted its 40-million-bit processing support. Because now they can:

- Assist you in building stronger neural pathways in your brain—retraining your way of thinking simply by revisiting them.

- Help to keep you consciously motivated and focused on your goal.

- Support you by resonating positive energy and vibrating with your goal, which strengthens the pattern within the Field because of the feelings and emotions the words create within you.

Without corresponding beliefs in your subconscious, or life-enhancing energetic patterns (similar to a blueprint) within your energy field to support the affirmation, the affirmation itself has no real power. In an effort to support this shift, the following tools are offered:

- The "Language of Creation," which not only speaks the language your subconscious mind can understand but also creates a life-enhancing blueprint within your energy field at the same time.

- The Chakra Belief Change Process, which allows you to program life-affirming beliefs into your subconscious mind while also infusing it into the energy field that surrounds you.

- Instructions on how to energize a life-enhancing pattern within your energy field to strengthen it, which quickens the manifesting of your goal in your life as well.

Two Most Powerful Languages of Creation: Visualization and Heart Coherent Emotion

We've been educated to use our mind, but we've not been educated on how to use our heart. The two most powerful languages of your subconscious mind are visualization and emotion. These are *vital keys* to creating an energetic pattern within the Field and to support your ability to manifest. They are part of the Language of Creation Process and create the frequency or wave of energy that transports the information into your system and into the environment that surrounds you. Auditory information is also considered to be a language of the subconscious mind, but because words themselves are abstract, it is not as powerful within the subconscious data system (as is evident with affirmations). Rather, auditory information *needs* the visual and emotional pieces to support it in order to have any real effect. For instance, unless you know the language spoken or written, the particular words you hear or read don't mean anything.

- Amor, sabiduría y verdad tendrían que ser compartidos con todos los seres. (Spanish)

- Liebe, Weisheit und Wahrheit sollten mit allen Lebewesen geteilt werden (German)

- L'amour, la sagesse et la vérité doivent être partagés par tous les êtres. (French)

- Ài, zhìhuì hé zhēnlǐ yào yóu suǒyǒu de rén gòngxiǎng. (Chinese)

- Lyubov', mudrost' i istina dolzhny byt' obshchimi dlya vsekh zhivykh sushchestv. (Russian)

- I agápi, i sofía kai i alítheia eínai na moirázetai me óla ta ónta. (Greek)

- Love, wisdom, and truth are to be shared with all beings. (English version of the above phrases.)

No matter what language you speak, when you see a cup, everyone on the planet knows it is a cup. No matter what language you speak, when you feel joy, everyone on the planet knows what joy feels like. The resonance of the frequency—the visual representation and the feelings of that information and energy—is what conveys the meaning behind the words, which is ultimately the language being communicated with the universe.

Think of your conscious mind as the navigator for creating your desired reality; your subconscious mind has a detailed road map with its huge resource databank and coordinates; and Heart-Coherence is your power source, the vehicle that will get you there.

With the Language of Creation Process, we have two very important tools to support us in living the life we want to create for ourselves.

1. We can take a general idea (or affirmation) that the conscious mind understands (such as, *"I am rich beyond my wildest dreams."*), and, using the Language of Creation Process, translate it and communicate it in the specific, literal, sensory-based language that the subconscious mind can understand and act upon. This is a vital step to the success of accomplishing conscious goals. This translation of any and all affirmations that speak to us can now support us at a deeper level than ever before. In addition, we can take a general idea for a goal (such as, *"I want to live a life filled with meaning and purpose."*) and use this process to become more specific and concrete about it with our conscious mind. Remember, if you can't get clear consciously on what these goals entail, how can you expect your subconscious mind to get clear and harness the power and resources that are available?

2. The second crucial tool relies on this truth: When we create anything in our life, we first have to have a 'pattern within the energy field.' When a pattern gets fully established—with enough energy for it to become dense enough to form matter—it then manifests into our current reality. Writing out and filling in the Language of Creation worksheet creates a resonance in the Field—a pattern in the Field—that, when energized sufficiently, becomes a reality. Everything in nature has a shape or form, and its vibrational structure comes into resonance with other like vibrational forms, which increases the possibility of manifestation.

The Language of Creation Process has an added benefit in that it can help us to create our own personalized, life-enhancing belief statements to aid our subconscious mind programming as well as create an energetic pattern in the Field. The beauty of this ability is that we can use the Language of Creation to improve most any area of our life. Essentially, what we are doing with this process is creating the mile-markers on a road map for our subconscious mind to follow, helping us to discern whether or not we are on the right path. Herodotus, a Greek historian, said, "The destiny of man is in his own soul." With this process, we become more involved with designing our own destiny and living a soul-filled life. I encourage you to share this process with every person you know, especially the young. The sooner they learn to communicate with their subconscious, the more empowered they will be, and the better their lives will become.

Step One: What You Want—The Importance of Phrasing

Expressing what you *DESIRE* works better than stating something you don't want. There is a tremendous difference between goals that are in alignment with your heart and goals that are based upon a sense of lack or scarcity. I'll share a story with you: There was a lady in one of my workshops who was in a wheelchair. I asked her what she wanted. She replied that she didn't want to be in her wheelchair.

I said: *"Okay, so you don't want to be in a wheelchair. What do you want?"*
She said that she didn't want walking to be painful.

I said: *"So, you don't want to be in a wheelchair, and you don't want walking to be painful. What do you want?"*

Well, at this point she was probably thinking I was a bit dim—after all, I kept asking her what she wanted, and she thought she was communicating that. The problem was, she had been telling me the whole time what she *didn't want*, focusing on the negative. Unfortunately, this is how many of us communicate in our everyday lives: "I don't like . . ."

- Traffic
- My boss
- How my clothes fit
- The rut I'm in
- Being frustrated all the time

This can be helpful information but not to the subconscious mind, which is responsible for helping us achieve what we *WANT*. If all we do is communicate negative statements, our subconscious can't be empowered to bring about what *we do want*.

Here's another way to think about the subconscious mind: Making negative statements is like going to the restaurant and telling the waiter that you don't want the pasta dish. The waiter then goes to the kitchen and tells the chef, *"Table 5 doesn't want the pasta dish."* Until you tell the waiter what you do want, you aren't going to be served. If your subconscious mind, with its million-to-one processor, cannot receive the core message of your desire, you are not going to get served a new reality.

Furthermore, our subconscious mind doesn't fully comprehend the word "don't." If we say, *"Don't think of a pink elephant,"* we immediately think 'pink elephant.' It's the mind's way of recognizing that it's supposed to think of something different.

With the Language of Creation, you are training your conscious mind to focus on, and communicating with your subconscious, what you <u>do</u> want. This enables you to create new blueprints or patterns within the Field to open up to new possibilities and to a new level of success in your life.

A Tip Before Completing this Process

Before creating your vision or goal, check to see if it is an overly inflated image of yourself, and, therefore, a concealed form of ego (such as wanting to become a movie star, a famous writer, or a wealthy entrepreneur). If these tendencies come naturally to you, then go for it. However, goals that are dynamic, rooted in an activity that you engage in and through which you are connected to your heart, are deeply fulfilling—much more so than ego-based identities. Instead of seeing yourself as a famous actor, you could see yourself inspiring countless people with your work and enriching their lives. Feel how that activity enriches or deepens not only your life but also countless others. All things can be taken in steps, building up to grander and grander visions for yourself. You may eventually become a movie star, a famous writer, or a wealthy entrepreneur, but you'll rarely get there if you start out with something that is an extreme or unrealistic stretch from where you are. Start out by creating success for yourself, then, when your subconscious experiences a sense of accomplishment, rather than continual defeat, it can more easily and readily manifest more meaningful and empowering life-fulfilling goals for you. But first, you want to build upon its success with steps it can accomplish.

The Secret Language of Creation

The Secret Language of Creation is about co-creating your reality. You begin by clearly describing what it is that you desire. Remember that your subconscious mind cannot distinguish between what is real and what is imagined because both concepts create internal emotions and chemistry tracking within the visual thought patterns.

Using paper and pencil or the downloadable Language of Creation worksheet from The Heart and Soul Academy (see Appendix II), write down what you want (your goal) and describe your end result.

Focus on one goal at a time. You can always come back and repeat this process again for each goal; however, by keeping it simple, you build your skillful use of this tool, as well as a solid foundation for future goals and life-changing experiences.

The Heart and Soul Academy's Secret Language of Creation   Date: _____

I now co-create my life's dream

Describe Your Dream: _____

"Your imagination is your preview of life's coming attractions." ~ Albert Einstein

...by Design:	...with Resonance:
Envision: This is your guidance system.	**Emotion:** This is your power system.
As best as you can, envision or imagine a mental movie where you are in it. Hold the vision of what is to come. What will you see in your life – that you don't see now – how will you know you've achieved your goal? Make this dynamic! Put yourself into the story. Imaginal cells begin to coalesce and guide your subconscious. Script your highlights: 1. 2. 3. 4.	Is this something you truly desire with all your heart? If so, close your eyes and allow yourself to really get into the emotion(s) of how you would feel when your goal manifests. Internal chemistry starts to track and align with your desire. Use emotion words that would best describe how you feel with your visualized goal. Write it down. (Are there any sensory experiences associated with this feeling – i.e. sounds, scents, body sensations, body temperature, colors, etc.?)

...and in Alignment: This is setting your course. It is your navigation system.

Life-Enhancing Statements: These are clear, concise statements (1st person, present tense, emotionally meaningful statements of fact) as if true right now. Brainstorm here and then choose the best one.

1.

2.

3.

Into Reality, for My Highest Wisdom and Benefit.

Embrace into Your Destiny: This is synchronizing your Energy Field with the universe.

Sacred Heart Alignment: Close your eyes.
- **Connect with Earth:** Envision the beauty of Mother Earth and feel the love and joy you have for nature. *Feel* this love in your heart and imagine sending a beam of love from your heart down deep into the earth. Notice that Mother Earth sends a return beam of nurturing love energy back to you. Breathe this energy up through your feet, draw it up your spinal column, and release this nourishing energy into the very center of your heart. Feel the flow of energy between you, the earth, and your heart.

- **Align with Spirit:** Envision the expanse of the heavens and the depths of space. Feel the awe, the wonder, and the love you have for the stars and all of creation. Imagine sending a beam of love from your heart up to your Soul Star and the heavens above. Immediately, your Soul Star sends a return beam of warm, golden energy of expanded consciousness to you. Breathe this expanded consciousness down through the top of your head and release this radiant energy into the very center of your heart. Feel the flow of energy between your soul star and your heart.

- **Center within Heart:** Feel both these energies flowing into your heart simultaneously – nourishing earth energy up your spine and expanded consciousness down through your head – swirling these shimmering energies into the center of your heart.

- **Remember a time when you felt deep, nurturing love and feel that love now.** Then, continue breathing as if through your heart and open to feelings of deep love, inner peace, harmony, and joy.

- **Recall your Life-Enhancing Statement now.** Imagine a miniature hologram of your desired goal and breathe with this image in your heart. Allow your heart's intelligence and wisdom to communicate and synchronize with the living essence of the Field for your highest wisdom and benefit.

Participate: Intend to take the action needed to bring this manifestation into reality. Determine the first step you need to take now.

Additional Life-Enhancing Statements: Create additional Life-Enhancing Statements to further support the alignment and resonance in creating your life's dream.

1.

2.

3.

4.

5.

Step Two: Envisioning Is Your Guidance System

Next, you are going to envision, which activates your guidance system. Visualization is a primary language of your subconscious mind and for manifesting. In your mind's eye, envision or imagine yourself in either a photograph or a mental movie. Hold the vision of what is to come. Be as specific or descriptive as you can. What will you see in your life that you don't see now? How will you know you've achieved your goal? Make this dynamic. Put yourself into the story. Imaginal cells begin to resonate and coalesce with the vision you are holding—they help guide your subconscious mind toward the life you desire to create. Imaginal cells lie dormant inside as little seeds of pure potential; they are activated and nurtured by our heart coherent consciousness that releases internal chemistry and opens us up to beautiful worlds of possibilities and our own transformations.

Write Out Your Highlights

Use literal, sensory based language that your subconscious mind understands. Your conscious mind understands the ideas of "seeing yourself content"—or living a life of "adventure," or one filled with "meaning and purpose"—but your subconscious mind does not understand what 'feeling content' looks like, nor adventure, meaning, or purpose. Use descriptive words when talking about abstract ideas.

What will you see in your life that you don't currently see, which will let you know you have achieved your goal?

Example: "To Own My Own Home"

If this is your goal, describe your home. How big is it? How will you be living in it? What's it like? Make it meaningful to you. Make this dynamic.

If the descriptions are too general, the results will be disappointing. Even such descriptions below won't help much:

- A four-bedroom "house"
- In a "nice" neighborhood
- Near a "good" school
- With a "small" yard

Generalizations are not meaningful enough to motivate action. If you cannot consciously get excited about it, how can you possibly expect your emotionally-driven subconscious mind to get motivated by it? Think of explaining it to a six-year-old child. Is it exciting? If so, your subconscious will be curious. If the description is too neutral, your subconscious won't put much effort forward. It will just keep sifting through those 280 quintillion bits of information, focusing on and being activated by the ones with the greater emotional or energetic charge—the ones with the most internal and external stimuli.

Come up with a list of three or four really good visuals that will help you see what life will be like when you have achieved your goal. List as many as you are motivated to write, but it does not have to be a long list. It just needs to give your subconscious a clear idea of what the goal is and what it looks like. See yourself in the picture—imagine someone filming a short video with you in it that shows everyone watching that you've accomplished your goal.

Some good descriptive examples might be:

- I see myself living in a home with an open floorplan for entertaining, three bedrooms, and another room for an office. It has beautiful wood floors and vaulted ceilings.

- I see us celebrating birthdays and holidays with decorations and friends and family gathered around the table. We're laughing and sharing good food. I look outside the window to see my grandchildren drawing chalk art on the cement patio.

- I see myself sitting beside the fire with a cup of tea in hand and watching the snow fall outside. I see myself snuggled on the couch with my love, watching a movie, and eating popcorn.

- When I come home and walk through the door, my dogs greet me, wagging their tails.

- I can see myself holding the title to the home in my name. The keys are hanging on a wall hook. My car is parked in the garage.

Turn the descriptions into life-enhancing statements that resonate with your heart and soul. Make them meaningful and dynamic . . . and put yourself in the picture!

Example: "To Find the Love of My Life"

Envision specific things you would be doing that prove you have found him or her. When envisioning 'the love of your life,' be sure to put the other person in the picture with you, even though you don't know who it is yet. Try envisioning the following:

- Walking hand-in-hand on the beach, watching the waves roll in.

- Laughing over a story told during your Italian dinner at Maggiano's, watching the sunset, and toasting to your love.

- Getting married and seeing yourself at your wedding or toasting to your 10th anniversary with a glass of champagne.

Describe your lives together: Children, grandchildren, travels, your home, and your pets—pick things that show you sharing your life with another person.

Example: "To Improve My Health"

Describe what it looks like to be trim and fit or lean and healthy. Describe what you would see in your life when your health improves as well as things you might be able to do that are off limits now. Examples could be:

- I see myself buying a smaller pair of jeans. I love the style and fit. They are so easy to zip up.

- I see myself enjoying eating lean protein, fruits, and vegetables instead of processed foods.

- I have more energy and enthusiasm to play with my children, grand-children, or dogs.

- I like how I move gracefully on the dance floor and how I look when I catch a glimpse of myself in the mirror.

- I enjoy the fresh air when taking our dogs for a walk, and we're walking three miles most days.

This is more dynamic and has more energy for change than saying, *"I don't like how my jeans fit,"* or, *"I need to lose weight."*

It's like painting a picture with the colors of our lives. In a world where too many individuals are not living the life they've dreamed of, we need to rewrite our vision of what our lives can be like and create potential, so we can live in greater joy, freedom, health, and creative expression.

Envisioning your goal, your end result—this is your guidance system.

Step Three: Emotion Is Your Power Source

How you feel is the other important language of your subconscious mind and the biochemistry it creates, so make this part juicy and enticing! Your subconscious mind either naturally pulls away from things when in protection mode, or it moves toward something when in a state of happiness and well-being. For your subconscious, this should be something it wants to move toward and what feels like the best feeling aspect if you were to accomplish this goal.

Ask yourself this: "Is your goal something you truly desire with all your heart?" If so, take some time and close your eyes. Allow yourself to really feel the emotion(s) you would experience when your goal manifests. How would you feel when you accomplished your goal? Write it down. Internal chemistry starts to track and align your desire with your emotions. Next, it starts to communicate with the living, pulsating essence that is the Source Field.

Use emotion words that best describe how you feel with your envisioned goal. Your job here is to feel really good. If you feel enthusiastic, then write it down. Whether it is joyful, accomplished, on-top-of-the-world, wearing a great big smile on your heart, or deep contentment, make it juicy and write it down.

Step Four: Additional Layers of Subconscious Communication

While visuals and emotions are the two most important languages of your subconscious mind, *and* for communicating with the living Field that surrounds us, other layers of communication that fill in the thought-form pattern you are creating include sound, scent, taste, and even color.

Take a moment to close your eyes and allow yourself to really get into feeling the emotions while you are envisioning your dream goal. Then, write down any additional sensory experiences you notice associated with how you are feeling. When you describe or clarify your feelings with greater detail, it turns your awareness inward and helps you tune in to your subconscious.

- Do you notice any sounds? Waves crashing on the beach? Children laughing in the background?
- Do you have a feeling like butterflies in the stomach, tingling, or goosebumps?

- Do you feel warm or cool?

- Do you see any colors? Write those things down.

Do you say anything to yourself, or do you hear someone saying something to you when you've accomplished your goal? If there is something, then write those things down. But keep it simple. The idea is to fill in your thought-form pattern and create juicy, feel good feelings of heart coherency.

- For example, *"Yes, I did it!" "Congratulations!" "Way to go!" "I love this job!" "I love my home!"*

Finding Your Heart Coherency

I guided one lady through the entire process where she described the beautiful three-bedroom home of her dreams in Texas. When I asked her to close her eyes and get in touch with her feelings, she said she felt lousy, and that she hated Texas. She said she grew up there and complained that it was too hot, with nothing but miles and miles of flat land. She said she loved the Puget Sound area of Washington. I asked her why she had written Texas. She said it was because she could afford a three-bedroom home in Texas but not in Washington.

She was letting her logical mind interfere with her heart. With her emotions, her body-mind energy field could not create internal chemistry to pull her toward her dreams but, instead, drew her away from her ideal home. She wasn't able to create any heart coherency to communicate with the essence of the Source Field to support her in drawing her to her desired goal. When she took the time to fill in the Language of Creation worksheet, she was able to focus and get really clear that what she truly wanted was to manifest a three-bedroom home in the Puget Sound area of Washington, which she eventually did.

Step Five: Create Your Life-Enhancing Belief Statement

This is a clear, concise (emotionally juicy) life-enhancing statement that is in the first person, as if it were true right now. It can be very similar to your goal statement. It could even be the same statement depending upon how it was worded, or it can be totally different. The key is to make it:

- Personal and in the present tense. Because your subconscious mind is timeless and doesn't distinguish between what is real and what is imagined, everything is here-and-now to your subconscious.

- Positive. Make it a positive expression of what you want, as if it were true in your life, rather than what you are trying to eliminate or avoid.

- Simple and concise. This makes it easy and uncomplicated and sums everything up. Your subconscious mind will remember it all. If we were to look up the description of what your life-enhancing, desired goal statement means in your personal dictionary, we'd see that it encompasses everything you wrote out, so keep it simple.

- Passionate and emotional. Because an emotionally charged, meaningful thought-form:

  o Gets the attention of your subconscious mind.

  o Generates positive chemistry in the body—strengthening the neural pathways.

  o Communicates (via heart energy) with the living essence of the Field that surrounds you.

  o Energizes and strengthens the pattern in the Field, bringing you closer to actualizing your goal.

If your goal was, *"I want to own my own home,"* drop the word 'want' to transform this into a life-enhancing belief statement because wanting something implies that you don't have it already. Your statement needs to be a statement of what *will* be true. Remember, once the subconscious mind accepts something as true, it continues to work toward the goal until it accomplishes it. And your goal is not to keep 'wanting' something.

You could say something along the lines of, *"I now own my own home,"* but that might not be emotionally charged enough. A better option would be, *"I now live in the home of my dreams."* Or, *"I love my beautiful home. It nurtures my soul."*

Other possible statements from the examples we used include, *"I now have a hot steamy love affair that will last a lifetime!" "I enjoy a nurturing relationship with the love of my life." Or, "I look great. I feel great. I love my healthy weight!"*

Adding Back the Affirmation

At this point, if you want to use a particular affirmation that you like, even if it is abstract, once you have defined it for your subconscious mind in the language it understands, it will become a useful and effective affirmation, creating a pattern in the Field for building your experience of reality. Understand, you can think positive thoughts or say affirmations all day long, but if they are too abstract or undefined, then it won't matter how many times or how emphatically you repeat them. There just isn't anything supporting their manifestation into reality.

The language of creation is not just about communicating with your subconscious mind in the sensory-based language it understands. It is also about heart-energy and the language of human emotion.

Step Six: Embrace Your Life-Enhancing Belief

The embrace step in this process is where you bring your life-enhancing belief into the energy field of you. It begins the process of communication, alignment, and synchronization of your energy field with the living essence of the universe to support it in becoming your reality.

It begins with the Sacred Heart Alignment. This helps create a heart-centered space that is aligned with your higher wisdom.

- Begin by closing your eyes.
- **Connect with Earth:** Envision the beauty of Mother Earth and feel the love and joy you have for nature. Feel this love in your heart and imagine sending a beam of love from your heart deep into the earth. Notice that Mother Earth sends a return beam of nurturing love energy back to you. Breathe this energy up through your feet, draw it up your spinal column, and release it into the very center of your heart. Feel the flow of energy between you, the earth, and your heart.
- **Align with Spirit:** Envision the expanse of the heavens and the depths of space. Feel the awe, the wonder, and the love you have for the stars

and all of creation. Imagine sending a beam of love from your heart up to your soul star and the heavens above. Immediately, your soul star sends a return beam of warm, golden energy of expanded consciousness to you. Breathe it down through the top of your head and release this radiant energy into the very center of your heart. Feel the flow of energy between your soul star and your heart.

- **Center within Heart:** Feel both of these energies flowing into your heart simultaneously, nourishing earth energy up your spine and expanded consciousness down through your head, swirling these shimmering energies into the center of your heart.

- With awareness in your heart area, remember a time when you felt deep, nurturing love and *feel* that love now. Breathe as if through the center of your heart. Breathing like this creates heart coherency, and this is a secret of greater synchronicity and flow in life.

- Relax. Open to feelings of deep love, inner peace, harmony, or joy.

- Recall your life-enhancing statement now. [*Pause.*]

- Imagine holding a miniature hologram of your desired goal in your heart's sacred space. Breathe with this image in your heart.

- Allow your heart's intelligence and wisdom to communicate with the living, pulsating essence of the Field for your highest wisdom and benefit.

- Next, determine if there is an action step you need to take. If something comes to mind, an idea, an image, or something to do, then set the intention to take the action needed to bring your manifestation into being.

- When you are ready, open your eyes and write down the action step you need to take and commit to doing it.

Congratulations!

With the Language of Creation Process, you have created a *very good* personalized blueprint in your energy field—a start of something wonderful to be co-created with spirit. While you have been helping your subconscious better understand what it is that you desire, let's find out if you have also enlisted its full support.

Discover If Your Subconscious Supports You

How do you know if you have also made a difference inside yourself? How do you know if your subconscious mind and energy field supports you in this goal? About half the time, once your subconscious mind understands what your goal is, it can easily assist you with this endeavor. The other half of the time your subconscious just doesn't have the programming in place to fully support you. This means it will need to be re-patterned in order for it to more fully support you in reaching your goal. You will want to verify if a subconscious change has been made with a simple energy test of your life-enhancing belief statement.

However the energy test turns out, whether your subconscious mind supports you at this moment in time or not, it is good to know. Because, then, at least you will know if you need to take any additional steps to program your subconscious mind for its support of your goal. Had I known how to do this back in the early days when I was doing hypnosis, I would have been better able to make necessary adjustments along the way for myself and others to benefit from subconscious programming. It would have been easier to know what parts of the guided process had taken hold and which ones needed adjustments.

Access Your Inner Wisdom

Using the protocol from Chapter 3, begin with the energy tests for accessing your inner wisdom, so that you know you are receiving reliable feedback. Say each with conviction.

Women	Men
"I am a woman."	"I am a man."
"I am a man."	"I am a woman."
Show me a YES.	Show me a YES.
Show me a NO.	Show me a NO.

- When you have received a YES response to your gender and 'show me a YES,' and a NO response to the opposite gender and 'show me a NO,' then proceed to test your life-enhancing belief statement.

- If your energy tests responded with a YES to everything, then your body-mind energy system is over-energized. You will need to de-stress with a calming practice from Chapter 3 then re-test.

- If your energy tests responded with a NO to everything, then you are dehydrated to the point where your internal electrical impulses are too weak to detect with energy testing at this time. Drink enough water to boost your electrical conductivity for clear feedback from your energy tests then proceed to the next step.

Energy Test: (Your Life-Enhancing Belief Statement here.)

If you received a YES response to energy testing your life-enhancing belief statement, it means your subconscious mind understands and can easily support you with achieving this goal.

If you received a NO response, it means it is not part of your subconscious programming. Therefore, with its million-to-one processor, each time you consciously attempt to accomplish your goal, your subconscious powerhouse would be working against you. It does not believe this statement is true for it at this time, which, again, is a good thing to know because now you know you need to take the next step in order to change this programming.

How to Program a Subconscious Belief

Inspired by the chakras and their ability to affect different types and different levels of consciousness, as well as their ability to affect different aspects of our psychology (and wanting to create a more effective change in the neuronal cells spread throughout our entire body, not just those found in the brain), led to creating a profound and highly effective process called the Chakra Belief Change Process. The beautiful thing about this process is that it not only harnesses the power of heart coherency, it is also communicating your goal with the living essence of the Source Field while it re-patterns your subconscious.

CHAKRA BELIEF CHANGE PROCESS

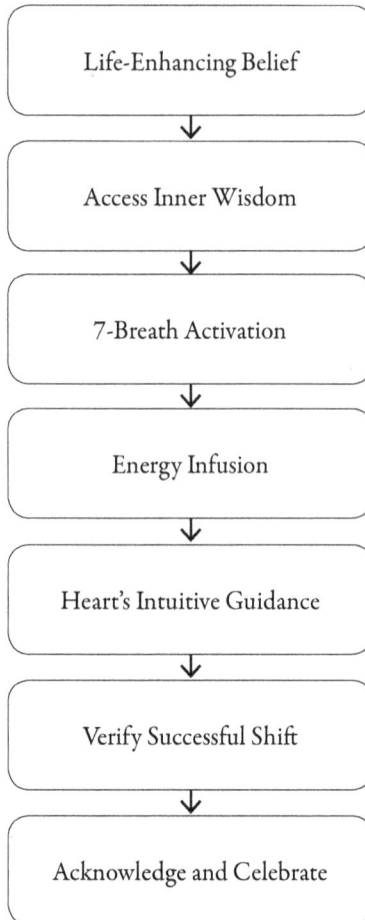

Life-Enhancing Belief

↓

Access Inner Wisdom

↓

7-Breath Activation

↓

Energy Infusion

↓

Heart's Intuitive Guidance

↓

Verify Successful Shift

↓

Acknowledge and Celebrate

Since you have your life-enhancing belief statement and have accessed inner wisdom, the next energy test you do if you have received a NO response is to energy test: *"It is in the highest wisdom and benefit to change this belief now."* We energy test this statement for the simple reason that your higher-self has a greater perspective and overview of what is in your best interest and how to guide you to your greatest joy, opportunities, purpose, and expression of you in this life.

If YES to this energy test, then proceed with the rest of the change process. If NO, then . . .

1. The wording needs to change slightly in order to be more in alignment with what is in your highest wisdom and benefit.

2. Your subconscious still does not fully understand what the belief statement means, and most often needs greater clarity with the vision of your goal, greater emotional connection, or some of the missing blanks filled in.

3. There may be another more suitable time to make this shift, and now is not the right time. Try again later.

When you have received a YES response that it is in your highest wisdom and benefit, then proceed to the next step with the shift process.

7-Breath Activation

This step activates heart-energy, moves it through your higher consciousness, and brings that energy into your power center.

- For 7 breaths: As you inhale, visualize beautiful heart energy flowing out from the back of your heart and up over the top of your head through your expanded consciousness. Then, as you exhale, imagine the shimmering heart energy flowing down the front of your body and into your second chakra, a center of power.

- Next, repeat your life-enhancing belief statement; for example, *"I am healthy and happy."*

- Envision or imagine the successful outcome in your mind's eye as if your belief is true for you now. Notice if there is any resistance or a feeling of constriction within. If there is, where in your body do you notice it the most? Make a mental note of this.

Energy Infusion

Channeling energy is one of the most effective ways to infuse your intention into your energy field as information is carried on the waves of energy and frequency. Energy flows where you put your attention. It is a life-force you allow to flow through you with your intention.

Starting the flow of energy is simply a matter of intending to do so. This focused flow of energy is not restricted by clothing, jewelry, watches, belts, or anything else. It easily flows where it is directed, and it flows to where it is most needed. Just allow and trust.

Your intention is to embrace your life-enhancing belief into your personal energy field and reality, accelerating the effects by infusing it with life-force energy.

- Close your eyes and start the flow of life-force energy.
- Begin spiraling or beaming energy into your 1st chakra, your root chakra.
- While flowing energy into your chakra, state your life-enhancing belief out loud; for example, "*I am healthy and happy.*"
- Follow with the phrase, "*I know it is true,*" until you notice a shift of some kind.

A shift can be any subtle, sensory-based signal that your subconscious sends you that tells you a change has taken place. It can be anything from feeling your muscles starting to relax, a sense of calm coming over you, maybe you see bubbles or a burst of color while your eyes are closed, or hear a shift of a tone in your ears. Each time you experience a shift, it could be the same way or different—it just depends on where the interference or restricting pattern in your energy field from past experiences had been stored in your body-mind energy system. In other words, if your limiting thought pattern from the past had been wired into your system while it was also linked to your sense of sound, smell, feeling, or taste, you might also experience your shift with subtle signals from one of these areas. The secret to this effective shift process is that it affects each of your body's unique energetic processing systems and configures the changes through your chakras. With energy channeling, it doesn't take long for a shift to happen. [Note: At first, if you are not sure you had a shift and find you're second guessing yourself, continue for a few moments more then proceed with the shift process. With time, you'll become more aware of these subtle signals. Rest assured that the energy test at the end of the process will verify for your conscious mind if the change has been made or not.]

- When you have sensed a subtle shift of some kind, move to your 2nd chakra. Spiral the energy through your fingertips in a clockwise motion, or beam it into your chakra. While continuing the flow of energy, state your life-enhancing belief out loud, followed by, "*I know it is true,*" at least three times or until you notice a shift.

- You continue upwards repeating this with each of your seven major chakras.

- When you have finished with your 7th chakra, your crown chakra, then once again envision or imagine the successful outcome in your mind. Notice an increased calm, peaceful feeling.

- Take a moment and feel the gratitude in your heart for this new shift in your subconscious programming, for coming into greater alignment with your essential nature and with your wholeness.

Ask Your Inner Wisdom

While still in this heart coherent state of being, ask your inner wisdom if there is another step for you to take. If nothing comes to mind, then simply enjoy the peace for a moment that comes when internal programs have aligned in greater harmony for your well-being. Everything flows more easily and effortlessly when you are vibrating with your higher emotions.

Verify Successful Shift

Once again, energy test your life-enhancing belief statement. This verifies that the successful shift has occurred. It should now be energy testing YES and confirm for your conscious mind, which likes to judge results, that the subconscious and your entire energy field is now supporting this reality.

Congratulations!

You have just created a life-enhancing shift for yourself and successfully programmed a new pattern into your body-mind energy field. Celebrate your win with a success gesture—the 'fist pump' is a great one to use. Curl your fist into a ball, then, with enthusiasm, pull your elbow down and slightly back, and say, *"Yes!"* This energetic motion is like a "score for the home team"—which is you. It not only signals your subconscious that you appreciate its participation with the successful completion of this change process, but also acts as an energetic anchor for this new pattern. It is like putting an exclamation point at the end of a sentence.

Little Known Secret Revealed

Life-enhancing beliefs support your positive outlook and your conscious evolution. They support you having the necessary programs by broadening the parameters of possibilities you have before you to create the life you dream of. They support your joy and emotional and mental well-being and also do a tremendous amount of good for your life experiences. Every time you make a change, you move into greater empowerment, and then everything is different for you as your horizons expand. However, the little known secret is, it is not *just* the life-enhancing beliefs that manifest the life you desire. This is where so many of the self-help, personal growth, belief change, Law of Attraction, and success seminars and methods ultimately fail in assisting your manifestation. Creating a pattern within the Field, *and* energizing your pattern with the best, appreciative, heart-based, feel-good emotions you can possibly feel, *is the secret to manifesting*. Your participation is where you focus and invest your energy—it is how you experience results. What you focus your attention on grows and expands. Your participation communicates with the living, conscious essence of the energetic field that surrounds you. These energetic patterns resonate, magnetize, and form the world around you. Programming or re-patterning your subconscious mind greatly supports you in your manifesting efforts. It makes a positive difference in how you experience your life, and this is their greatest benefit. Each time you program another life-enhancing belief into your body-mind energy field you are strengthening the pattern you have created there.

Henry David Thoreau said, "As a single footstep will not make a path on the earth, so a single thought will not make a pathway in the mind. To make a deep physical path, we walk again and again. To make a deep mental path, we must think over and over the kind of thoughts we wish to dominate our lives."

Learning how to program the subconscious with a new pattern greatly lightens the burden of having to "think over and over again the kinds of thoughts we wish to dominate our lives" in order "to make a deep mental path." While I firmly believe in the *significant benefits* of programming our subconscious mind, and the world of difference it makes in our lives, my 32+ years of experience working with the subconscious has also shown me that active participation (i.e. investing your energy on your goal) helps support and strengthen not only the pathways in the mind, making them the more dominant pathways, but also builds and strengthens the pattern in the energetic field until it becomes manifested and you experience results.

"Today I want you to ask yourself this one question. Why not you?
Why not you to do something for work that you love?
Why not you to have a healthy body?
Why not you to be, have, or do anything you have ever dreamed?
We are so quick to think others are deserving over ourselves.
The truth is that we are all deserving, so why not you?"
~ Jillian Michaels

See Appendix II for instructions about how to download 2 Minds in 1 Brain, the Language of Creation form, and the Chakra Belief Change Process at: www.theHeartAndSoulAcademy.org/resource-page/

CHAPTER 7

Beyond Programming Beliefs

---

*"Destiny is not a matter of chance; but a matter of choice.
It is not a thing to be waited for; it is a thing to be achieved."*
~ *William Jennings Bryan*

Importance of Participation

The universe requires your participation and manifesting does, too. There is a relationship between you and your goals, wants, desires, and dreams. Relationships also exist between you and other individuals, the environment, the world, and the universe. Energy and matter are also connected—it is the bridge between the visible and the invisible. Everything is about relationships.

Think of yourself and the universe as a partnership where you are working together. Participation in one form or another is required on your behalf, in addition to the communication, if you desire to manifest *anything*. Sometimes it requires being proactive and taking steps toward your goal, such as making phone calls, gaining skills, and putting what you know into action.

If you wish to learn a new skill like flying, even if you have programmed your subconscious mind by saying, *"I am now a licensed pilot,"* you will still need to take the time and go through the classes and learn how to fly with precision and safety before you will be allowed to fly on your own. If you wish to improve your health, in addition to life-enhancing beliefs programmed into your subconscious, you will still need to prepare nutritious meals, drink water, exercise, and get adequate rest.

Energizing the Pattern

Often, for many of your manifestations, your participation might very well take the form of what I call, "energizing the pattern." Remember, you created a pattern, a blueprint in the Field during your Language of Creation Process. When you energize the pattern, you are building and strengthening the energy field around you until it becomes manifest. It is the flow of energy coming into your body and energy field that powers your health, your life experiences, and your state of consciousness. While learning how to fly took time, and you could see progress with each new skill, some manifestations you need to do over a period of time, and you cannot always see the progress being made until it finally arrives in reality. Such as a synchronistic event that leads you to find the love of your life, your dream home, your dream job, or making a connection with someone that has the information you were seeking. It is as if your destination is just off your radar screen—you can't see it yet, but you *are* getting closer and closer. You can connect with anything to which you can tune your vibration and resonate with.

Understand that our reality is condensed light and energy. Once energy reaches a certain threshold where the molecules vibrate in unison, they become more solidified. As this light and energy become more and more condensed, they eventually become solidified enough that we can begin to see, feel, and experience them in our third-dimensional reality.

Boost Your Success

You energize the pattern you created by channeling heart coherent life-force energies into it. Imagine holding your goal in the palm of your hand. You could imagine that you are holding a miniature hologram of your goal if you like. Whether it is the love of your life, your beautiful home, your dream job, radiant health, or an empowered, self-assured you, it is the intention that is important.

Internal chemistry and imaginal cells, which lie dormant within our heart and soul, are like seeds of pure potential and start to track your intention. They are activated and nurtured by our heart coherent consciousness that releases internal chemistry, which then opens us up to beautiful worlds of possibilities and our own transformations.

Begin with the Sacred Heart Alignment. Then, with your intention, simply start the flow of life-force energy, allowing it to flow from your heart, through your arms, and down into the image of the goal you are holding in the palm of your hands. I like to get into a space of feeling really good, appreciative feelings, and I imagine that I am sending a beam of shimmering energy to my goal. I get better results in life than most anyone I know—though, I do remember a time when this wasn't always the case.

How It Worked for Me

I did this when my husband and I wanted to buy a specific piece of land in Ashland to build our home. We found a location we absolutely fell in love with, but it seemed out of our price range, and we hadn't looked for funding or even started the process of finding a lender. I had picked up a rock and a small pine cone to symbolize the property, plus I had taken pictures to help me visualize. I would hold the rock or pinecone in my hands to help me connect with the land, though many times I would just imagine I was holding a small hologram of the property in my hands and would send loving appreciation and life-force energies to it. Unbeknownst to us, there were five other people who were interested in the property and could easily qualify, but because we had this heart-felt, energetic communication going on between us and the property, everything lined up perfectly, and we became the new owners.

Greater Understanding of Appreciation

Appreciation has a wonderful, expansive energy signature all its own. It isn't just a feeling—it's one of the most natural and empowering forms of energy there is. Think about it: the term 'appreciation' is used in the financial world to describe an *increase of value* in an investment or asset portfolio. The energy of appreciation has the power to actually attract, increase value, and unlock the fullness of your life—for what you focus on expands.

Practice:
- When you express appreciation, you *really need to feel* it. It is the emotion—the energy in motion—that communicates with the living, pulsating essence of the Source Field. Practice feeling and expressing appreciation until it becomes as natural to you as breathing.

- Appreciate what you have. It tells your higher self that you are thankful for what you have already created in your life and that you still continue to receive value from those creations. Therefore, you are open for more to come your way because you will be appreciating that, too. Your higher self and the Source Field support you in achieving your goal.

- Express appreciation for specific creations first. Do this for what you want as if it were already true. Those feelings communicate with the Source Field, and it begins to coalesce, becomes more palpable, and shows you signs that let you know you are moving closer to your goal, creating your reality. And, since appreciation is a form of expansive energy, this energy is being applied to the pattern you have created, strengthening it, solidifying it, adding to it until it becomes a third-dimensional reality.

- You have an endless supply of the empowering energy of appreciation. Every time you express it, your *capacity to express and receive* appreciation expands, too. This means that the energy of appreciation that you have available to you is increasing, and it is adding value to your life in the form of all the wonderful things you'd like to enjoy as part of your life's experience.

Imagine It, Pattern It, and Energize It

Participation is all about playing with the Source Field. It is about us taking an active role to create the life we want to live. It means that after you have created the pattern in the Field, you continue to be involved until your goal has manifested.

Your job is to keep participating frequently, and with duration, until you reach your goal. It's like you and your spirit have decided to go into business together—you are partners in a 'Destiny Factory' that is just for you. You are both committed to this venture, and you each have specialized tasks that are required in order for your factory to run smoothly. The part of the factory you are working in with your tasks is the solid third-dimensional world that you can see, and the other part of the factory is in the spirit world, in invisible dimensions. You still have to do your share of the work (focusing on your goal with appreciative, joyful, happy, excited, enthusiastic, juicy, feel-good emotions while vibrating it out into the universe frequently and with duration), and your spirit is doing its share of the work (that you can't see; '*Taking care of the HOW*' and syncing up the matching vibrations in your environment and the world). Then, when that dream goal is nearing completion, you can see it more clearly in reality, but not until then because it is still in the invisible side of the factory just prior to its entrance into this three-dimensional world.

Let's think of the relationship as a tree. When you plant a seed, it takes time to grow, and it won't grow any faster with you tugging on its shoots. Your job is to keep energizing your goal into manifestation. You are changing your relationship with your goal until you are united with it. Manifesting takes place in the 'in-between' spaces of the unseen dimensions that are filled with all possibilities. Wondrous things are happening that are beyond the bounds of human reasoning.

Destiny Under Construction

What does "frequently and with duration" mean? It means as often as possible, for as long as possible, or for as long as you can maintain the juicy, heart coherent feelings that come to you when you think of how sweet it will be when your goal becomes your destiny. Feelings of:

- Enthusiasm
- Anticipation
- Excitement
- Joy
- Admiration
- Accomplishment
- Happiness
- Pleasure
- Being unstoppable
- Triumph
- Empowerment

This is the 'sweet spot' for magical things to happen. These not only create positive, healing bio-chemical reactions in your body, but they also create magnetic vibrations out into the world around you that put you in a time and space of synchronicity and flow. When you are no longer able to hold those good-feeling emotions in, then let them go and come back to your participation with them later.

Participate by envisioning your desired goal combined with the 'sweet spot' of heart coherency as often as possible throughout your day.

- When you wake up in the morning and while getting out of bed.

- When you are in the shower.

- When you are brushing your teeth.

- When you are driving somewhere, especially when you are stopped at a red light—this is the perfect time to stop, take a deep breath, and focus on your goal.

- When you are standing in line at a check-out counter.

- When you are taking a walk.

- When you are watering your plants or gardening.

- When you are drifting off to sleep at the end of your day.

The more often you do this, the more you are not only strengthening the neural pathways in your brain, but you are also energizing, strengthening, and magnetizing your goal into reality. It is literally becoming a more and more solidified pattern in the energy field until it becomes manifested in this dimension and reality.

Let Go of the 'How'

That is spirit's job. That is spirit's expertise. You take care of your job: focusing on your desired goal with excited, feel-good emotions, as often as possible for as long as possible. 'Know' that it will be coming. Stay curious, and it won't be long before you notice the signs that things are aligning for you. It will happen in the right place at the right time. You don't need to know when: every goal you have will have its own incubation period. You don't know how long that will be. While you may have an idea of what you'd like it to be, there's no exact date. It is like a birth process. Some goals will take longer than others. It doesn't matter how big your goal is either. Just because it is big doesn't necessarily mean it will take any longer to manifest. For example, it doesn't take any more gravity to hold an elephant to the earth than it does a mouse. It works the same for both of them. So, the size of your goal doesn't really matter. It will happen when everything is in perfect alignment and when and how it is supposed to happen. Stay curious. Trust this process, and life becomes magical.

Manifestation of a goal takes place when a strong energetic pattern has been built and established because it is the fabric of the universe. Rupert Sheldrake, a biologist and prolific author, introduced us to the idea of morphic fields and their structure and form. When enough thought and emotion wave-form energy has been woven into the substance of reality, it finally becomes dense enough with its specific resonance that it forms and eventually becomes a visible, tangible 'thing' in our third dimension. It is the pattern within the morphic field that has enormous potential and creates our possible realities, and this is where the science of our so-called magic occurs.

"Heroes take journeys, confront dragons,
and discover the treasure of their true selves."
~ Carol Lynn Pearson

See Appendix II for instructions about how to download the Energize a Pattern Process at: www.theHeartAndSoulAcademy.org/resource-page/

CHAPTER 8

Finding the Elusive Belief

"So oftentimes it happens that we live our lives in chains
and we never even know we have the key."
~ Lyrics from Already Gone, performed by the Eagles

We've discussed how to come up with a belief that you want to program into your subconscious, how to communicate with the subconscious in the language it understands, how to program a belief into your subconscious, and even how to energize the belief pattern in your energy field to quicken and strengthen its results. But how do you go about finding a belief that is not so obvious, the one that is secretly, or not so secretly, sabotaging your best efforts? How do you find the elusive belief that you are consciously unaware of that is holding you back?

Practical Lessons with Powerful Results

A 12-year-old boy who I worked with had been diagnosed with Oppositional Defiant Disorder. Energy testing to discover the message that this behavior held led us to 'Beliefs'—specifically those having to do with his spiritual connection and the universe around him. Further energy testing revealed his lack of feeling nurtured and supported. That is a pretty powerful message for one so young—that he was feeling abandoned and alone in the universe. The belief we ended up programming into his subconscious that was in his highest wisdom and benefit was, "*I am nurtured and supported through my connection with the universe.*" A couple more beliefs were added to support this new pattern, and within less than 24 hours, his mother reported that her son was no longer displaying any of the previously negative behaviors. Her son was putting dishes away from the dishwasher when she asked him to; he was putting on socks and shoes to go to school when he was asked, and he was brushing his teeth and getting ready for bed in a timely manner. Gone were the long, drawn-out tantrums, resistance, and anger with being asked to do simple chores. Furthermore, his defiant behavior never returned—all because of a hidden belief that no one would have been able to consciously come up with.

Messages Within Your Grasp

I have found that the elusive belief you are looking for will always be within arm's reach, most often in the same room as you are in, or in resources you regularly use. It is not going to take you on a world voyage to the far reaches of mysterious, hidden places on earth. Your soul wants you to get the message, grow, and move on to more exciting things. Your subconscious mind, with its million-to-one data processor containing approximately 280 quintillion bits of information gathered over a lifetime, knows where to locate that information. Your higher wisdom, which has a greater perspective than either your conscious or subconscious, easily guides you to the perfect, insightful resource.

Finding the Source

If you have book shelves containing many books, you could easily energy test to find out if the source of wisdom with the message is in one of those books. If YES, start narrowing it down to smaller and smaller groups of books until you get to one book. Is it on the top, middle, or bottom shelf? Next, is it on the first half or the second half of the shelf? When you get to the book itself, you could then further narrow it down with energy tests to smaller groups of pages (within the first 50, between pages 50–100, and so on). When you have narrowed it down to one page, read the page and see what catches your attention, then energy test to confirm that the sentence (or two or three) insights from the page contain the gist of the message.

When you have received the message, create a positive life-enhancing belief that is in your highest wisdom and benefit and program it into your subconscious and energy field. Voila—it is easier than first imagined! It is surprisingly accurate given the vast knowledge contained within the subconscious, and the higher wisdom you have access to, which guides you each step of the way. It will always be tailored to your needs because of the personal circumstances you face in each situation.

Energy Tests in Action

My dear friend and colleague Darryl Gurney most often uses a single source to get incredibly accurate and insightful messages for his clients. His source is a big, thick book, *Messages from the Body: Their Psychological Meaning (The Body's Desk Reference)*. Last I saw it, his book was well-worn and completely falling apart due to the amount of use it gets.

Darryl doesn't necessarily look up the symptom and use the message that coincides with the problem or issue—he energy tests which page the most appropriate message can be found on by narrowing it down bit by bit until he comes to the exact page and exact paragraph. He then reads what is there to discover the message that higher wisdom has to convey.

As impressed as I am with that book, I personally never got around to actually purchasing it. At first, it was because of the price. Believe me, it is well worth the price! Though, back then, I just didn't have the money to spare. As time wore on, I learned that I was getting messages for myself and my clients that were just as accurate and insightful despite using other sources of knowledge and wisdom. The resources I most often use are oracle cards, which is a special type of card deck designed for exploring oneself, divining inspirational truths, and seeking inner wisdom. I'm fond of two sets in particular:

- *Wisdom of the Hidden Realms Oracle Cards and Guidebook* by Colette Baron-Reid (or you can use any other oracle deck of Colette's that speaks to you; they are all good.)
- *The Faerie's Oracle Cards and Guidebook* by Brian Froud and Jessica Macbeth.

These are often used with *The Healing Runes* (by Ralph Blum and Susan Loughan) or a reference book from my shelves. I find them fun and also filled with different perspectives, containing knowledge and wisdom that has always captivated me with their deep insights.

Use the Source that Speaks to You

Any source that speaks to you can be used as a source of wisdom and insight. Whether it is a deck of oracle or tarot cards, the *I Ching*, runes, affirmation books, or *Notes from the Universe*, use what your higher self draws you to. A participant in one of my workshops exclusively uses her church hymnal. This is something I would have never thought to use, but, for her, it is perfect. She said she allows spirit to guide her to a specific page, then she reads the page and gleans the insights and message. The important thing is that your higher wisdom will use what is in the room, or easily accessible, to guide you to the most appropriate message.

Messages from Your Higher Wisdom

We will be pulling all the pieces of this L.E.E.P. System together, though for now, if you would like to play with a little self-discovery piece, give this a try:

- Energy test, *"There is a message my higher self has for me."*
- If YES, energy test if the message can be found in a nearby resource, such as your book shelf, or gather 2–3 sources together ahead of time to find if there is a message in one of them.
- Hold the intention to receive a message.
- Energy test to discover which resource your message can be found in.
  - If it is a book, energy test to discover which page the message is on.
  - If it is an oracle deck, divide the deck into two or more piles and energy test to discover which group your card is in. Narrow it down until you come to one card.
- Reflect on the message.
- Determine whether or not you would like to create a life-enhancing belief to program into your subconscious. This, too, could be done with an energy test.

I like to discover if my higher wisdom has a message to share with me that I can contemplate over a cup of tea in the morning. It starts my day off with sacred moments I cherish.

*"The real voyage of discovery consists not
in seeking new landscapes but having new eyes."*
~ Marcel Proust

*See Appendix II for instructions on how to download a Flow Chart
at:* www.theHeartAndSoulAcademy.org/resource-page/

CHAPTER 9

Healing Emotional Wounds

"We are kept from the experience of Spirit because our inner world is cluttered with past traumas . . . As we begin to clear away this clutter, the energy of divine light and love begins to flow through our beings."
~ *Father Thomas Keating*

Along the journey of self-empowerment and conscious evolution, we often discover that we are also on a journey of self-healing. It may not have been our first intent when we started out, though we end up discovering that some of our greatest hindrances are due to long forgotten, past emotional wounds that have created what we now recognize as emotional interference patterns. In resolving these detrimental patterns within, we discover that our emotions are the language of life and a reflection of our soul. By being in touch with our emotions, they guide and lead us to a deeper understanding and more authentic relationship with our self. This chapter is about learning how to find and resolve emotions within yourself or others that create the emotional interference patterns that play a part in holding you back in an area of your life.

All of us experience negative or unhealthy emotional extremes that at times can feel overwhelming. The duration or intensity of these emotions may cause them to not fully resolve or process themselves completely. In these cases, the stress they create not only causes an obstruction within the physical body by sending out a continuous interfering resonance that wreaks havoc with our health, but they also hijack our peace of mind, slowing down our personal growth. Instead of moving beyond our sense of betrayal or insult, or a temporary bout of anger or grief, this negative emotional energy can remain lodged in our body-mind energy field, potentially causing considerable physical and emotional distress.

Remember, emotional interference patterns are created by repressed, denied, or unresolved emotions that distort and block the natural life-force energy of our body, and we need our healthy, heart coherent emotions to manifest the life of our dreams.

The Trouble with Lingering Distress

Do you ever feel overwhelmed by something you can't quite put your finger on? Have you ever been consumed by a past event or felt a rising resentment that you just couldn't let go of? Have you ever regretted certain experiences in your life but felt powerless to move beyond them?

Some of the adverse emotions you've experienced in the past may still be creating problems for you in subtle, yet very damaging ways. Many people are afraid of what they might find if they spend any time analyzing their old emotional wounds. But you have to discover what's holding you back, and your past is buried in your subconscious. Studies in neuroscience indicate that as much as 95–99 percent of our consciousness is actually below our level of awareness. The energetic patterns behind our emotions create our experience of reality, though we have trouble recognizing them.

Circumstances that often initiate internal emotional conflict include:

- Abandonment, rejection, neglect, or adoption
- Loss of a loved one, giving up a child for adoption, miscarriage, or abortion
- Trauma, injury, or physical abuse
- Mental, verbal, or sexual abuse
- Relationship problems or divorce
- Financial hardship or struggling to survive
- Work or home stress (or long-term stressors)

- Natural disaster or witnessing/experiencing a traumatic or abusive event and feeling powerless to do anything about it
- Mental or physical illness
- Negative talk or beliefs about yourself or others and the need to gossip

Emotional interference patterns hinder our freedom, our happiness, our health, and our tendency to love. We operate from a reality that we perceive through our emotional pain—a reality of injustices, which are emotional poison. The more we deny or repress something, the greater the build-up of emotional toxicity, which often takes the form of an explosive release of pent-up emotion—emotion that can be damaging to both yourself and others.

Emotions Significantly Influence Conditions or Effects in Our Lives

Out of our emotional reactions to life, we create our beliefs:

- The world is safe or unsafe.
- I am a good person or a bad person.
- I am lovable or unlovable.
- I am worthy or unworthy.
- I am a winner or a loser.

Our emotional reactions to life govern our thought patterns, our beliefs, and our attitudes, and send out vibrations that resonate with other energetic fields, drawing those matching ones to us.

From our beliefs come our behaviors in life—whether we are easy going, generous, kind, and helpful; or unkind, confrontational, underhanded, or bitchy. Our behaviors then create results in our lives:

- Whether we get the promotion or not.
- Whether we've created loving, supportive relationships or stressful, challenging ones.

- If we have a neat, clean, and organized environment or are clutter-laden pack rats.

Then, of course, the results we get—either good or bad—influence how we feel, creating this continuous cycle *until we alter it*.

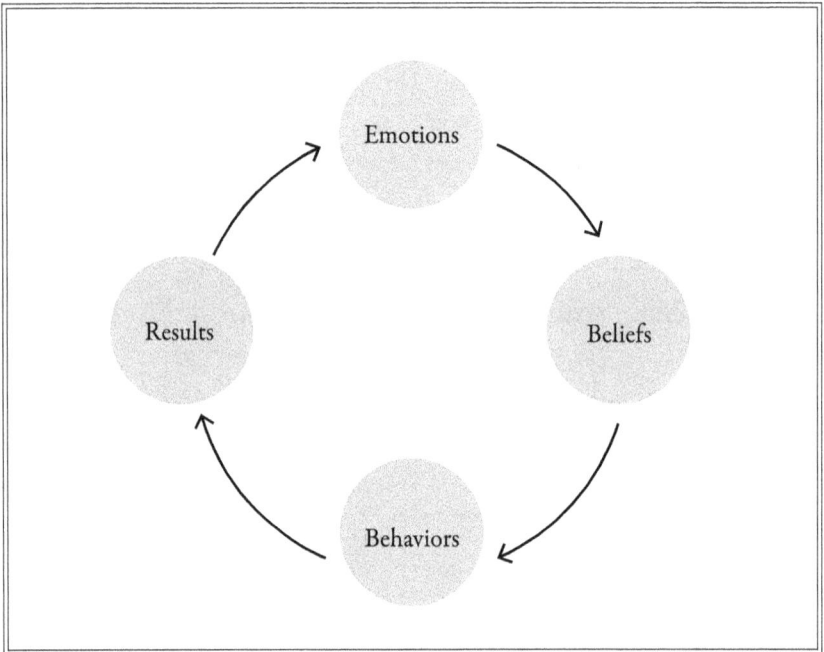

According to Dr. Candace Pert, neuroscientist, "our emotions are constantly regulating what we experience as reality." Our emotionally driven subconscious mind has the uncanny ability of bringing people and situations into our lives that force us to face, and feel, whatever we have previously resisted, denied, or suppressed because that is what it has stored there. **That emotional vibration is what the subconscious is experiencing on a continuous basis.** It is what drives our subconscious because those are the programs it is familiar with. The unresolved emotions are the ones attracted into our experiences over and over again. Until we change the patterns, they have an energetic charge to them and will continue to trouble us.

Feelings Create Biological Changes

In his talk on Heart Intelligence, Joseph Sundram, Ed.M., states that your perceptions immediately generate feelings and thoughts, and this includes all of your life experiences. If we are feeling stressed, it is not from the events themselves, but from our emotional reactions to those events—it doesn't matter what set them off.

Common stressors are:

- Time—the perception of never having enough time or that everything takes too long
- Pressure—taking on more than you can handle or a job that never ends
- Frustration—relationship problems, hostility, blaming others, edginess
- Unresolved conflicts, being confrontational
- Feeling victimized—lack of control over situations, a job you don't like, constant care-giving
- Perfectionism—expecting too much
- Financial matters—hardship, struggle to survive
- Negativity—resentment, bitterness, aggression, anxiety, worry, apprehension, depression
- Inadequacy—not enough quality time or rest and relaxation

The perceptions we have can be positive, negative, or neutral. Neutral perceptions barely affect us because we don't really care one way or the other about them—they just don't have much energy attached to them. But our positive and negative perceptions have stronger feelings, emotions, and energy connected to them. At the speed of your feelings, you begin to create biological changes—changes in hormones, tension in muscles, and changes in respiration, blood pressure, and heart rate. Like when we unexpectedly see a dear friend we haven't seen in a long time—from the moment we see that person, there is an upwelling of feelings. Biological changes start taking place, tracking that feeling. On the other hand, when we see someone who stresses us out—someone who we believe has done us wrong—there is an unmistakable sinking feeling. This emotion creates immediate biochemical changes of toxicity inside the body.

Repetition Equals Habit

While it is our decision to resent or love someone, if we do it long enough it becomes wired into our system and our neuro pathways and highly influences our behavior. Our capacity to be resentful or loving becomes a hardwired, automatic response. We all know people who are quick to judge, anger, blame, or feel victimized—their neurological pathways have been ingrained into them through internal repetition.

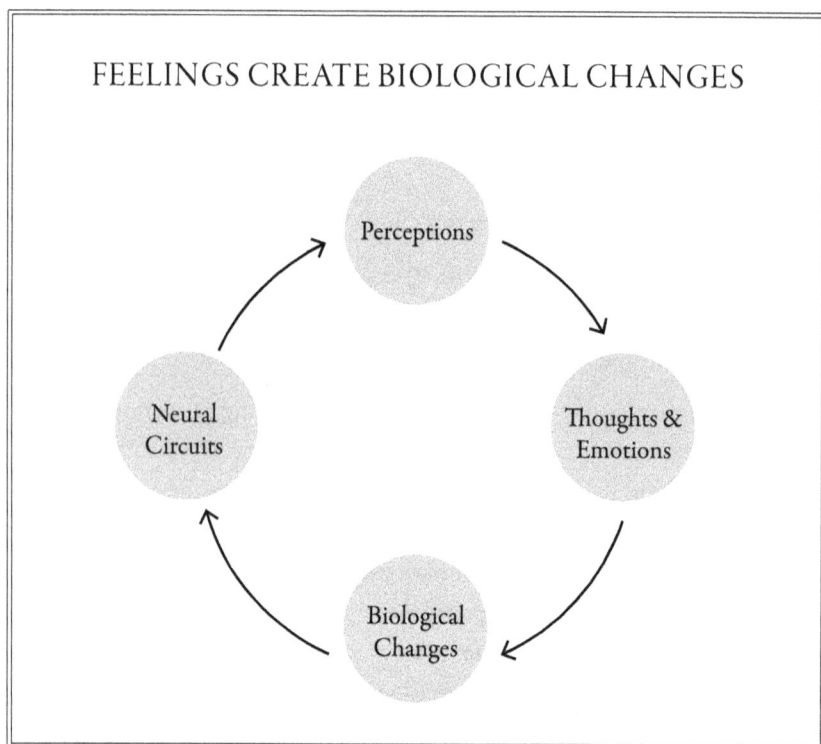

FEELINGS CREATE BIOLOGICAL CHANGES

Perceptions

Thoughts & Emotions

Biological Changes

Neural Circuits

This model was developed by researchers at the Institute of HeartMath.

This diagram demonstrates that emotions, thoughts, or habits literally create new pathways. Why is this important? Because whatever you do habitually creates neural circuitry, or pathways, and the way that the brain and the body are hard-wired together is by the way you perceive. This neurological structure underlies our capacity to access our intelligence—these circuits can open up our ways of thinking and ways of being, as much as they can close us off.

Ask Yourself

- What emotional interference patterns are holding you back?
- What have you unintentionally created for yourself?

Those outdated neural pathways were developed at a time that had emotional meaning for us, but now they hinder us from achieving fulfillment as adults. Fortunately, we can learn how to resolve those outdated ways of being that no longer serve us and no longer serve who we are becoming.

Your Emotional States and Your Health

Repressed, denied, or unresolved emotions affect us in two distinct ways. They cause us to feel an exaggerated emotional response because they are buried in our subconscious mind and seem controlled but, in actuality, are building with continuous unseen impulses until they eventually implode. Our perception of reality becomes skewed and reactions happen before we know it.

Anxiety, depression, fear, nervousness, resentment, uneasiness—all these feelings that we can't seem to shake—have detrimental effects on our lives. They prevent us from achieving goals, short-circuit our relationships, limit our happiness, and diminish our ability to love. They suppress our natural and healthy sexual expressions, and they cause us to make assumptions, often hurting the ones we love.

Many individuals struggle under the weight of the accumulation of bruised emotions and emotional wounds without ever saying a word. Too often, we tend to be afraid that we'll suffer if we explore our emotional wounds, not realizing that the ongoing fear of suffering is worse than the time it takes to explore the cause of that pain. When our emotions are blocked due to denial, repression, or trauma, we become stuck—we are unable to respond appropriately or authentically to the world around us.

Unfortunately, these emotional interference patterns cause us to misinterpret behavior. They cause us to overact to innocent remarks and can trigger our everyday, minute-to-minute choices and behavior. Unresolved feelings create the challenges, the uneasiness, the pain, and the crisis situations in our lives.

The other way that emotions affect our health is physically. They can cause physical pain because they generate specific, constant, low-level vibrations that create toxins in our blood and irritate our body's tissues. Over time, continuously distressed tissues begin to dysfunction. Since our emotions are directly connected, and inseparable from, our body's physical responses, it is important to find and resolve emotional interference patterns as they can interfere with the proper function of our body's organs and tissues, causing pain, fatigue, and illness due to the chemical changes that create a toxic environment of biological waste and inflammation.

It is a conservative estimate that 90 percent of all physical problems have psychological roots. Emotional interference patterns can block the flow of life-force energy in the body. They lower the immune function, making the body more vulnerable to disease, and they interfere with the way our DNA expresses itself. The good news is, our body has an incredible ability to heal itself when the disruptive patterns are eliminated and life-force energy can flow freely once again.

A Blueprint for Health

Deepak Chopra, MD, a prominent advocate for alternative medicine, states that we only have an energetic blueprint for health—there is *no* blueprint for disease. This concept has greatly influenced my work over the years as well as my research into how information and energy influences our health. Dis-ease is caused by energetic disturbances—waveforms with an intensity and duration that cause distortions, interrupting the natural flow of life-force in the energy fields that makes up *You*. Chopra says we have a body-wide information network that is ever changing, dynamic, and infinitely flexible. A 'mobile brain' that moves throughout our entire body, located in all places at once and not just in the head that consists of:

- Neurotransmitters that carry very basic messages, either 'on' or 'off', referring to whether the receiving cell discharges electricity or not.

- Peptides that are more likely to move through extracellular space, sweeping along in the blood and cerebral fluid, traveling long distances in the body, and causing complex and fundamental changes in cells whose receptors they lock onto.

Emotions Reside Everywhere

Since emotions cause bodily functions and changes in tissues, and are often associated with certain organs or body parts, do emotions start in our body ... or in our head? Candace Pert, neuroscientist and pharmacologist, explores in her book, *Molecules of Emotion*, whether the ultimate source of emotions originates in the body and then gets perceived in the head, or if they originate in the head and trickle down into the body. The answer, she discovered, is both.

Emotions cause natural changes in our body and its associated organs. Those organic modifications are chemistry signals—neurotransmitters that carry information and energy that gets conveyed as an emotional state. It can be perceived either consciously or subconsciously. Therefore, every change in our mental emotional state is accompanied by a corresponding change in our physical body. And our body responds automatically, not intentionally, to environmental situations, which our mind interprets as emotions (such as surprise) based on context. It is a simultaneous two-way street. Neurotransmitters associated with emotions link our body and mind together with information and energy that profoundly influences how we respond to, and experience, our world.

Emotions create a chemical process in our body that is then transmitted from the surface of the cell into our cell's interior, where the message can change the functioning of the cell dramatically. A chain reaction of biochemical events begins to occur, either to the benefit or detriment of our health, and a number of activities within our body take place. These chemical signals play a wide role in regulating practically all of our life's processes because emotions are the link between our mind and body. They greatly influence the body-wide biochemical network of information that is communicated throughout our internal systems, such as the endocrine, neurological, gastrointestinal, and immune system. This information alone should be enough to convince most individuals that learning to resolve the emotional interference patterns we have within us is a necessary skill to have.

Emotions are essential in reaching the greatest possible understanding of who we are and what we want, and they make themselves known primarily through internal sensations. The more attuned we grow to these internal sensations, by resolving the disruptive emotional patterns, the wiser and more consciously aware we become.

The Good, the Bad, and the Ugly

There is a difference between resolving our disruptive emotional interference patterns and experiencing uneasy emotions, such as anger, grief, sadness, frustration, or fear from time to time. Oftentimes, we refer to these sensations as 'negative,' and I'd like to take a moment to clarify this a bit. Feelings or emotions themselves are not negative or positive—they are just natural responses to situations. Some emotions are more pleasant than others, that's for sure, but most often they are valid and appropriate for our changing circumstances. Some of our uneasy emotions alert us to danger and warn us to take a different course of action. That doesn't necessarily make them 'bad,' 'wrong,' or 'negative'—as a matter of fact, it's a good thing and an appropriate response for those circumstances. In most cases, we move through them. Now, if we act out with our anger, fear, or uneasiness by behaving in inappropriate ways, that is what makes the expression of them bad, negative, or even problematic because we are still held accountable for our actions. And we do have the choice of how to act upon the emotions we feel.

Anger, grief, and fear are not negative in themselves; in fact, they are vital for our survival and have beneficial value. In the proper amounts, even our unpleasant feelings help us stay on course toward health and happiness. Negative emotions can motivate us to learn more and to do better. We need anger to define our boundaries, grief to deal with our losses, and fear to protect ourselves from danger. If we lacked these feelings, we wouldn't know when we were veering away from our goals, values, beliefs, comfort zone, physical health, happiness, and soul's purpose.

The Glory of Letting Go

It's only when our feelings are denied, such that they cannot be easily and rapidly processed through our system and released, that they become toxic. The more we deny them, the greater the toxicity. We need to allow all of our feelings to be felt and to move through us, regardless of whether we think they are acceptable or not, and then let them go. By acknowledging them and letting them run their natural course, the so-called 'bad' ones are transformed into 'good' ones, and we are liberated from suffering with them any longer than necessary. By lovingly accepting our anger, grief, and fear, we become assertive, compassionate, and resourceful. We release pent-up tension, and our body chemistry shifts into a healing mode.

Dr. Hamer, who developed the German New Medicine method, states that when we resolve our internal conflicts it evokes tissue repair and restores the loss of bodily function—our body shifts toward a healing and regenerative mode once again. This complements Candace Pert's view, that "every change in the psychological state, either conscious or unconscious, is accompanied by an appropriate change in our physical body." So, when making changes in our emotions, we also make changes in our biology—either toward decay or toward regeneration.

Our emotions play a vital role in our ability to create the life of our dreams—they unite our mind with our body. The good news is, you get to influence these shifts toward wholeness, and it is easier than you may think. When you have discovered the emotion that has been contributing to an interference pattern within you, you will have learned a message your life experience was sending you through its signals.

Transforming Emotional Interference Patterns

We begin with a series of energy tests to discover the primary emotion that is causing the interference pattern. Consciously identifying the emotion is the first step toward its resolution as it acknowledges its validity and right to expression. This alone creates a softening, an opening, for release to take place.

EMOTIONAL INTERFERENCE PATTERN RESOLUTION PROCESS

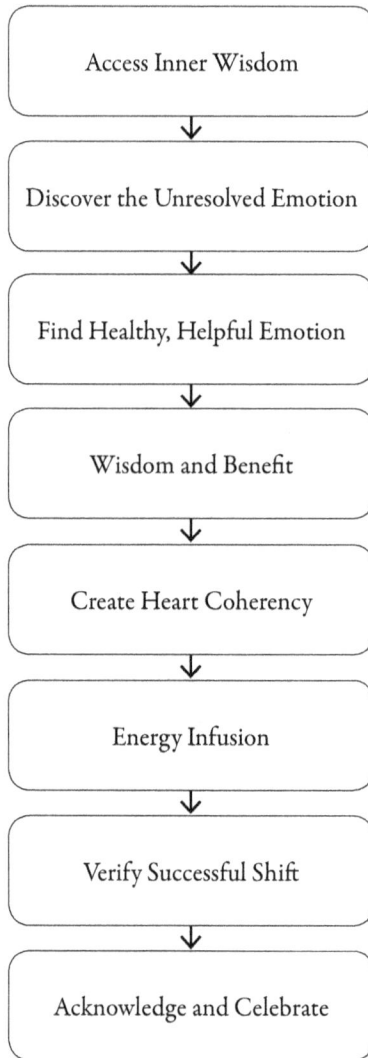

Access Inner Wisdom

↓

Discover the Unresolved Emotion

↓

Find Healthy, Helpful Emotion

↓

Wisdom and Benefit

↓

Create Heart Coherency

↓

Energy Infusion

↓

Verify Successful Shift

↓

Acknowledge and Celebrate

Here is your step-by-step process for resolving emotional interference patterns.

Access Inner Wisdom Communication Systems:

[See Chapter 3 for full description, or download full process from The Heart and Soul Academy website.]

Discover the Emotional Interference Pattern:

Energy test one of the following (whichever is most appropriate for your situation) unless you already know it is an emotion that needs to be resolved.

- *"There is an unresolved emotion to shift at this time."*
- *"There is an emotion blocking me from (name the issue)."*
- *"There is an emotional interference pattern manifesting as, or contributing to, (name the issue or situation)."*

If the response you received was YES, then you will energy test to find the unresolved emotion that is involved.

Finding Emo—Energy Test to Discover the Unresolved Emotion:

In this exercise, you'll have your higher wisdom locate the unresolved emotion using the Finding Emo Chart. There may be more than one emotion involved, and, if so, then one will have a higher priority than another. Since consciously we may have a difficult time *knowing exactly* which emotion it is that needs to be resolved, we energy test for it as our higher consciousness knows exactly what needs to be resolved.

Using the Finding Emo Chart (found on the next page), energy test:

- *"The highest priority emotion to resolve can be found on the left-hand side of the chart."* If YES, then it is in the 7th, 5th, or 3rd chakra group. If NO, then it is in one of the other groups.
- *"The highest priority emotion to resolve can be found on the right-hand side of the chart."* If YES, then it is in the 6th, 4th, or 2nd chakra group. If NO, then it is in the 1st chakra group in the center of the page at the bottom.
- If it was on either the left or right side of the chakra groups, you simply energy test each of the three groups listed to discover which chakra group the unresolved emotion can be found in.
- Once you have found the group that you can find the unresolved emotion in (let's say it was in the 1st chakra group), then energy test to discover which side of the group it is in: *"The highest priority*

FINDING EMO:
UNRESOLVED EMOTIONAL WOUNDS

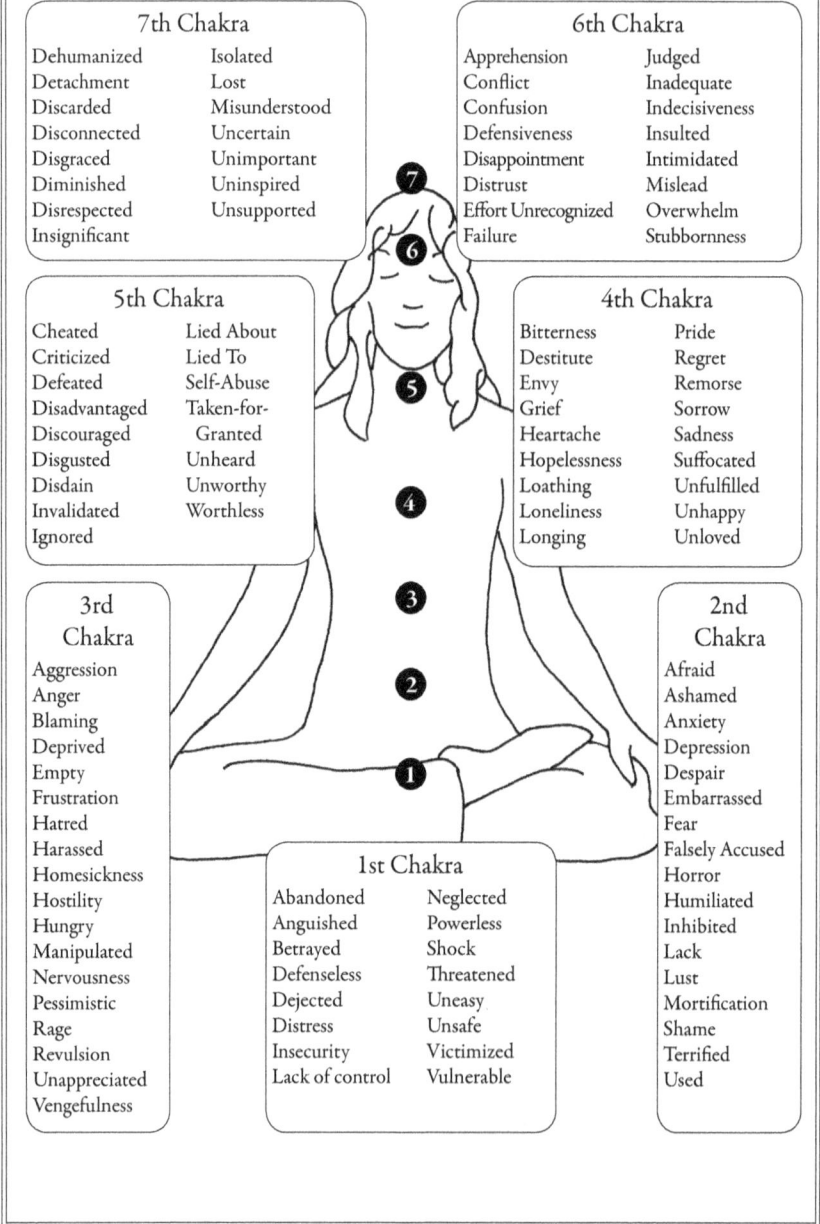

7th Chakra

Dehumanized	Isolated
Detachment	Lost
Discarded	Misunderstood
Disconnected	Uncertain
Disgraced	Unimportant
Diminished	Uninspired
Disrespected	Unsupported
Insignificant	

6th Chakra

Apprehension	Judged
Conflict	Inadequate
Confusion	Indecisiveness
Defensiveness	Insulted
Disappointment	Intimidated
Distrust	Mislead
Effort Unrecognized	Overwhelm
Failure	Stubbornness

5th Chakra

Cheated	Lied About
Criticized	Lied To
Defeated	Self-Abuse
Disadvantaged	Taken-for-
Discouraged	Granted
Disgusted	Unheard
Disdain	Unworthy
Invalidated	Worthless
Ignored	

4th Chakra

Bitterness	Pride
Destitute	Regret
Envy	Remorse
Grief	Sorrow
Heartache	Sadness
Hopelessness	Suffocated
Loathing	Unfulfilled
Loneliness	Unhappy
Longing	Unloved

3rd Chakra

Aggression
Anger
Blaming
Deprived
Empty
Frustration
Hatred
Harassed
Homesickness
Hostility
Hungry
Manipulated
Nervousness
Pessimistic
Rage
Revulsion
Unappreciated
Vengefulness

2nd Chakra

Afraid
Ashamed
Anxiety
Depression
Despair
Embarrassed
Fear
Falsely Accused
Horror
Humiliated
Inhibited
Lack
Lust
Mortification
Shame
Terrified
Used

1st Chakra

Abandoned	Neglected
Anguished	Powerless
Betrayed	Shock
Defenseless	Threatened
Dejected	Uneasy
Distress	Unsafe
Insecurity	Victimized
Lack of control	Vulnerable

Note: Emotions can lodge anywhere in the body, regardless of what chakra or organ they may have originated from.

emotion to resolve can be found on the left side of the 1st chakra group," or *"The highest priority emotion to resolve can be found on the right side."* If YES, narrow it down further: *"The highest priority is found in the top half"* or *"the bottom half."*

• You keep energy testing portions of the chart that you get a YES response to until you get to the point where you can be very specific. The unresolved emotion can be found on the left hand side of the chart in the 1st chakra group list on the right hand side in the bottom half. Energy test the last few at a time until you find the one that energy tests YES. For example: *"The highest priority emotion to resolve is victimized."* YES.

Yay! With the help of your inner wisdom, you found the highest priority emotion to resolve the problem, challenge, or issue you are experiencing. This is the message your higher wisdom has been signaling for you to discover, so that it can be released and can free up your life-force energies for a better life experience.

Body Awareness:

Emotions can lodge anywhere in the body, regardless of what chakra or organ they may be associated with. This step finds where the unresolved emotion resides within you. Close your eyes, take a deep breath in, and as you release your breath notice where in your body your attention is being drawn. Project your consciousness into that area. Make a mental note of where it is and what you notice.

Optional Exploration:

Your subconscious mind has stored all the details of how and when this unresolved emotion became stuck within the body. It knows who was involved and how it is affecting your health, mind, and behavior. Most often, you won't ever need to know more than which emotion it is in order to release it. Should your higher wisdom determine there is more for you to consciously know, it will push information up to your conscious level of awareness. You could energy test, *"It is important to know more about this emotion."* If NO, then move on to discovering the healthy, helpful emotion to replace the emotion causing the interference pattern. If YES, then there is more for you to consciously explore and discover.

Finding out when it occurred and how it happened often results in a more in-depth understanding of the event or situation. Your subconscious will not connect the unresolved emotion with chronological age so much as it will associate it with a specific emotionally charged event, circumstance, situation, or person(s). You can use age references as markers for narrowing down your search to a specific year or event. There are many ways to use the process of deduction to get this information, and there is no right or wrong way to find out how or when the emotion became stuck. Follow your intuition and energy test it. You could energy test, *"The emotion became stuck between birth and 10 years of age."* (Or *" . . . between 10 and 20," " . . . 20 and 30,"* etc.).

Find the Healthy, Helpful Emotion

Whether or not you choose to further explore the origination of the emotional interference pattern, the next step is to find the healthy, helpful emotion that will replace the one that had been causing the disturbance in your energy field.

You will use a series of energy tests and work with the Healthy, Helpful Emotions Chart to pin down the specific emotional energy that would best resolve the interference pattern and restore healthy, life-force flow in the body-mind-spirit.

Using the Healthy, Helpful Emotions Chart, energy test:

- *"The best emotion to have instead would be found on the left-hand side of the chart."* If YES, then it is in the first two columns. Energy test to discover which it is.

- If NO, then it is in one of two columns on the right-hand side. Energy test to discover which it is.

- Then energy test, *"The best emotion to have instead is in the first 11."*

If YES, then narrow it down to discover which one. If NO, then it is between 12 and 22.

• Keep energy testing portions of the chart that you get a YES response to until you get to the point where you can be very specific. Example: The healthy, helpful emotion can be found in the second column of the chart in the top half between 1 and 5. *"The healthy, helpful emotion is #1."* NO. *"The healthy, helpful emotion is #2."* NO. Energy test the last few at a time until you find the one that energy tests YES. *"The highest priority emotion is Courage."* YES.

Yay! You found the emotion that your higher wisdom, with its expanded perspective, considers to be the best emotion to replace Victimized in your energy field. You might have *consciously* chosen Empowered, Respected, In charge, or something else that would make sense, but might not be the best choice, which your higher wisdom can more easily see would be in your best interest. This is the message your higher wisdom has been signaling for you to discover, so that it can help you transform and empower yourself.

HEALTHY / HELPFUL EMOTIONS LIST

1	2	3	4
1. Accepted	1. Connected	1. Happiness	1. Productive / Useful
2. Acknowledged	2. Contentment	2. Heard	2. Proud
3. Admired	3. Courage	3. Helped	3. Rapture
4. Adored	4. Delight	4. Helpful	4. Reassured
5. Affection	5. Desired	5. Hope	5. Recognized
6. Amazement	6. Eagerness	6. Important	6. Relief
7. Amused / amusement	7. Elation	7. In control / In charge	7. Respected
8. Appreciated	8. Ecstasy	8. Included	8. Safe
9. Approved of	9. Empowered / Powerful	9. Inspired / Inspiration	9. Satisfaction
10. Arousal / aroused	10. Enthusiasm	10. Listened to	10. Secure
11. Attractive	11. Enthusiastic	11. Jolliness	11. Sexy / Sensual
12. Awe	12. Enthrallment	12. Jovial	12. Supported
13. Believed in	13. Enjoyment	13. Joy	13. Tenderness
14. Bliss	14. Euphoria	14. Jubilation	14. Thrilled
15. Capable	15. Excitement	15. Loved / Lovable	15. Treated fairly
16. Caring / cared for	16. Exhilaration	16. Needed	16. Triumphant
17. Cheerful	17. Fondness	17. Noticed	17. Trusted
18. Cherished	18. Forgiven	18. Optimistic	18. Understanding
19. Clear (not confused)	19. Forgiving	19. Overjoyed	19. Understood
20. Compassion	20. Free / Carefree	20. Passionate	20. Valued
21. Competent	21. Fulfilled / Full	21. Pleasure	21. Worthy
22. Confident	22. Gladness	22. Private	22. Zeal / Zest

Higher Wisdom Support

Now that you've found the unresolved emotion, and a healthy, helpful emotion to replace it with, let's find out if it's in your highest wisdom and benefit to make this change. Simply energy test: *"It is in the highest wisdom and benefit to make this change now."* If YES, proceed with creating heart coherency to make the shift.

Sacred Heart Alignment

[See Chapter 5 for full description.]

Energy Infusion:

Your intention is to embrace the healthy emotion (*name it, i.e.: Courage*) in your personal energy field and reality, accelerating the healing effects by infusing it with nourishing, healing energy.

With eyes closed, energize the area (spiraling energy through your fingertips in a clockwise motion) into the part of your body you had felt the unresolved emotion the most and had projected your consciousness into. Imagine filling up the space with the healing energy of the healthy emotion and continue until you sense a shift in the energy there—a transformation indicating that the dense energy has dissolved.

Then, starting with your 7th chakra, in a clockwise motion, spiral the healthy emotion with nourishing energy. Spin the energy into the chakra at least three times or until you sense a shift. Move from the 7th chakra down to the 6th and repeat this spiraling of energy and healthy emotion until you notice a change. Do this with each consecutive chakra, feeling the changes in each one, until you sense a shift in the final chakra—your root chakra.

Bring your awareness to the area of your body you had originally projected your awareness into. Notice the difference. When you are ready to bring your focus back to this present moment, you may open your eyes.

Verify Change:

Verify and confirm that the emotion has been fully resolved. Energy Test: *"This shift is complete."* If NO, repeat the process, so that the shift can completely resolve the emotion. If YES, then acknowledge and celebrate.

Celebration Fist Pump:

Take a moment to gratefully acknowledge your inner strengths and capability. Gratitude is a very powerful emotion. Celebrate by anchoring this new energetic shift within you with the celebration fist pump!

Determine if there is another emotion that needs to be changed:
Since there may be more than one emotion contributing to an interference pattern, and you will want to resolve all that are involved, energy test: *"There is another unresolved emotion to shift."* If YES, then repeat the earlier process by following the same steps. If there is no other emotion to change at this time, then energy test: *"This emotion has been resolved."* It should be testing YES.

Congratulations

You have learned a time–tested heart coherent, Life-Enhancing Energetic Process to resolve emotional interference patterns within the subconscious, easily and effortlessly. Because it affects different types and levels of consciousness flowing through your chakras, its power is beyond anything previously known to shift the energy of emotional patterns stored within the brain cells distributed throughout your entire body, not just in the brain.

Traumatic Stress Release Process

Another time-tested process we have used successfully for many years now has been specifically designed to shift and release the traumatic stress held deep within the body-mind energy system to evoke a state of peace and detachment. This process does not block your memory of the event; it simply releases the emotional stress from the body-mind energy system that the event created.

The Traumatic Stress Release Process is based off the original Brain Gym Posture called Hook-ups, which Dr. Paul Dennison discovered could be used to release emotional stress and alleviate learning difficulties. According to Dr. Dennison in his 2010 edition of *Brain Gym Teacher's Edition*, he said, "Hook-ups shift the electrical energy from the survival centers in the hindbrain to the reasoning centers in the midbrain and neocortex, thus activating hemispheric integration, increasing fine motor coordination, and enhancing formal reasoning." Wayne Cook, an expert in electromagnetic energy, invented the posture variation that we use for traumatic stress release, from which Hook-ups are adapted (see drawing). While in this posture, "the tongue is pressed into the roof of the mouth to stimulate the limbic system for emotional processing in concert with the more refined reasoning in the frontal lobes." Working with higher wisdom to guide the process, it has become invaluable for working with post-traumatic stress disorder.

This process moves the hurtful energy away from the survival centers (where trauma gets stuck), processes it via the limbic system (the emotion processor of the brain), and passes it on to the more efficient higher brain functions in the neocortex for resolution. As your body's life-force energy circulates through these blocked areas, it connects with the electrical circuits in the body containing the disorganized energy.

This flow of energy allows your subconscious to shift to a state of peace regarding the entire experience. Within minutes, the chaotic stress is deactivated—it does not take long to neutralize the distress. It appears that 25 minutes is the longest that the subconscious mind can hold onto a stressor while in the Hook-up Posture—though experience has shown that emotional stress has been released between 3–5 minutes and up to 12 minutes, on average. Since everyone is different, you just allow the shift to take however long it needs to take for that person's system to work out the internal distress. Even if it should take up to 25 minutes to process this distress at the subconscious level, it would still appear to be a better choice than living with it for any longer than a person needs to.

Permission was given by Brain Gym to use the Hook-up Posture.

Step-by-Step Process for Traumatic Stress Release

It Takes Two:

Always do this process with another person present. One person (Facilitator) helps another (Recipient) with the traumatic stress release.

- Facilitator: Have a box of tissues on hand for recipient's comfort.

Vital for Accurate Energy Testing with a Partner:

Facilitator sits to the side of the person being energy tested.

- Facilitator's thumb supports the other person's wrist with one hand and lightly rests their other hand on the person's shoulder to complete an energy circuit.

Recipient sits with his or her arm extended in front (parallel to the floor), using only the small amount of energy it takes to keep the arm raised.

- Recipient keeps his or her body relaxed, chin parallel to the floor, eyes open and focused downward.

When energy testing with someone else, the Facilitator will have the other person repeat each of the following energy tests out loud. Just as soon as the person you are working with says the statement with emotion and conviction, while he or she is still connected with that statement, say, *"Hold firm"* before gently applying pressure to his or her arm. This is the cue that you are going to gently press downward on the outstretched arm. Facilitator says, *"Hold firm"* then applies gentle downward pressure for about two seconds or until the other person's arm either 'locks in place' or 'is easily released and pushed down.'

- Avoid bouncing the other person's arm by using gentle, steady pressure.
- Ask the person you are working with if the pressure is comfortable. Adjust the pressure (more or less), as required, to his or her satisfaction and comfort level.

Women	Men
"I am a woman."	"I am a man."
"I am a man."	"I am a woman."
Show me a YES.	Show me a YES.
Show me a NO.	Show me a NO.

TRAUMATIC STRESS RELEASE PROCESS

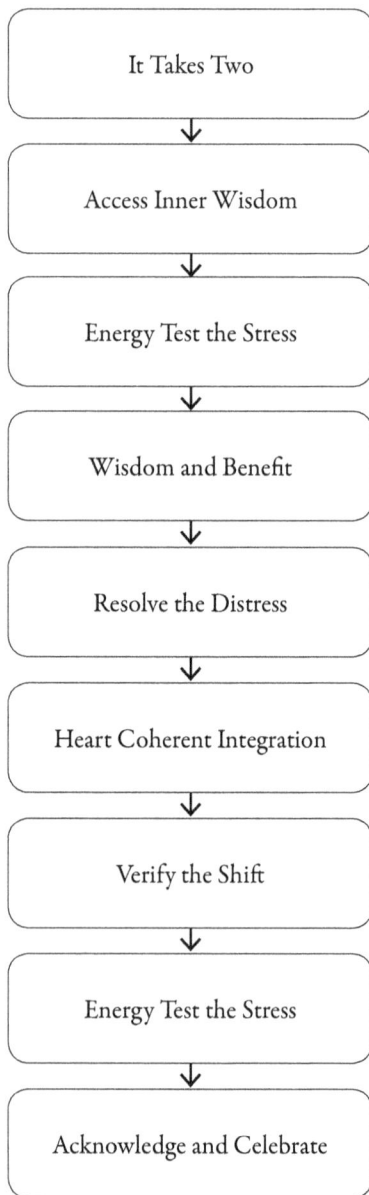

It Takes Two

↓

Access Inner Wisdom

↓

Energy Test the Stress

↓

Wisdom and Benefit

↓

Resolve the Distress

↓

Heart Coherent Integration

↓

Verify the Shift

↓

Energy Test the Stress

↓

Acknowledge and Celebrate

Energy Test with Your Partner:

- Facilitator, say, *"Repeat after me with emotion and conviction, 'I am a woman.'"*
  - Just as soon as the Recipient has said, *"I am a woman,"* Facilitator says, *"Hold firm"* then gently applies pressure to Recipient's arm for two seconds.
- Facilitator, say, *"Repeat after me, 'I am a man.'"*
  - Just as soon as the Recipient has said, *"I am a man,"* Facilitator says, *"Hold firm"* then gently applies pressure to Recipient's arm for two seconds.
- Facilitator, say, *"Show me a YES.—Hold firm."*
  - Gently apply pressure to Recipient's arm for two seconds.
- Facilitator, say, *"Show me a NO.—Hold firm."*
  - Gently apply pressure to Recipient's arm for two seconds.

Facilitator asks Recipient if the energy tests were Strong (arm locks in place) or Weak (arm let's go or takes more effort to hold outstretched).

NOTE:

- If the person you are working with received a YES response to correct 'gender' and 'show me a YES' *AND* received a NO response to the 'opposite gender' and 'show me a NO,' then proceed to the next step.
- If your energy tests responded with a YES to everything, then your partner's body-mind energy system is over-energized; he or she will need to de-stress with heart coherent breathing or calm his or her system by putting a hand on his or her forehead, then re-test 1–3 minutes later.
- If your partner's energy tests responded with a NO to everything, then he or she is dehydrated to the point where the internal electrical impulses are too weak to detect with energy testing at this time. Have him or her drink enough water to boost the electrical conductivity for clear feedback from the energy tests then proceed to the next step.

Energy Test the Stress:

Facilitator, energy test with the person you are working with: *"Think of the stressful situation or memory, and when you have recalled the event, nod your head."* The beautiful thing about this step is that the person you are working with does not have to reveal all the details of the ordeal with you or even say them out loud. Private matters can remain that way, and your partner can keep it private if he or she wishes. When your partner nods his or her head, say *"Hold firm"* and gently press downward on his or her extended arm.

- If weak, continue to the next step because the distress is wreaking havoc inside.

- If strong, the person may already be in a place of detachment about the entire event at the subconscious level. Or, if it is apparent that your partner is consciously affected by the event, he or she may have triggered an over-energized state (fight or flight) that is affecting the energy test. His or her over-energized system will calm and relax with heart coherent breathing. Re-test again in a few minutes.

Higher Wisdom Support:

Energy Test: *"It is in the highest wisdom and benefit to make this change now."* If YES, proceed to the next step. Do not proceed if you do not receive a YES to this step—it would not be in the highest wisdom and benefit to do this process at this time, and your partner does not need the added stress of going through the motions without the benefit of relief.

Resolve the Distress:

- Recipient sits in the Hook-up Posture with ankles and wrists crossed in a way that creates comfort. [Variation: With wrists crossed and fingers interlaced, the person may rest his or her hands in his or her lap instead of against the chest.]

Facilitator, while holding sacred space for this transformational shift to occur, say to Recipient, *"Breathing deeply, and with your eyes closed, place your tongue on the roof of your mouth. Think about the stressful situation. [Pause.] Attempt to feel the stress for as long as you can . . . until you no longer feel bad . . . no matter how hard you try. When you come to a place of peace or detachment, you may open your eyes."*

Facilitator, remain silent during the Recipient's processing; although, you may wish to remind him or her to take as long as necessary. This reassures your partner to stick with the exercise. Have patience and trust the process because you received confirmation from his or her inner wisdom that this process was in the highest wisdom and benefit to release this traumatic stress now. You know the success of this procedure is already assured; otherwise, you would have received a NO energy test response.

Remember, while this process usually takes only a few minutes, 3–12, on average, it has been known to take up to 25 minutes for the subconscious mind to process and deactivate the distress from within a person's system. The stress works itself out below the conscious level of the mind where energetic shifts reconfigure the electrical circuits that are involved with the blocked emotional stress. The energy flows of the body naturally shift; they ebb and flow, relax and energize, and ultimately release the interference pattern during this process.

Let the person you are working with know you have tissues, just in case they are needed. Have compassion but don't interfere with the Recipient's process. Your partner has everything necessary to resolve this traumatic stress interference pattern. Once the stressful emotions are no longer sending out their distress signals, an individual then experiences peace or detachment regarding the experience. Have patience and trust that everything is unfolding as it should. When your partner opens his or her eyes and has come to a place of peace, proceed with Heart Coherent Integration.

Heart Coherent Integration:

Creating heart coherency allows this energetic shift to be integrated and infused into the whole body-mind energy system. While still in the Hook-up position, have the Recipient close his or her eyes and guide him or her through the Sacred Space Alignment. [See Chapter 5 for full description or download the full process from The Heart and Soul Academy website.]

When the Recipient's eyes have opened, tell him or her to relax— uncrossing the ankles and wrists, bringing the palms to his or her heart—and take a moment to embrace the new shift in his or her whole being.

Verify the Shift:

Energy Test: *"This emotional stress has been successfully released—Hold firm."* If YES, continue to the next step. If NO, have the Recipient drink some water and retest. The amount of energy shifting through his or her internal circuits may have caused dehydration. If the Recipient still tests NO after a few sips of water, then repeat the Traumatic Stress Release Process to resolve any residual energetic disturbance.

Energy Test the Stress:

Energy Test: *"Think about the stressful situation or memory now, and nod your head when you have recalled it."*

When the Recipient has nodded, say, *"Hold firm."* Apply gentle, downward pressure on his or her outstretched arm. The energy test result should be strong, indicating there is no stress associated with this traumatic event weakening the body-mind energy system.

Celebration Fist Pump:

Have your partner take a moment to gratefully acknowledge his or her inner strengths and capability. Gratitude is a very powerful emotion. Then, celebrate by anchoring this new energetic shift with the celebration fist pump! Hugs are always nice, too.

The Hook-up posture may be used anytime to naturally de-stress your body-mind energy system for emotional centering. As Dr. Paul Dennison and Wayne Cook discovered, it is considered to be a most effective way to address the feeling associated with being emotionally overwhelmed.

The Blessings of Forgiveness Process

Much has been written about the value of forgiveness, although the concept has often been misunderstood when we simply believe it's something we're supposed to do. The thought of forgiveness changes nothing when we are only jumping through a socially acceptable hoop. There are times when working with individuals when 'Forgiveness' has come up in energy testing as the highest priority for them to shift in order to move forward. When it does, it carries the message that this plays a significant role in what's been holding them back. The Blessing of Forgiveness Process is about how to go deeper and more fully into forgiveness when the conscious decision to forgive has not been working as well as you'd hoped due to resistance at the subconscious level.

I'd like to share with you a deeper understanding of the blessing that comes with forgiveness for those times when the circumstances you endured had such an impact that it was carried into the depths of your being. The greatest gift of forgiveness is that we free ourselves from allowing the experience to adversely affect our lives. Leonard Laskow, MD, author of *Healing with Love*, says that, "Forgiving is for giving yourself love and freedom. It is an act of self-love." The act of forgiveness is a course of action, a catalyst, which frees us from the emotions of the actions we have experienced or witnessed. It rescues us from the things that have hurt us in the past. It helps us reclaim the power to decide how that past event will affect our life in the present and permits us to move forward, so we can get on with the venture of living a joyful life. Until you forgive, you still have an energetic connection to the past person or event.

Blessing is a quality of feeling, emotion, and thought that Gregg Braden, author of *Walking Between The Worlds*, says allows us to clear out our anger, judgments, and pain regarding specific events in our lives. It does so without condoning the action, pardoning the behavior, or absolving what had happened. It simply acknowledges that the event occurred. Forgiving does not mean the other person is no longer held accountable for his or her actions because those do have consequences. Nor does it relinquish responsibility. It simply means that when we bless and forgive the people, circumstances, and events that hurt us in life, we are acknowledging their existence, and by doing so, it allows the hurt to move out of our being.

Bodily Harm

The distressful emotions generated by the unforgiven situation or event create a chemistry shift within the body. Because the amygdala is tuned into *all* of our emotions, it is considered to be the emotional processing center of the brain. Unfortunately, it can easily create unending cycles in the breakdown of signals to the frontal cortex, cutting off access to our intelligence, as well as restricting the life-force energies moving through our body. The only way we sense this inability to heal is that the body creates adverse effects in our life, such as:

- Increased frustration, conflicts, resentment, bitterness, and anger
- Inability to fully relax, unwind, and decompress
- Headaches, fatigue, inflammation, and sleep disturbance

Many individuals using this Blessing of Forgiveness Process have experienced that the emotional charge associated with the stressful event can be transformed and even completely released. This, in turn, releases the energetic interference patterns that would have otherwise drained you of your life-force energies and contributed to illness or dis-ease.

When we are able to completely and wholeheartedly forgive, shifting our emotions around the entire event to those of peace or detachment, it releases the emotional charge surrounding what happened. That emotional shift contains an electrical charge, which, in turn, creates a biochemical change within the body that heals the fear, the anger, the judgment, and the grief that had been stored within the subconscious. The release of subconscious resistance frees up the life-force energy to flow through you once again. You still have the memory itself, only without the attachment or detrimental, biochemical responses. You've transformed from a constricted way of being into a more expanded state of being, which affords you greater peace, love, harmony, and joy.

The L.E.E.P. Blessing of Forgiveness presented here includes and honors all parties that were involved:

- Those who inflicted the suffering
- Those who suffer
- Those who witnessed the suffering

Let's break this down and take a closer look at each part.

Forgiveness of Others

This can be tricky because we get into our heads and find all the reasons why people should be punished for their actions. This is where pseudo-forgiveness usually shows up. We feel we ought to forgive because it's the right thing to do, or it's the spiritual thing to do. Unfortunately, it lacks authenticity because it is just a concealed form of judgment and resentment masquerading as forgiveness. The real reason we forgive those who have hurt us is not because they deserve to be forgiven, but because we don't want to suffer and hurt every time we remember what they did. As Don Miguel Ruiz says in his book, *The Four Agreements*, whatever anyone did to you has nothing to do with you. It's about acknowledging that the actions of the offending person were the learned behaviors of that person at that time. They were dealing with their own inner anguish and torment. The words and actions that hurt you were merely a reaction to the turmoil that played out in that person's own mind, and that they acted upon while involving you. *Nothing anyone ever does is because of you . . .* it is because of that person's perceptions of the world. They simply act out upon their perceptions and the pain that they carry within them.

Once we have this awareness, it helps us to not take this personally, and, then with compassion and understanding, it will lead us to forgiveness. By forgiving others, we are simply acknowledging the existence of their actions, and by doing so with heart-consciousness rather than the mind alone, it allows that hurt to be released from the body. We can rationalize all we want, but until we forgive in our heart, the person, event, or circumstance will haunt us again and again. And, if we say, *"I just can't forgive,"* then what we are really saying is, *"I prefer to live with my emotional poison, with my pride and my anger. I prefer not to move from this place of suffering."* Our justifications are ways we put forgiveness aside in order to not deal with it. When we forgive, it frees us from limitations to live in greater joy and happiness.

Forgiveness of the Witnesses to Suffering

In this forgiveness process, we will bless those who have witnessed suffering. They have a need to make sense of all they have seen, and they carry a part of the energetic imprint of the event within them. Many people suffer from their inability to comfort or lend a hand and see the events of their world unfolding before their eyes, feeling powerless or helpless to prevent the pain and suffering of others. When we bless those who have witnessed the suffering, it releases their energetic cords or connection to the situation.

Forgiveness of Yourself

Often, the people we most need to forgive are ourselves. Resentment and anger are emotions that actually bind us to the events that cause our suffering. Debbie Ford says that mostly we have to forgive ourselves for taking whatever happened to us too deeply—to the depths that shut us down—for keeping us in our smallness, and paralyzing us from living fully in this present moment.

Consider the following questions. Do you . . .

- Judge yourself harshly?
- Put yourself down?
- Diminish yourself in any way?

- Do things to harm yourself?
- Overeat?
- Drink too much?
- Have an addiction?
- Overspend?

You may wish to forgive yourself if you experience this reality and inwardly beat yourself up over it. These are all ways we inflict self-harm. Resisting forgiveness only hinders our growth and draws more unwanted experiences to us. It is time to make peace with the past—all of it. It is the key to freedom and inner peace, and it starts within you.

Forgiveness Begins Within

It is time to release the negative effects associated with those transgressions. It is time to love yourself and reclaim the power that has been binding you to negativity. We need to forgive if we wish to live in greater joy, peace, and harmony. Doing this mentally is just not enough. We have to do this from the heart in order to free the energy that has paralyzed us and bound us to the past. When we release and let go, it frees our life-force and inner light to shine forth more fully and realigns us to our wholeness. We won't forget or lose our sense of discernment; we simply release our emotional suffering and distress, freeing up the energy for our own healing and evolution.

Energy Centers for Transformation

The L.E.E.P. Blessing of Forgiveness Process will make use of two very powerful energy centers within you—the Hara and the heart.

Your Hara center, also known as the Dan Tien, is a special power center approximately two inches below your navel, and sits inside toward the center of your body. You can imagine this center as an energy conversion portal . . . a powerful energy vortex where you can send *any and all* distress or unwanted thoughts and feelings for transformation and release. There isn't anything that this center cannot handle for it is stronger than any distress you can possibly send to it.

Your heart generates a powerful electromagnetic field all around you—the largest energetic field of your body. This luminous energy field is alive and flowing. Your heart's energy field has a vortex, a portal that can be used as a doorway into the sacred space within your heart. This is the seat of your soul and a timeless dimension of consciousness that holds such enormous potential. In this space, you have access to your higher wisdom, expanded consciousness, and infinite compassion. It is filled with your soul and divinity, which is nurturing and safe, along with all possibilities, dimensions, and realities, including compassionate forgiveness.

Life-Enhancing Energetic Process for Forgiveness

This is a guided process, and, therefore, it is recommended that it be facilitated, so it can move along at a pace that is right for you. If you do not have someone to help you with this, you may do your best following along with the instructions below, or you may visit the Heart and Soul Academy website and listen to the guided process there if you would prefer. (See Appendix II for instructions.)

Energy Test:

"It is in the highest wisdom and benefit to do the Blessing of Forgiveness Process now." If YES, continue.

Close your eyes. Search your heart for any unresolved hurt, resentment, bitterness, or disagreements. Choose now to forgive and release either a specific event or all those who have caused you pain and grief in the past, including yourself, and just let it go. It is time to release the negative effects around those situations. It is time to love yourself and reclaim the power that has been binding you to negativity, draining you of your life force, and diminishing your inner light. You choose to forgive if you wish to live in greater joy, peace, and happiness because forgiveness is a tremendous way to clear the body of emotional pain. Decide who or what circumstances you are choosing to forgive.

Sacred Heart Alignment:

- **Connect with Earth:** Envision the beauty of Mother Earth and feel the love and joy you have for nature. Feel this love in your heart. Imagine sending a beam of love from your heart down deep into the earth. Notice the return beam of nurturing love that Mother Earth sends back to you. Breathe this energy up through your feet, bring it up your spinal column, and release this it into the very center of your heart. Feel the flow of energy between your heart and the earth.

- **Align with Spirit:** Envision the expanse of the heavens and the depths of space. Feel the awe, the wonder, and the love you have for the stars and all of creation. Imagine sending a beam of love from your heart up to your soul star and the heavens above. Immediately, your soul star sends a return beam of warm, golden energy of expanded consciousness to you. Breathe this consciousness down through the top of your head and release this radiant energy into the very center of your heart. Feel the flow of energy between your soul star and your heart.

- **Center within Heart:** Feel both these energies flowing into your heart simultaneously—nourishing earth energy up your spine and expanded consciousness down through your head—swirling these shimmering energies into the center of your heart.

- These energies symbolically represent the fusion of spirit with matter—the divine feminine and divine masculine joined in pure love within you. Remember a time when you felt deep, nurturing love and feel that love now. Then, continue breathing as if through the center of your heart.

Now is the moment where you are empowered to break the cycles that have led to your suffering. Ask yourself if you truly are willing to forgive and move beyond your habitual responses to the person or event that caused hurt or suffering in the past. If so, nod your head or say, *"Yes."*

Activate Your Hara's Power Center:

Next, activate your Hara center, approximately two inches below your navel in the center of your body. Imagine this point as an energy conversion portal . . . a powerful energy center where you can send *any and all* distress or unwanted thoughts and feelings for transformation and release. Feel its power. Know that there isn't anything that this center cannot handle. Know that it is stronger than *any* distress you can possibly send to it. To activate your Hara center, focus your attention on this area. Breathe into this center and imagine it being filled with violet and golden light with each breath. Take at least three deep breaths through your Hara's energy conversion portal, relaxing more with each exhalation.

Sacred Heart Space:

Imagine or sense your heart's energy field all around you, alive and flowing. Become sensitive to the movements of your heart's energetic movements.

Feel yourself moving with the currents of this field. If you cannot sense or feel the currents, relax and just pretend that you can.

Your heart's energy field has a vortex, a portal that can be used as a doorway into the sacred space of your heart. In a moment, you will be guided into this sacred space. There, you have access to your higher wisdom, expanded consciousness, and infinite compassion.

Bring your attention to your heart's energy field and imagine or pretend you are there. With your consciousness, follow the vortex of energy—this portal, which will lead you to the sacred space within your heart.

With your next breath, breathe in and hold it for a moment. [*Pause*.] Then, as you exhale, trust your inner resources to take you directly through the portal's doorway of your heart's most sacred space—a place filled with your soul and divinity. [*Note to Facilitator: let your partner fully exhale and soften your voice.*] You are now within your heart's sacred space . . . a place that is warm, nurturing, and safe.

This space is the seat of your soul and a timeless dimension of consciousness that holds enormous potential. A space filled with all possibilities. All dimensions and realities are available to you here—including compassionate forgiveness.

Establish a Breathing Pattern:

Now, you are going to establish a breathing pattern between your heart's sacred space and your Hara's powerful conversion portal. Inhale love and light through your heart, then exhale love and light through your Hara. Inhale through your heart and exhale through your Hara. Continue this process for a few deep breaths.

[*Facilitator, allow for at least three complete breaths.*]

This breathing pattern is a powerful tool for moving through and releasing any distressful events, thoughts, or feelings in your body-mind energy system. Just let go of anything that no longer serves you.

Bring your attention back to your sacred heart space. Now, bring to your awareness the person, people, or circumstances you are choosing to forgive.

Take a moment as you consider your commitment to forgive and release the emotional suffering you've been holding onto, freeing up your energy for your own health and well-being.

Communicate with those who you are forgiving anything that you have been holding onto that has caused your suffering. Don't hold back. Whether it is hurt feelings, a sense of betrayal, anger you've held onto, love you've withheld, or even revenge you've desired.

Send any hurt or stressful thoughts or feelings to your Hara's conversion portal for transformation and release by simply breathing in through your heart and exhaling out through your Hara. Continue to express to each being whatever was done that has caused you suffering and distress until you feel a sense of completion—releasing all harm you believed was ever done to you at any time, by any person or set of circumstances. Send *any* and *all* distress out through your Hara for transformation and release until you feel a sense of peace or detachment associated with the entire experience.

Take your time. Breathe love. Allow the violet light of transformation and the golden light of expanded consciousness to transform and release all. Take all the time you need for transformation and release. Then say, *"Okay"* when you have finished or feel complete.

Softly repeat to yourself three times with feeling and meaning, *"All is blessed, forgiven, and released."*

Bring your attention back to your heart's sacred space. Breathe through your heart and feel the nurturing love of the soul essence you have within you and relax. To all those who have witnessed any part of your suffering, send gratitude for their care and compassion. Allow the violet light of transformation and the golden light of expanded consciousness to release their energetic cords or bonds to the situation. And breathe love. Then say, *"Okay"* when you have finished or feel complete.

Softly repeat to yourself three times with feeling and meaning, *"I bless those who have witnessed my suffering."*

Bring your attention back to your sacred heart space. Breathe through your heart and feel the nurturing love of the soul essence you have within you and relax. *[Pause.]* It is now time to lovingly express forgiveness for yourself, for all you did or *didn't know to do* in the experience. Forgive yourself for all you regret and for all the ways you were unloving to yourself or others. Forgive yourself for all of the ways you diminish yourself, put yourself down, or harm yourself in any way. *[Pause.]*

Forgive yourself for having taken whatever happened to you too deeply—to the depths that shut you down and have kept you in your smallness, limiting you from fully living in the now, the ever present moment.

Send *any and all* hurt or distressful thoughts or feelings to your Hara's conversion portal for transformation and release by breathing in through your heart and exhaling out through your Hara until you feel a sense of peace, release, and forgiveness for yourself, completely setting yourself free. *[Long pause.]*

Forgive yourself for any harm you believe you have ever done to anyone, including yourself, in this lifetime and all lifetimes, in this dimension and reality, and all dimensions and realities.

Take your time. Breathe love and allow the violet light of transformation and the golden light of expanded consciousness to transform and release all—sending any and all hurt or stressful thoughts or feelings to your Hara for transformation and release. Take all the time you need to forgive, transform, and release. Then say *"Okay"* when you have finished or feel complete.

Integration:

Now, bring your hands to your heart, resting them on your chest, and feel the love and warmth you have inside. Softly repeat to yourself three times with feeling and meaning, *"All is forgiven."*

When you are ready, point your fingertips inward toward your heart.

Simply breathe love through your heart's sacred space for a few breaths. Allow love to fill every cell of your body and every space between every cell. Radiate love and light through every atom of your being, so that you shine and shimmer like stars within. Your essential nature is the seat of your soul and a timeless dimension of consciousness that holds enormous potential. A space filled with all possibilities, filled with so much divine love and light that it overflows, and you radiate this love and light out to surround and embrace yourself fully.

Repeat after me, and say to yourself:

"All is forgiven."

"I bless and release all."

"In this lifetime and all lifetimes."

"In this dimension and reality and in all dimensions and realities."

"For the highest wisdom and benefit of all, including myself."

Once again, fill yourself with so much divine love and light that it overflows—radiating out from the center of your heart. Then spread your arms upward and outward, as if tracing a big heart shape in the air, radiating love and light from the center of your heart, sharing this forgiveness and release without limitation throughout the world. Conclude by pointing your fingertips downward toward the earth, anchoring it for the highest wisdom and benefit for all.

You may open your eyes when you are ready.

There you have it! The three biggest secrets for resolving emotional wounds and releasing traumatic stress from your body-mind energy system, allowing you to move into greater peace, joy, and flow in your life. As we heal our emotional wounds and traumas, we raise our personal frequencies to a more expanded, evolved consciousness for ourselves. Be good to yourself. Love yourself. Heal your emotional wounds.

*"The moment you have in your heart this extraordinary thing
called love and feel the depth, the delight, the ecstasy of it,
you will discover that for you the world is transformed."*
~ Jiddu Krishnamurti

*Please see Appendix II for instructions about downloading these process and chart resources
at:* www.theHeartAndSoulAcademy.org/resource-page/
*Emotional Interference Pattern Resolution Process—Finding Emo Chart—Healthy, Helpful
Emotions Chart—Traumatic Stress Release Process—The Blessings of Forgiveness Process*

CHAPTER 10

Essential Human Needs:
Uncommon Knowledge

"Our deepest wishes are whispers of our authentic selves.
We must learn to respect them. We must learn to listen."
~ Sarah Ban Breathnach

Is there an essential need in your life that's not being met or expressed?

As you learned in the previous chapter, your emotions carry messages. Disharmonious or distressed emotions can either be emotional wounds that need to be healed, or perhaps they are signaling us of an internal unmet need.

We all have basic needs that are universal and significant to all of humanity. They have a life-force of their own and show up in different and important ways. While all humans share these, each person's needs vary, just like their need for water, food, or sleep. One person may require more personal freedom and independence, where another may crave more connection and closeness. Some people want more opportunities for expression and creativity, while others have a greater desire for play and humor. This chapter is about how to find a need that is not being met, and which may be holding you back, and how to take steps to integrate it back into your life's experience.

The Impact of Unmet Needs

When our needs are not being fulfilled, we can easily feel discouraged, frustrated, resentful, disconnected, or invalidated. When we lose touch with this vital part of ourselves, we have a greater tendency to be disappointed with the actions and behaviors of others. It is easier for us to think of what is wrong with them, to misinterpret their intentions, or make false accusations against them. It is not so much about them, or their behavior, as much as it is about us and our feelings of discontent. It undermines not only our own lives, but also impacts how we relate to others. When we are living lives that fulfill our needs, we have less reason to find fault with others.

The problem is, when our needs go unrecognized, it makes it that much harder to go about fulfilling them. Unfortunately, most of us have never been taught to think in terms of our needs—it is largely uncommon knowledge. As Howard Thurman says, "Don't ask what the world needs. Ask what makes you come alive, and go do it. Because what the world needs is people who have come alive." Self-knowledge and awareness is what makes us come alive as we move toward fulfilling our needs. From the moment we begin communicating what we desire, rather than finding fault with someone else, the possibility of finding ways to meet our needs is greatly increased. Then, in turn, we can more easily help others to acknowledge and fulfill their own unmet needs.

FEELINGS ASSOCIATED WITH ESSENTIAL HUMAN NEEDS

Feelings When Needs Are Not Fulfilled		Feelings When Needs Are Fulfilled	
Aggravated	Hostile	Absorbed	Fascinated
Agitated	Hurt	Adventurous	Free
Angry	Impatient	Alert	Friendly
Anguished	Indifferent	Alive	Fulfilled
Annoyed	Irate	Amazed	Glad
Anxious	Irritated	Amused	Glorious
Apprehensive	Jealous	Animated	Glowing
Bewildered	Leery	Appreciative	Good-natured
Bitter	Lonely	Blissful	Grateful
Bored	Mad	Buoyant	Gratified
Chagrined	Miserable	Calm	Happy
Concerned	Mournful	Carefree	Hopeful
Confused	Numb	Cheerful	Inspired
Dejected	Overwhelmed	Comfortable	Interested
Depressed	Passive	Confident	Intrigued
Detached	Perplexed	Content	Invigorated
Disenchanted	Pessimistic	Curious	Involved
Disappointed	Reluctant	Delighted	Joyous
Discouraged	Resentful	Eager	Jubilant
Disgruntled	Restless	Ecstatic	Mirthful
Disheartened	Skeptical	Effervescent	Optimistic
Displeased	Sorrowful	Elated	Peaceful
Distressed	Spiritless	Enchanted	Radiant
Exasperated	Suspicious	Encouraged	Refreshed
Fidgety	Troubled	Energetic	Satisfied
Frustrated	Uncomfortable	Enlivened	Stimulated
Furious	Upset	Enthusiastic	Thankful
Helpless	Uptight	Excited	Upbeat
Hesitant	Weary	Exhilarated	Wonderful
Horrible	Withdrawn	Expansive	Zestful

This chart was inspired by Marshal Rosenberg's Non-Violent Communication Training course.

Exercise: Discover What You Need

Becoming more aware of these essential needs is the first step toward helping ourselves lead more fulfilling, enlivened, and satisfied lives. Whether we are out of touch with what our specific needs are in a given situation, or whether we want to elicit the help of our higher wisdom in becoming more aware of our needs in general, discovery is only an energy test away.

Energy Test:

In varying degrees, each according to his or her own unique nature, we each have natural needs. Complete this simple energy test: *"There is a need in me that is not being met."*

If YES, energy test each of the following six groups of needs, then use the Essential Human Needs chart to find out what specific need is not being met. For example, *"The unmet need can be found in (physical nurturance)."* This would be a message for you that nurturing this need back into your life would be beneficial and would serve you well.

- Physical Nurturance
- Autonomy
- Interdependence
- Celebration and Play
- Integrity
- Spiritual Communion

Keep energy testing each of these groups until you come to a YES response, then narrow it down in that group until you come to the unmet need.

ESSENTIAL HUMAN NEEDS

1
Physical Nurturance

Air
Clothing
Financial Security
Food
Health
Intimacy—to know that
  at least one other person
  accepts us totally for who
  we are
Movement / Exercise
Personal Safety / Security
Protection—from life-
  threatening forms of life:
  viruses, bacteria, insects,
  predatory animals, especially
  human beings
Rest
Safe environment
Sensuality
Sexual expression
Shelter
Touch
Water
Well-being

2
Autonomy

Sense of Achievement
Sense of Being in Charge
Sense of Competence
Having option of making
  responsible choices
Independence
Choosing dreams, goals,
  values
Choosing plans for fulfilling
  ones' dreams, goals, values
Personal Freedom
Personal Growth
Privacy—opportunity to
  reflect upon, process, and
  contemplate experiences
Sense of Status within social
  settings

3
Interdependence

Acceptance
Appreciation
Closeness
Community
Connection
Consideration
Contribute to the enrichment
  of life
Emotional safety
Empathy
Honesty (the empowering
  honesty that allows us to
  learn from our limitations)
Love reassurance
Respect
Support
To be seen, recognized for
  who we are
Trust
Understanding, and to be
  understood
Valued

4
Celebration / Play

Adventure
Celebrate the creation of life
  and dreams fulfilled
Celebrate losses: loved ones,
  dreams, mourning
Friendship
Fun
Humor
Romance
Spontaneity

5
Integrity

Authenticity
Attention—to give and
  receive it, a form of
  nutrition
Creativity
Meaning
Purpose
Security in an environment
  that allows us to develop
  fully
Self-worth
Significance

6
Spiritual Communication

Altruism
Beauty
Being of service
Consciousness
Harmony
Inspiration
Order
Peace
Self-transcendence

*This chart was inspired by Marshal Rosenberg's Non-Violent Communication
Training course.*

Once we acknowledge, understand, and are consciously aware of our needs, solutions are easier to find and carry out. We now have more choices in how to bring them into our life experience and ways to honor them more fully. You could communicate with your subconscious what your life would be like if you were living that need fulfilled within you.

- What would you *see* that would let you know you've made this unmet need a greater part of your life?

- How would you *feel* if this unmet need were a greater part of your life?

- What might be *different* in your life if this need were fulfilled?

You could enlist the support of your subconscious with the Language of Creation Process to help you become more aware of fulfilling your needs and recognizing that they are important. Maybe you would like subconscious support for overcoming a fear that you'll be judged, criticized, or ridiculed for identifying and revealing your needs. Gently remind yourself that the interpretations or obnoxiousness of others says more about them than it does you, then program your subconscious for your success and worthiness with the Chakra Belief Change Process. You won't be able to meet your needs at the expense of others—this would be emotional slavery. When we accept full responsibility for our needs, it is easier for others to respond compassionately and respect them.

Helpful Action Tips

- Create a list and a plan of action to support you as you take the necessary steps.

- Communicate your needs to others in order to fulfill them. Other individuals are not always able to read our minds or interpret our words. In this case, we need to make a clear request of others, with specific actions, in order to fulfill our needs.

There is an excellent formula used by Non-Violent Communication to consciously communicate our needs. It is a conscious strategy process.

First: Identify the feelings that are going on inside you about an experience or concern you are having—be a witness to what is going on without the need to immediately react.

> *Example:* "I feel a sense of frustration when I am being micro-managed. I feel resentful that I am not being trusted to manage my time and responsibilities on my own."

Second: Be with the feeling for a bit, then identify and clarify the needs you believe are not being met for you—a basic human need that anyone might have.

> *Example:* "I need to be treated with respect and to be trusted that I know how to manage my time on my own terms. I also need to be given the chance to prove my competency and have a sense of 'Being in Charge.'"

Third: In any set of circumstances, there is the 'Self' and there is the 'Other.' So, the next step is to feel empathy for the 'Other'—try to understand his or her feelings and needs. Ask yourself, "Why is he/she choosing to do this?" Name the need that you are sensing.

> *Example:* "The 'Other' may be under a lot of stress and feel a sense of pressure. He/she may not be feeling supported in the moment."

Fourth: With an open mind, create an empathetic connection with the other person and then communicate your needs.

> *Example:* "I am feeling a sense of frustration and resentment because I have a need to 'be in charge of my own time' that is not being met. I need to be trusted that I can make competent, responsible choices. I have a sense that you are under pressure and may be feeling unsupported."

Listen: Be present and listen from your heart to the other person's response. The other person will sense that you care even if your best guess wasn't completely accurate—this invites him/her to clarify specific needs and feelings, (plus, the other person will feel heard because you listened).

Needs Met: Once both individuals' needs are acknowledged and understood, solutions are easier to find and carry out as ideas pop into the mind for taking action to resolve the problem. Everyone feels good because it is our natural inclination to make life more wonderful for ourselves and others.

Tune In and Be Present

A daily practice of being present and focusing inward for a few moments on what you are feeling helps you to notice, acknowledge, and identify what your needs in life truly are.

There's a huge benefit when you take the time to discover, acknowledge, and honor your needs. Your life experience will become more carefree and enlivened. You'll feel good. You'll be more content and satisfied. And, when you honor your needs as well as those of others, you enrich humanity.

"We must make the choices that enable us to
fulfill the deepest capacities of our real selves."
~ Thomas Merton

Please see Appendix II for instructions about how to download the Essential Human Needs chart.

CHAPTER 11

Influences of a Distant Past

"Everything can be taken from a man
but the last of the human freedoms—to choose one's attitude
in any given set of circumstances, to choose one's own way."
~ Victor Frankl

Past Lives

There are times when the distant past, which consists of past-life experiences and ancestral lineage influences, affects current-life circumstances. This occurs when there is a carry-over interference pattern that needs to be resolved. When this is brought to your attention, you will have a life lesson to learn, and, by doing so, it will help you resolve the problems you are working through. Let's begin with taking a look at past lives.

Evaluating the Benefit of Past-Life Exploration

It is estimated that up to 44 percent of the world population believes in reincarnation, and many individuals believe it is possible that some part of our consciousness continues on after death. Whether you personally believe or not is not the question at hand; it is whether or not the therapeutic benefits from past-life exploration resolve the interference pattern. If so, then it is of value.

Exploring the Unexplainable

There are many cause and effect forces that play a part in our life that we don't always understand. A past-life influence is often the cause of a problem or symptom that does not respond to modern day treatments, therapy, or common sense approaches. What should normally work simply doesn't. Unexplained illness or unexplained chronic pain are good examples of past-life influences. The doctor says, *"I can't find anything wrong with you"* and gives you a clean bill of health. Yet, for no apparent reason, the warning signals continue to trouble you. Take fibromyalgia, for example. The physical symptoms may make it difficult to diagnose, but it is possible that they stem from past-life resonance memory where the body had been so impacted with suffering, trauma, and weariness that a person simply doesn't function well until having extended periods of rest.

Past lives store unfinished or incomplete issues that are etched into our soul's journey. Some may be self-inflicted, like blame, abuse, and self-loathing, while others may be the result of great atrocities, such as murder, rape, drowning, being fed to the lions, or scalped alive. A past life may also be filled with regret, betrayal, fear, resentment, or incomplete challenges or life purpose works that weren't fully realized.

Perpetual Energy and Its Purpose

While the physical body may die, the energy of the consciousness itself cannot be destroyed—it remains long after the body is gone and is taken with us into future lives. When energetic distortions are not resolved, they create the same themes in our lives in order to give us the opportunity to heal them. They can come back to haunt us in recurring dreams and nightmares, strange memories, unexplained fears and pains, and destructive habits.

A Lifetime of Past Lives

My whole life I have remembered parts and pieces of several past lives. For me, they seemed to get touched off at certain ages or by similar sets of circumstances that trigger the memories or the interference pattern.

Dying from starvation in India—One of the very few lifetimes I was ever male corresponded with my having life-threatening pneumonia when I was six years old. From this memory/experience not only was I aware of death from a very young age, but I've always wanted to have a storage of food supplies on hand.

Dying in a gas chamber—I missed Thanksgiving with my family because I was deathly ill with pneumonia when I spontaneously had a vision of myself dying in a German concentration camp in 1942 (and then felt a deep sense of relief that the suffering in that lifetime was finally over). Within just a few hours, I began to feel better. My lungs cleared, and I regained my strength. After that past-life recall, I've not had a cold or flu since.

Temporary survival—I remember being on a hillside field, gathering herbs and having Viking-like raiders beat, rape, and leave my tortured body for dead. I survived, and, after a few days, was able to make it back to my village only to discover that everyone was dead. Everyone I had ever known had been brutally murdered, including my only child. I remember holding her lifeless body, not moving, until I myself, eventually died. This memory has made me deeply appreciate being a mother and genuinely cherish my children in this lifetime.

My Daughter's Past Life Entwined with Mine

When my daughter Danika was almost three years old, she briefly remembered a past life with me in it. I was nine months pregnant with my son and had asked Danika to bring me her shoes, so I could put them on her feet, and we could go to the store. She brought them to me then got this far away look in her eyes, stared off into the distance, and said, *"When I was your mom, and you were my little girl, we had to take horses into town because there were no cars."* From my hypnotherapy training I remembered to ask her what country or year she lived in. Unfortunately, the sound of my voice brought her back to the present. She looked at me in surprise and said, *"You again?"* then burst into a great big smile, wrapped her little arms around me in a big hug, and exclaimed, *"Oh, it's you again!"* Keep in mind, this happened when she was barely three years old and had no knowledge that there was ever a time when cars didn't exist.

It was during that same lifetime where she was my mother that I remember her taking me by horse and cart and leaving me at a nearby abbey in an attempt to save my life. At around age 15 in that lifetime, I became a nun in order to escape a marriage to an older man who had already drunkenly beat two previous wives to death (which was not a crime at that time) for not working hard enough on his farm. That lifetime's imprint made me further cherish the opportunity to be a mother in this life.

The Allure of Past Lives

Most of us can't help being captivated by the compelling allure of past lives. There are:

- Scientific protocols and investigations into the past lives of children who remember them spontaneously.
- Adults who vividly remember past-life experiences while under hypnosis.
- The talents of young children who display amazing abilities in music, art, and foreign languages without ever having a single lesson.

It is such an intriguing subject that much has been written and explored from many different angles. The Past Life Process started to come into the L.E.E.P. System years ago while I was working with a woman in her late 60s who had unexplained back pain. During one point in the session, I asked her to go back to the time of origin when her back pain started. While on the massage table, she started arching and writhing about—it looked very much as if she was in agony and being tortured on a medieval stretching rack. Her flashes of memory recall, along with energy testing, confirmed this fact and solidified my belief that past lives can set into motion a memory in your energetic field of consciousness that needs to be healed, or it will continue playing an unexplainable or puzzling role in your present-life experiences.

Energetically, this L.E.E.P. piece of the puzzle gives you the opportunity to:

- Resolve certain interference patterns in the subconscious
- Heal the distorted energy configuration that has been put into motion
- Resolve "unfinished business" to release past karma and to move on for soul growth
- Achieve a different perspective about being human

Self-Discovery Process

Have you ever wondered how to hone in and explore a past life? When working with a past life, begin with energy testing a series of questions to discover the past-life circumstances, dynamics, and storyline that is meant to be uncovered. For example, energy test periods of time.

- "Is the past life before or after the Christ era?"

Once you've determined whether the lifetime was before or after the time of Christ, according to the Julian calendar, then you can begin narrowing it down to discover the specific time period when the past life took place.

- Between 1-500 AD. Between 500-1000 AD. Between 1000-1500 AD. Between 1500-1950 AD.
- Between 500-1 BC. Between 500-1000 BC. Between 1000-3000 BC.

Keep narrowing it down until you get an approximate time frame—the exact year is not as important as the time frame itself. It could be a relevant lifetime in the mid-800s, and that would be sufficient enough for the purpose of exploring this past life.

Discover Who You Were:

- Energy test to discover the age you were during that lifetime.
  - Between conception/birth and 10 years old. Between 10-20. 20-30. 30-40. Etc.
  - Keep energy testing until you discover the relevant age during that lifetime.
- Were you male or female?
- On a scale of 1-10, what was your social status in life?
  - 1 being the lowliest of society and 10 being royalty or a member of the hierarchy.
- On a scale of 1-10, what was your financial status?
  - 1 being dirt poor and 10 being extremely wealthy.
- Optional exploration: Country or continent the lifetime took place on; though, this is not always necessary or vital to know.

Determine Who Was Involved:

It's important to find out who was involved in this influential event and where the energy is most conflicted. In role playing, for example, both of the individuals involved play a part in creating the conflict. They do so in order to learn a lesson from it from different perspectives. In every conflict there is the side that explores what it is like to lend weight to the problem, and the side that agrees to, and explores, what it's like on the opposite end by receiving the burden of the problem. What's it like to play the part of an Oppressor versus a Victim? The Betrayer or the Betrayed? The Fortunate or Less Fortunate? This is not done as a punishment, but it is meant as a way to learn from and experience different viewpoints. Discover which perspective you played a part in by energy testing:

- Self-to-self. This lets you know you created the interference pattern on your own.
  - Example: Individuals who were sickened so much by the atrocities witnessed in war that they shot themselves in the foot in order to get released from duty—they inflicted the harm due to an internal emotional struggle.
- Self-to-other(s). In this case, your actions created the interference pattern while causing suffering to another person or multiple people.
- Other(s)-to-self. Here, someone (or several people) harmed you, thus creating an interference pattern.

Most often the inflicted suffering was intentional, though, on rare occasions, it could be unintentional. An example might be a situation when you had to betray another person in order to protect your child or spouse, or to face death by not choosing to betray the other. The harm inflicted was not intentional. It was simply an act of desperation.

Find Out Who Else Was Involved:

- Energy test to discover the age the other person was during that lifetime.
  - Between conception/birth-10 years old. Between 10-20. 20-30. 30-40. Etc.
- Keep energy testing until you discover the relevant age during that lifetime.
- Were they male or female?
- On a scale of 1-10, what was the other person's social status in life?
  - 1 being the lowliest of society and 10 being royalty or a member of the hierarchy.
- On a scale of 1-10, what was their financial status in life?
  - 1 being dirt poor and 10 being extremely wealthy.

Reason Behind the Suffering:

Energy test to discover the main reason that created the conflict and suffering.

- Begin by discovering which chakra is impacted—this will give insight into the set of circumstances and also carries a portion of the message.

  - 7th: Spiritual connection, insights, psychic abilities

  - 6th: Worldly vision, trust, intelligence, and psychic vision

  - 5th: Self-expression and expressing one's own truth

  - 4th: Deals with matters of the heart, love, and relationships

  - 3rd: Deals with personal power and self-worth

  - 2nd: Deals with sexuality, fertility, and creative expression

  - 1st: Deals with survival issues and physical expression in life

In order to determine the original cause of the conflict, energy test the following topics:

- Power / Business Dealings

- Money / Wealth

- Relationship / Family / Heartache

- Acts of Atrocity / Acts of Natural Disaster

- Health: Illness / Accident / Poisoning

- Spiritual / Religious

- Other—use intuitive guidance to explore another area of life if it's not listed above

Healing the Past

Now that you have a basic understanding of the storyline, it is time to heal the past. Experience has shown me that it is most always a belief that needs to change or an emotional wound that needs to be healed. Energy test to find which L.E.E.P. will be of highest priority to use in order to resolve the interference pattern, then follow the instruction steps for that process.

- Belief Change

- Resolve Emotional Wound

- Blessing of Forgiveness Process

- Traumatic Stress Release

Your skills and confidence will grow as you learn to work with, and piece together, past-life influences. Rest assured that there is no need to get caught up in *the drama* of the past life, only to heal the distorted energy caused by it.

Ancestral Lineage Influences

Many indigenous cultures teach that we are placed on earth to be the caretakers of all that is here—that each generation has a responsibility to "ensure the survival and thrival for the next seven generations." They believe that what we do today affects future generations, and we must always remember our responsibility to them and act accordingly. Not only does what we do today affect generations upon the planet, but scientific research is also proving that genetic memory is being passed onto us from past generations.

Epigenetics is an area of science that studies the epigenetic (above genetics) expression of our genes *and* how the cellular memory effects of past generations affect present and future generations. Epigenetic influence can be accumulated and added onto DNA throughout our lives, setting off a chain reaction of cellular changes that result in health changes and life experiences. Geneticists discovered that epigen-change could be passed down from parent to child, one generation after the other. Since energy is never lost and is still contained within the family's group consciousness, behavioral epigenetics can influence our strengths, resiliencies, and talents, as well as our weaknesses, deficiencies, and limitations.

An Indirect Imprint

Our ancestor's experiences, beliefs, and emotions leave an impression, a molecular scar or adhesion, on our DNA and in our lives. Those adhesions that permanently attach to the DNA can be replicated right along with it through the next generations. If someone in your ancestral lineage experienced hardships, tremendous trauma, world disaster, Holocaust, famine, injustice, a scalping, or suffering of some kind, the chemistry from that stressful experience, to some degree, becomes imprinted on your DNA. The molecular residue becomes part of us, ingrained in the energetic makeup of who we are. This means people can inherit some level of negative interference patterns that adversely influence their life experiences, perceptions, behaviors, personality, and outlooks in life without knowing it, including:

- Relationships and Social Behaviors
- Prosperity and Success
- Health, Well-being, Birthmarks, and Receding Hairlines
- Phobias, Sleep Patterns, and Aging

Once we understand that our ancestral stress has been transferred to us, in part or in whole, we can take steps to heal the past and prevent it from affecting the future as well. And, when we make the choice to heal our ancestral wounds, we bring a higher level of consciousness into our lineage line.

I facilitated the ancestral lineage healing process for a woman in her mid-50s who had been struggling in her business ventures. During the session (which involved visualization), she said she noticed a cloud of dark, heavy energy along her father's side while doing the clearing process. Afterwards, she recalled hearing stories of her crotchety, stubborn, old grandfather who had lost a fortune during the Great Depression. About six weeks later, she called to say that everything in her business had been lining up and falling into place, that she felt like it was flowing without any difficulty or hold-ups, and that she was getting recognition where she hadn't before.

Looking for the ancestral interference pattern can be a daunting search for a needle-in-the-haystack if you don't have effective tools at your command. The outline formula given for honing in on a past life works for ancestral lineage, too, though, the following guided shamanic process will energetically clear both lines of generational imprints and move healing energy forward into future generations in one powerful, grace-filled session.

Life-Enhancing Energetic Process for Healing Ancestral Lineage:

This process is a guided process, and, therefore, it is recommended that it be facilitated, so it can move along at a pace that is right for you. If you do not have someone to help you with this process, do your best by following along with the instructions below, or you may visit the Heart and Soul Academy website and listen to the guided process there.

Energy Test: *"It is in the highest wisdom and benefit to do the Healing Ancestral Lineage Process now."* If YES, proceed.

Sacred Heart Alignment:

[*NOTE to Facilitator: As you guide a person through this process, be sure to speak in a calm, relaxing voice.*]

Close your eyes.

- **Connect with Earth:** Envision the beauty of Mother Earth and feel the love and joy you have for nature. Feel this love in your heart and imagine sending a beam of love from your heart down deep into the earth. Notice that Mother Earth sends a return beam of nurturing love energy back to you. Breathe this energy up through your feet, draw it up your spinal column, and release the nourishing energy into the very center of your heart. Feel the flow of energy between you, the earth, and your heart.

- **Align with Spirit:** Envision the expanse of the heavens and the depths of space. Feel the awe, the wonder, and the love you have for the stars and all of creation. Imagine sending a beam of love from your heart up to your soul star and the heavens above. Immediately, your soul star sends a return beam of warm, golden energy of expanded consciousness to you. Breathe this expanded consciousness down through the top of your head and release the radiant energy into the very center of your heart. Feel the flow of energy between your soul star and your heart.

- **Center within Heart:** Feel both these energies flowing into your heart simultaneously—nourishing earth energy up your spine and expanded consciousness down through your head—swirling these shimmering energies into the center of your heart.

These energies symbolically represent the fusion of spirit with matter joined in pure love within you. Remember a time when you felt deep, nurturing love and feel that love now. Then, continue breathing this feeling of love as if through the center of your heart.

Sacred Heart Space:

Imagine or sense your heart's energy field all around you. This energy field is alive and flowing. Become sensitive to the movements of your heart's energetic movements. Feel yourself moving with the currents of this field. If you cannot sense or feel the currents of your heart's energy field, relax, and just pretend that you can.

Your heart's energy field has a vortex, a portal that can be used as a doorway into the sacred space of your heart. In a moment, you will be guided into this sacred space. There, you have access to your higher wisdom, expanded consciousness, and infinite compassion.

Bring your attention to your heart's energy field within you and imagine or pretend you are there. With your consciousness, you will follow the vortex of energy—this portal, which will lead you to the sacred space within your heart.

With your next breath, breathe in and hold it for a moment. Then, as you exhale, trust your inner resources to take you directly through your portal's doorway to your heart's most sacred space—a place filled with your soul and divinity. [*NOTE to Facilitator: Let your partner fully exhale and soften your voice.*] You are now within your heart's sacred space—a place that is warm, nurturing, and safe.

This sacred space is the seat of your soul and a timeless dimension of consciousness that holds such enormous potential. A space filled with all possibilities. All dimensions and realities are available to you here . . . including your entire ancestral lineage.

Imagine you have wings of light extending from the back of your heart—these wings represent your ancestral lineage going back generation upon generation into the past. The left side represents your mother's lineage line; the right side represents your father's.

Access Your Mother's Ancestral Lineage:

Focus your attention on your mother's lineage—the wing of light extending from your left side. This wing represents your mother, her parents, grandparents, great-grandparents, and so on, extending back through the generations. This wing of light includes all their siblings—all your aunts and uncles, extending back three, four, and five generations and more.

Bring your attention back to your sacred heart space. Breathe into this space and imagine it being filled with the violet and golden light of transformation and expanded consciousness with each breath. When you are ready, allow your consciousness and higher wisdom to hone in on any and all areas of distress on your mother's side that need to be transformed, healed, and released. "Breathe into" these areas, sending them love, light, and healing

energy. Send compassion and understanding for their hardships and struggles, for their loss of possessions or abandoned belongings while escaping
abuse or catastrophe. Breathe love, light, and healing energies into the areas
of loss of a loved one, sending compassion and understanding for a financial
struggle or trauma. Send the energy of forgiveness to *wherever* it is needed
for these things in the past, helping free them.

Send love and gratitude. Thank them for their gifts of courage. Honor
them for their strengths. Bless the past with love, light, and healing energies
for a brighter, more abundant future of the family line with greater freedom
and expression of the human spirit.

Open your eyes when you've finished or feel complete. Energy Test:
"This side of my ancestral lineage is transformed and healed." If YES, proceed to the next step. If NO, repeat this step.

Access Your Father's Ancestral Lineage:

Close your eyes. Focus your attention on your father's lineage—the wing
of light extending from your right side. This wing represents your father,
his parents, grandparents, great-grandparents, and so on, extending back
through the generations. This wing of light includes all their siblings—all your
aunts and uncles, extending back three, four, or five generations and more.

Bring your attention back to your sacred heart space. Breathe into this
space and imagine it being filled with the violet and golden light of transformation and expanded consciousness with each breath. When you are ready,
allow your consciousness and higher wisdom to hone in on any and all areas
of distress on your father's side that need to be transformed, healed, and
released. "Breathe into" these areas, sending them love, light, and healing
energy. Send compassion and understanding for their hardships and struggles, for their loss of possessions or abandoned belongings left while escaping abuse or catastrophe. Breathe love, light, and healing energies into the
areas of loss of a loved one and compassion and understanding for a financial struggle or trauma. Send the energy of forgiveness to *wherever* it is
needed for these things in the past, helping free them.

Send love and gratitude. Thank them for their gifts of courage. Honor
them for their strengths. Bless the past with love, light, and healing energies
for a brighter, more abundant future of the family line with greater freedom
and expression of the human spirit.

Open your eyes when you've finished or feel complete. Energy Test:
"This side of my ancestral lineage is transformed and healed." If YES, proceed to the next step. If NO, repeat this step.

Unite the Past with the Present:

Close your eyes. Bring your attention to your life here and now. Feel the renewed love and light energy in your wings of light. Sense how much clearer and brighter they are, how radiantly they shine. Feel the love and gratitude your ancestors have for you. Feel your wings of light wrap around you in a great big hug, embracing you in the warmth of your ancestors' love. The blood that pumps through your body is because of the love, courage, steadfastness, determination, resilience, adventure, and lives of many past generations who came before you and stand behind you. Breathe as if through your heart, infusing this potent energy within you. Bask in it and carry this beneficial energy forward into your life. Allow it to radiate out through your entire body, filling every cell and every space between, becoming so full that this love and light begins to radiate out, filling your entire field of energy.

Blessing Future Generations:

Set your attention on future generations. With your intention, send the healing energies of love and light forward to your children, grandchildren, great-grandchildren, and beyond (even if you never have children or grandchildren.) Send it to future generations to support humanity with love, light, and compassion. Strengthen your lineage and the lives that are touched with greater freedom of spirit to play, enjoy, and express life more fully—to be, do, have, or experience their heart's desire. To create heaven on earth.

Ground Yourself in the Here and Now:

The ancestral lineage healing process can leave you with a sense of timelessness and a feeling of being ungrounded. To anchor and ground yourself in the here and now, imagine sending a beam of energy down into the earth. Allow your energy to extend down through the ground, through the layers of rock, and all the way to the very center of the earth where it instinctively goes to a special grounding spot just for you. Then say out loud three times, *"I am grounded, fully present, and free to experience life to its fullest."*

Healing past-life experiences and ancestral lineage influences are little-known, though highly-valued, processes that are missing from traditional therapies that support personal growth. They free up energy that prevents you from carrying out your life's purpose and your soul's mission, freeing your energy for greater peace, joy, fulfillment, and conscious awareness. Exploring past lives gives insight and a deeper awareness of who you are as a human being.

"The future belongs to those who believe in the beauty of their dreams."
~ Eleanor Roosevelt

See Appendix II for instructions about how to download the Past Life Discovery and Ancestral Lineage Healing Processes at:
www.theHeartAndSoulAcademy.org/resource-page/

CHAPTER 12

Reclaiming Disowned Selves

"Most of the shadows of this life are caused
by our standing in our own sunshine."
~ Ralph Waldo Emerson

Throughout history it has been said that inside each of us is a community of personalities, each with their own voices and points of view. As we grow and develop our personality, we begin to experience life through our perceptions and conditionings. At some point along our journey there comes a time where we uncover hidden parts of ourselves we've disowned that we don't want to face—the shadow portions of ourselves.

We tend to fear these disowned parts because we don't like seeing the undesirable, unattractive, and distasteful aspects of our personality. We don't want to identify with them. We want to believe we are better than that. The only thing is, we can't really get rid of any part of ourselves because it is part of who we are. Yet, the shadow is one of the most important but least understood aspects of humanity because of its obscure nature.

How the Shadow Develops

These disowned selves are fragmented pieces of the personality that linger in the shadows, fragments of yourself that have been pushed away or shunned in some fashion every time they have emerged. They are not evil or bad, just everything you have denied or repressed because they were deemed unacceptable by your family, community, religion, or society. Your shadow gets created by what you reject—what's not okay, forbidden, or taboo. All of us have parts of disowned selves buried within us that have a profound influence in our lives, whether we realize it or not.

We disowned these parts because they were socialized out of us—we were conditioned by all the right/wrong, good/bad, should/shouldn't, and either/or situations that created internal conflict.

- It's good to behave, sit still, and be quiet. It's bad if you don't.
- It's bad to act out or draw attention to yourself. It's good if you are subdued.
- You shouldn't touch yourself there—that's shameful.
- Either you conform or you are shunned.
- It's wrong to tell a lie. It's right to tell the truth.

We push these parts away because, ultimately, we want to fit in, be accepted, and belong.

Masks, Hats, and Personalities

In order to cover up our insecurities, uncertainties, and inabilities, we identify with a certain set of shadow personas. They insulate us from aspects of life we perceive as threatening and unfamiliar. The masks help us cope or gain attention when dealing with our situations. You may recognize some of these:

- The People Pleaser wants to make others happy.
- The Perfectionist wants to get things right.
- The Responsible is accountable and does what needs to be done.
- The Follower wants to belong.
- The Rebel is willing to fight for freedom and a good cause.
- The Manipulator wants to direct, arrange, and be in charge of the circumstances.
- The Pusher needs to be doing something and has a never-ending 'to-do' list.
- The Free Spirit is spontaneous and wants freedom of expression.

The drawback is, deep down inside we know these are disguises we hide behind. We don't recognize that we've been conditioned this way to safeguard our vulnerability. We have forgotten that these masks were only meant to be temporary, and, therefore, we come to believe it is who we really are. The deception grows deeper within us as we lose touch with the full range of our being. When this happens, we feel empty inside and look for ways to fill that void with food, drugs, alcohol, sex, or material items. We become workaholics or seek out co-dependent relationships. For example:

- The driven, accomplished man who has everything going for him; a workaholic who excels at the office, is competitive in the gym, strives to be a good husband, provider, and father and has proven and re-proven his masculinity while secretly fearing he is not man enough, so he has an affair to prove his manliness and suffers from outbursts of aggressive anger while slowly drinking himself to death.

- The twenty-something beautiful, vivacious woman obsessed with wearing the latest fashions, watching every calorie she eats, hanging out at the local clubs while wanting to be everybody's best friend, yet engages in casual sex because she's afraid that she is unloved, unattractive, and not good enough.

- The stay-at-home mother who sacrifices all her needs for her children, does her best to take care of her husband, keeps a spotless house (okay, a near spotless house), and resents not being able to pursue her career interests while longing for freedom and envying others' achievements while she slowly shelves all her dreams.

- The divorced father who wants to be there for his children, does his best to take the time and make the plans, yet over the years has been undermined by his ex-wife in front of their children so much that invisible barriers have grown between them. In his good nature, he puts up a brave front yet secretly hurts deep inside while growing more detached with every passing holiday, missed birthday, and loss of time, tired of putting himself out there and being overlooked until he no longer tries.

The Inner Rules We Must Follow

The disowned aspect of our self operates under our radar and imposes all kinds of rules that get stored in the subconscious. A good example is a child who receives 98 percent on a test and proudly shows his dad. His father questions him, *"What happened to the other two percent?"* The child experiences a feeling of disenchantment and, consequently, believes that in order to get his dad's approval, and maybe deeper still, his love, *"I have to be perfect."* Then from this rule, the subconscious mind judges mistakes as "bad," and the person becomes identified with the primary identity as the Perfectionist begins to take shape. Or, another rule could be, *"Why even try? Humans aren't perfect."* This then creates procrastination.

If you have a rule that says, *"It's not okay to make mistakes,"* then your inner critic, the law enforcement officer of the primary identity, takes over in these situations, saying:

- For the People Pleaser: *"You can't put your own needs first."* The inner critic judges you as selfish.

- For the Perfectionist: *"You can't make mistakes."* The inner critic judges you as careless.

- For the Responsible: *"You can't be self-indulgent."* The inner critic judges you as irresponsible.

- For the Pusher: *"You can't take a break."* The inner critic judges you as lazy.

- For the Achiever: *"You have to achieve your goals."* If you don't, the inner critic judges you as useless.

- For the Spiritual: *"You can't get tied to worldly pursuits."* The inner critic judges you as unenlightened.

Every time the inner critic attacks, it is your sensitive inner self (often referred to as the inner child) who takes the abuse. The inner critic requires a target, an ego-based construct, to justify its role in order to keep the suffering going, so it is never out of a job. The more your inner self is attacked, the more it becomes wounded, until it finally goes deep into hiding.

The inner self carries your vulnerability, but it also carries sensitivity, intimacy, playfulness, wonder, magic, curiosity, joy, and enthusiasm—all wonderful traits. When this inner self with its childlike qualities goes away, we lose these virtues. But, if we can learn to separate from the judgmental part of ourselves and acknowledge that it is okay to make mistakes, which we can learn from, then we can be gentle with ourselves. If there is no suffering or wrong, then there is nothing for the inner critic to attack, judge, or impose upon. Shifting the energy pattern eliminates the loop and heals the wound, so there is nothing for the inner critic to do. Consequently, when we see someone make a mistake, because we have separated from that as part of ourselves, we understand and no longer judge. After all, what would there be to judge? We can now relate to that person on a deeper, more compassionate level. So, if we want to have the magical, wonderful qualities of our inner self available to us, we need to separate from the inner critic.

Who Do You Judge or Resent? Are You Projecting?

The people we judge usually possess a similar character trait that mirrors part of us we have disowned. That is why we get triggered by them. When an individual carries the reflection of a shadow persona that we have pushed away, we feel uncomfortable and get judgmental. What the other person is unknowingly doing is vibrating out a frequency that activates within us the very part we ourselves have disowned, which in turn makes us feel uneasy, but, in essence, is showing us something we need to embrace and welcome back into our body-mind energy system in order to become whole again.

When you project your disowned identity onto others (by superimposing qualities or characteristics onto them), it harms your relationships. What you can't be at peace with within yourself, you can't be at peace with in others, so you limit yourself and sour your relationships. This is part of why opposites attract. When you push something away, it creates an energetic vacuum, which has the effect of attracting that same energy back into your life. It mirrors what you have to integrate in order to become more whole. But, since we are unfamiliar with our shadows, we don't necessarily comprehend that and act out against that part we can't be with. We don't recognize what's going on and end up projecting our judgment toward others.

Let's say you identify yourself as being *responsible* because you get things done, receive approval from others, and feel like everything is good. *Responsible* has become your primary identity. This is when you say to yourself, *"I can't ever be seen as being irresponsible.*" Now, life becomes less fun. You identify with getting your 'to-do list' done, doing what needs to be done for everyone else, and putting your enjoyment last. The part of yourself that just likes to play and have fun, the part that isn't worried about everything being in its place, gets pushed away and deemed irresponsible. Life becomes too serious and a bit of a drag. Then, when you see someone taking time off to play, going skiing, taking weekend getaways at the beach, or playing hooky, you start judging them (*"They should be at work, mowing the lawn, etc."*). You judge them because you can't be at peace with that part of yourself. You might even be jealous.

Judging others makes it difficult for us to be at peace with ourselves because some of the emotions that come up can be quite strong. When we identify with them, they cause a lot of conflict in the world and in our relationships.

The Good and the Bad

All the identities exist in polarity. Personal/Impersonal. Strict/Lenient. Rebel/Pleaser. Optimistic/Pessimistic. From the perspective of the primary identity, it sees the disowned identity as bad. If we liken the identities to the elements, we could say that one of them is like water. From the perspective of the primary identity, water may be seen as bad because it could drown you. Yes, it could, but what else can it do? You could also say that water is good because it helps to grow plants and food, quenches thirst, and cleans dishes. It's the same with fire. It may be bad because it could burn you and destroy forests and homes. But what else can fire do? You could say it's good because it cooks our food, keeps us warm, and gives us light. These energies are not good or bad; though, if you become identified with one of their polarities, you put yourself in duality, then judge these energies as either good or bad or right or wrong, depending on your viewpoint.

How Shadows Harm Us

When you push your disowned identity underground, it can destroy you while draining your energy at the same time. Like a hydra (a monster in Greek mythology) that can grow two heads after one is cut off, each time we attempt to get rid of a shadow aspect of our self, it comes back with more tenacity. It takes a tremendous amount of energy to push your shadow away. Have you ever tried to hold a beach ball underwater? You push it down, and the longer you hold it down the more it wears you out, then, as soon as you let go, the ball pops up with gusto. It's like people who have disowned their anger; all of a sudden, they throw a temper tantrum, blow-up, and explode. But when you embrace your shadow, it goes from being a tsunami in the ocean to a ripple across a pond.

Non-Verbal Communication Harms Others, Too

The greatest harm of disowning our shadow may very well be the effects it has on our society. Psychologists tell us that 95–99 percent of all communication is non-verbal, and people pick up on that communication at a subconscious level and can feel uneasy. Each society has its own set of unspoken rules, morals, and behaviors that it believes are normal. While we disown our shadow and push this energy away from us, it goes out into the living, flowing energy fields of the collective consciousness that surrounds us. It is possible that someone who carries tremendous emotional wounds, who would customarily be considered problematic, and who has very few barriers or boundaries protecting them from the onslaught of cast-off negative energies, could easily detect this energy. Then, without having a strong defense system, they are more apt to act out these negative aspects. They become society's scapegoats, expressing and acting upon the fears we have been afraid to own and tame for ourselves. But, when you own your disowned qualities, you are able to make decisions and take actions that are free from judgments and defensive emotions.

The Benefits Disowned Selves Provide

When looking at an inner self from a distorted perception, one side of things looks bad for one reason or the other. But from the other side, they look good for other reasons. When the shadow is made conscious, it gives us great gifts. We have to recognize what the benefit of the disowned qualities would be— what gift it has to offer us.

- The People Pleasers are more concerned with satisfying others, rather than themselves, and often at the expense of their own well-being. This can lead to feelings of resentment and being taken advantage of. When disowned, a People Pleaser appears to be self-serving and inconsiderate of others. When reclaimed, you can achieve a cooperative balance between pleasing others and pleasing yourself without feelings of guilt or resentment.

- The Perfectionist doesn't want to make mistakes, so it can end up setting unrealistic standards for excellence that inhibit completion of projects and tasks, leading to feelings of frustration and not being good enough. The other extreme is disowning the Perfectionist. When this happens, a person can become careless, negligent, or even overly nitpicky about details. But when you can reclaim both polarities of the Perfectionist, you can be impeccable when the details make every difference, such as performing surgery or engineering a plane, and also be okay when making mistakes because they are part of learning, experimenting, and discovering new ways of doing something to pursue your personal best.

- The Responsible does whatever needs to be done but can become overly burdened by the obligations of everyday life, thinking he or she is the only one who can do the job and get it done right. When disowned, a person can become unreliable, irresponsible, and resistant to being held accountable. The opposing identity challenges the status quo, is open to new experiences, and doesn't always take things too seriously. When both polarities are reclaimed, the Responsible is more conscientious and can balance between what is urgent or important and what can wait until later without sacrificing obligations.

- The Follower is a loyal and dedicated personality, who easily helps, and willingly supports, others to fulfill their aspirations. These people can become so focused on fulfilling the wants of others that they neglect their own interests and end up feeling inferior or resentful. When the Follower is disowned, the person can become stubborn, rebellious, or obstinate. When reclaimed, this person helps the success of leaders, teams, or organizations without sacrificing his or her own goals.

- The Rebel has a fiercely independent nature and non-conforming spirit that often challenges authority. When out of balance, a Rebel can become defiant, stubborn, and argumentative, and can also alienate others. When disowned, the Rebel is passive, reluctant to question authority, and suppresses his or her own voice. When the polarity is reclaimed, a Rebel fights for what he or she believes despite what everyone else says. These individuals help set new levels of freedom, truth, and expression, such as saving our environment and endangered species and by exposing hidden agendas.

- The Manipulator, with its underhanded or deceptive ways, uses methods that can be considered exploitive, or uses ulterior motives for gain at the expense of someone else. But, when you own your inner Manipulator, it's harder to be manipulated or taken advantage of because you can spot the deception more easily. You are not as naïve. If you identify with being innocent or naïve, then you can more easily be taken advantage of. Too, when you own your inner Manipulator and use it consciously, it is easier to create win/win scenarios instead of win/lose situations.

- The Pusher is overly driven and has a difficult time turning the on-switch off. Pushers are known for having never-ending 'to-do' lists, which often leaves them feeling exhausted. When disowned, they can feel indifferent about getting things done and may wish they had the energy to fulfill their goals and dreams. When you use your inner Pusher, it is easier to excel at multi-tasking. Your motivation and sense of accomplishment will also increase.

- The Free Spirit is another non-conformist, who is great for inspiring spontaneity and having the ability to express one's individuality. When disowned, daily requirements can make life feel stifled or restrictive to the Free Spirit. When reclaimed, you can act upon impulses and inspiration while feeling a greater sense of personal freedom and openness.

Every energy has its value, but we don't see the value when we identify with only one polarity. We have to separate from it in order to see its worth, which will reveal itself when you take a deeper look. Darryl Gurney, originator of *Shadow Energetics,* says our job is to look at all these shadow energies, to discover what their value is, and to use these inner aspects wisely in order to become energy masters. We must also use them with consciousness. When you embrace these energies, bringing them to conscious awareness, it transforms them, and they stop being monsters.

Gurney goes on to say that these energies want to be part of our lives and embraced for the gifts they have to offer. You can have favorite parts, but you don't want to leave any part out because there are times where you want to access a particular energy for the strength it gives to your life experience. They offer their unique perspectives, thoughts, feelings, and opinions. They add more juice, adventure, and vibrancy to our lives and enrich our experiences. We want to learn how to dance with these energies and become more purposeful in our choices. There are times where you can:

- Be irresponsible and have fun and play, especially when making sand castles with a child.

- Experience wild passionate lovemaking without feeling guilty or ashamed.

- Be assertive when need be, so you are not taken advantage of.

- Have your emotions and compassion available when connecting with children, your spouse, or other people.

All energy has value. It is all part of the universe and of the Divine. Even lying can be a noble thing when used properly. Could you imagine being in Nazi Germany and helping hide a Jewish family? It would be a very beneficial thing to have your liar persona available to help you and others in hostage situations. You may not like some of your dark qualities showing up at inappropriate times, but, when you own them, you can use the energy in the way it was meant to be used—with consciousness.

Why We Need to Reclaim Disowned Qualities

Owning our polarities is about balance. It is impossible to be in a place of unconditionally loving yourself when there are parts of you that have been pushed aside. You'll be triggered internally, which means your energy patterns will be activated, and you'll know something is out of balance. You want to love yourself unconditionally because when you have that relationship with yourself, then you are aligned with the living essence of the Field (because the essential nature of the Field is love). Your intentions become that much more powerful because they are aligned like a laser—they go out and come back with that much more power for manifesting because of your connection with the Field of all possibility.

Everything has a gift, and it is our job to figure out what the gift is. You can only find that answer from a neutral place within yourself that doesn't carry judgment. Take a look at sexuality. The inner critic might say that it is shameful, dirty, and sinful. But look at the gift in sexuality. It is a creative life-force. It gives us pleasure, boosts our immune system, and creates connection in our relationships. When we push our sexuality into the shadows, we lose all those wonderful things that it can bring us. Once we can see the value, then we can see why we want that part available to us.

Power is another energy that is often in shadow. Let's say a person was abused by one of his or her parents. It's easy to draw a conclusion that power is bad and want to push it away. Though, if you ask, in the tradition of Byron Katie, *"Is this true?"* and *"Can I absolutely know this is true?"* you have to admit that not all power is bad. Power used with consciousness has the ability to set boundaries, such as the ability to say 'No' and mean it. Until you embrace your power, you will attract people who use their power purposefully because the world is going to mirror what you need to learn. After all, the universe is focused on us becoming whole.

"Out beyond the ideas of wrong-doing and right-doing there is a field.
I'll meet you there."
~ Rumi

How to Reclaim Our Disowned Qualities

In the past, doing shadow work meant a drawn-out search, focusing on the unpleasant and unflattering aspects, motives, and actions of your personality. It was an energy-draining process that could take up to two years or longer to resolve. Fortunately, there are easier ways of finding our shadow and reclaiming it in very little time.

It takes courage to face your shadow and to reclaim the parts that you judge, resent, and condemn. It takes willingness to be honest and to free yourself from these perceived faults. You may already be aware of a shadow personality you need to work with and embody, one that pushes your buttons or makes you twinge. Though, if you are not already consciously aware, you can energy test to find out which shadow is a priority for you to work with and reclaim.

Self-Discovery Process

Energy test the following to receive insight into a shadow quality for you to reclaim:

- *"There is a shadow quality that would be of benefit for me to reclaim at this time."*
- *"There is a shadow quality operating within me that is responsible for the (conflict/problem) in my life."*
- *"There is a shadow quality that I am projecting onto a situation in my life."*
- *"I am expressing a shadow quality outside of my conscious awareness."*
- If YES to any of the above, then energy test: *"The highest priority can be found in column #1 of the Shadow Polarity Chart."*
  - If YES, then narrow the column down into portions until you come to the specific shadow polarity to reclaim.
- If NO, then the priority can be found in column #2 of the Shadow Polarity Chart.
  - Narrow it down until you come to the specific shadow polarity.
- When you have found the specific shadow polarity, energy test to discover which half of the polarity needs to be reclaimed (i.e.: Liar / Honest / Lazy / Productive).
- Energy Test: *"It's in the highest wisdom and benefit to change my relationship to a shadow quality now."* If YES, proceed to discover which statements below would be of greatest benefit for you.
- Insert the specific shadow quality you have identified that is in your benefit to reclaim into the statements below and energy test them. If you receive any NO responses to the life-enhancing belief statements (meaning it is not already a part of your subconscious mind belief system), then use the Chakra Belief Change Process to transform them.

SHADOW POLARITIES

1		2	
1. Doing	Being	1. Common Sense	Intuition
2. Mental	Emotional	2. Frigid	Amorous
3. Impersonal	Personal	3. Perfectionist	Carefree
4. Vulnerable	Powerful	4. Lazy	Productive
5. Not good enough	Magnificent	5. Traitor/Betrayer	Loyal
6. Bad	Good	6. Dumb	Intelligent
7. Ordinary	Special	7. Ignorant	Wise
8. Loser	Winner	8. Intolerant	Acceptant
9. Failure	Successful	9. Passive/Aggressive	Forthright/Direct
10. Cautious	Risk Taker	10. Compulsive	Laid-back
11. Irresponsible	Responsible	11. Untrustworthy	Trustworthy
12. Undisciplined	Disciplined	12. Pompous	Respected
13. Rule Follower	Free Spirit	13. Cheater	Faithful
14. Rule Maker	Form-breaker	14. Better than/Arrogant	Humble/Respectful
15. Selfish	Pleaser	15. Abuser	Caregiver
16. Liar	Honest	16. Energy sucker	Vivacious
17. Disorganized	Organized	17. Insensitive/Thoughtless	Caring
18. Manipulative	Caring	18. Stingy	Generous
19. Controlled	Free	19. Shameless	Fearless
20. Dependent	Independent	20. Blamer	Compassionate
21. Co-dependent	Separatist	21. Immature	Mature
22. Introvert	Extrovert	22. Serious	Playful
23. Idealist	Accept Things	23. Pessimistic	Optimistic
24. Pragmatist	Visionary	24. Unforgiving	Forgiving
25. Conservative	Rebel	25. Spineless	Courageous
26. Loner	Community	26. Trashy	Classy
27. Earthiness	Spirituality	27. Judgmental	Forgiving
28. Sinner	Saint	28. Unlovable	Lovable
29. Lower Self	Higher Self	29. Shyster	Trustworthy
30. Elitist/Snob	Warm-hearted	30. Man/Woman Hater	Loving

Life-Enhancing Shadow Quality Belief Statements

1. *"I have complete separation from . . . shadow quality."*

2. *"I am free from . . . shadow quality."*

3. *"I embrace my . . . shadow quality."*

4. *"I love myself when I am . . . shadow quality."*

5. *"I am worthy of . . . shadow quality."*

6. *"I deserve to be . . . shadow quality."*

7. *"I see the value in . . . shadow quality."*

8. *"I am capable of . . . shadow quality."*

9. *"I forgive myself when . . . <u>shadow quality</u>."*

10. *"I accept myself when I am . . . <u>shadow quality</u>."*

11. *"I give myself permission to be . . . <u>shadow quality</u>."*

12. *"I allow myself to be . . . <u>shadow quality</u>."*

13. *"It is okay for me to be . . . <u>shadow quality</u>."*

14. *"It is safe for me to be . . . <u>shadow quality</u>."*

15. *"I am loved when I am . . . <u>shadow quality</u>."*

16. *"I can relax and be at peace with my . . . <u>shadow quality</u>."*

17. *"I learn, grow, and become wiser with my . . . <u>shadow quality</u>."*

18. *"I forgive others when they are . . . <u>shadow quality</u>."*

19. *"I love others when they are . . . <u>shadow quality</u>."*

20. *"I accept others when they are . . . <u>shadow quality</u>."*

Freedom and Empowerment

When we shift our relationship with a shadow identity and take responsibility for our judgments and our reactions to another's behavior, we can say to ourselves, *"I am being affected, but it really has nothing to do with this person. It's about how I am seeing myself in his or her actions."* When we do this, we become aware of our imbalances and recognize that they are not about someone else's behavior.

Once you have embraced your disowned identity, you no longer have this provoking polarity. It opens you up to greater choices, greater personal freedom and empowerment, and a greater sense of being in charge of your life. If you are a People Pleaser, and it comes to a holiday (where you are *expected* to go to your in-laws but don't want to), you believe you *have to go*, that *you have no choice* in this situation because you think you must put other people's needs first. When you are in touch with the other side of this polarity, though, then you would say to yourself, *"No. I don't want to go. I don't enjoy myself, and it doesn't support my well-being,"* which translates to, *"It's not going to work out for me this time for I have chosen (or have committed) to do something else instead."* In this case, you would experience no guilt and have no inner critic attack.

When you separate from the polar energy of the People Pleaser, you could say to yourself, *"Part of me wants to go because it believes we should go, but another part of me would rather not go"*—and, therefore, a conscious choice can be made. The choice itself doesn't matter; it is where the choice is coming from that does. This greater awareness is *consciousness* because there is free choice. It is very liberating. When we embrace all these parts of ourselves, we have greater freedom and understanding, and it is much easier to love ourselves unconditionally.

Love is the impulse toward unity and oneness. It is the energy that is everywhere. When you align with this frequency, you are no longer in this duality of us versus them, but experience unity, which is part of your spiritual journey, and a greater sense of connection where everyone is your brother and sister. And everything is part of a larger eco-system, which we all depend upon.

When we bring our shadow qualities to conscious awareness, up to the light, they transform and add richness to our life. Learning to recognize our own talents allows us to appreciate and love everyone else's unique gifts.

"I will love the light for it shows me the way, yet
I will endure the darkness because it shows me the stars."
~ *Og Mandino*

See Appendix II for instructions on how to download the Shadow Polarity Chart and Shadow Discovery Belief Change Process at:
www.theHeartAndSoulAcademy.org/resource-page/

CHAPTER 13

When Lifestyle Choices Are at Fault

*"What we call the secret of happiness is no more a secret
than our willingness to choose life."*
~ Leo Buscaglia

There are times when your higher wisdom and subconscious mind will lead
you to the source of the problem, which may or may not have anything to do
with subconscious interference patterns. It can, however, have something to
do with a lifestyle choice you've made.

We're human—we like to have fun and enjoy life to its fullest. Somewhere, sooner or later in this exploration, we may find that health challenges
force us to take a closer look at lifestyle, health choices, and practices. Being
responsible for our own health and well-being is a basic necessity to living a
satisfying life. These days it is more important than ever to be diligent about
our lives because of all the deception there is in the marketplace, toxins in the
environment, and a healthcare system that is a dreadful failure.

The focus of this chapter has to do with lifestyle elements that contribute
to a problem in your life. Much of it is common sense, and you have heard
it before. Though, when your inner wisdom brings your attention to these
choices and options, they carry a message that plays a part in your health and
wellness.

I once read that Deepak Chopra said there is no blueprint for disease. I
found this to be a profound truth for me in that we only have a blueprint for
health, and that disease is only an interference pattern disrupting the healthy
blueprints in our lives. This interference pattern creates the illusion of separation within us that alienates us from our essential nature and that of the

Divine essence of who we are at the core of our being. When we resolve that interference pattern, life-force energy returns and flows freely. It reconnects us to the parts that had been shut down and begins supporting and restoring healthy functioning once again.

There Is Only One Disease

It may be labeled with many different names, but, essentially, there is only one disease. How the disease is named depends upon where the interference pattern is located that is disrupting your health and causing chaos inside your body. Yet, they have the same symptoms in common, those of toxicity and nutrient deficiency. The simplified solution is to:

- Cleanse your body of toxins
- Feed your body the nutrition it needs
- Heal the illusion of separation by reuniting with your essential nature using L.E.E.P.s

Whether your inner wisdom leads you to the message of lifestyle choices and one of the following categories, or whether you choose to include a few of the following elements as part of your decision-making process, it will make a world of difference in how you look and feel. Plus, it may very well be part of the resolution to the problem you are seeking to solve.

Our health has two main sides:

1. The part we can see and experience physically through our body.
2. The part we can't see. The mental and emotional aspects that we experience through our conscious and subconscious thought processes.

Toxins

Toxins in the body are one of the main reasons we feel bad and develop disease. We get toxins from the foods we eat, the water we drink and bathe in, and the air we breathe. Another major source comes from pharmaceutical drugs, either over-the-counter, prescription, or in vaccines. Here are several things that may surprise you:

Artificial Food Coloring can cause allergic reactions, hyperactivity, and ADD in children and may contribute to visual disorders, lead to significant reduction in I.Q., interfere with brain-nerve transmission, and cause nerve damage and tumors.

Aspartame is an excitoneurotoxic carcinogenic sweetener added to many food and beverage items. It contains three particularly dangerous neurotoxins: methanol, aspartic acid, and phenylalanine. Aspartame breaks down into formic acid (which is used as a pesticide), formaldehyde (which is an ingredient in embalming fluid), and diketopiperazine (which is a brain tumor agent). Even at extremely low doses, it causes gradual damage to the neurological and immune systems and permanent genetic damage.

Chemtrails are visible trails left in the sky by an aircraft but differ in nature from most airplane trails in that they don't disappear within minutes but continue to spread, creating a thin layer of cloud cover. Unlike the other toxins, this one cannot be avoided. Investigations into these sprayings state they consist of biological, chemical agents and weaken the immune system of the general population. Spray samples that have been analyzed have revealed many deadly and highly toxic biohazard substances from the chemtrail residue, including Mycoplasma Fermetans Incognitus, the bioengineered pathogen associated with the Gulf War Illness. It is sad that our planet has had such a long history of exposing individuals to hazardous pathogens without their knowledge or consent.

Chlorine is an inferior water treatment that is used to control microbial contamination, but it reacts with organic matter in the water and forms dangerous, carcinogenic trihalomethanes. According to Dr. Joseph M. Price, MD, in Moseby's Medical Dictionary, "Chlorine is the greatest crippler and killer of modern times. It is an insidious poison." Dr. Herbert Schwartz of Cumberland County College in Vineland, N.J. says, "Chlorine has so many dangers it should be banned. Putting chlorine in the water supply is like starting a time bomb. Both mental and physical conditions, such as cancer, heart trouble, and premature senility are attributable to chlorine treated water supplies. It is making us grow old before our time by producing symptoms of aging, such as hardening of the arteries." The good news is, the most practical and efficient method for removing chlorine, chlorine by-products, and taste and odor problems is to filter it with granular activated carbon (GAC) or other suitable chemical-removing filters. Consider using a water filter system for your home. It will help to eliminate toxins before the water is used to cook, clean, shower, and bathe.

Fluoride is an extremely neurotoxic chemical added to drinking water and toothpaste that interrupts the basic function of nerve cells in the brain, causing docile submissive behavior and I.Q. devastation.

MSG: Monosodium Glutamate, used to enhance food flavors, is an excitotoxin that has been found to dramatically promote cancer cell growth and metastasis and is a major source of cardiac irritability. Excitotoxins literally stimulate neurons to death, causing brain damage to varying degrees and are dangerous to human health.

Sodium Nitrate is a food additive used as a preservative in a variety of processed foods. The problem is that when you eat it, nitrosamines are formed, and these dangerous compounds are highly carcinogenic.

This is only a small list of toxins intentionally added to our food, water, and air supply that we should avoid as much as possible. It should be considered a crime for any company or organization to do this; unfortunately, it is legal and all done in the pursuit of profit at our expense.

Toxins and pharmaceutical drugs create interference patterns within your energy field that weaken your ability to concentrate and to transmit vibrations necessary for communicating, manifesting, or co-creating with the environment and universe around you. The more drugs someone can get you to take, the more powerless you become, and the more it reduces your ability to create the life you want. The solution is to take as many precautions as you are able to in order to prevent toxins from entering your body in the first place, and you can do things to rebalance your body as a whole as well.

Detox Your Body

Even though your body has an extraordinary internal detoxification system, it needs your help. Here's a brief look at three critical organs involved with your natural detoxification system:

Liver: This is your first line of defense and acts like a filter, preventing toxic substances in food and beverages from passing into your bloodstream.

Colon: The colon produces both healthy and unhealthy chemicals. You want to keep your colon functioning regularly since its main role is to flush out toxins before they can do you any harm.

Kidneys: Like clockwork, these hard-working organs are constantly filtering your blood and getting rid of toxins in the form of urine.

In a highly polluted world, the liver and kidneys, especially, are so overworked that they never have a chance to rest. The practice of cleansing the body to get rid of unhealthy toxins has been around for centuries, though very few people actively do it. Hippocrates recommended cleansing to improve health and purify the spirit. Fortunately, our society has begun a return to natural remedies and therapies. Dr. Bernard Jensen said, "In a world where dietary choices are poor, environmental pollution is heavy, stress levels are high, and exercise is often a last priority, internal cleansing is more important than ever for optimum health."

Build Up Your Immune System

A sufficiently strengthened immune system can tolerate a far greater biological threat or incident than most of the governmental programs and pharmaceutical organizations would have us believe. It's important to remember that any detrimental organism, whether it is a virus, bacteria, fungus, or parasite, has to reproduce itself inside your body in order to harm you. This includes those weapons grade 'super killer microbes' created in the laboratory. Yet, there are ways for us to build protection that are easy enough to utilize to improve and enhance immune system functions.

Decrease Stress

Stress is your body's way of responding to certain life experiences and is an adverse reaction to mental and emotional attitudes or physical experiences that affect overall well-being. It is the perception that the situations we are dealing with are greater than the amount of time, ability, or energy we have to cope with them. Prolonged stress generates a constant, low-level vibration within the body that creates toxins in the blood and irritates the body's tissues. It is estimated that 80–90 percent of visits to primary healthcare physicians are due to stress-related disorders because the stress symptoms often mimic symptoms of other problems. Stress-related ailments and complaints range everywhere from headaches and upset stomachs to high blood pressure, chest pain, and sleeping problems. Research shows that stress can not only bring on certain symptoms, but also aggravate existing health problems and diseases. It could easily be affecting your health, wellness, or even work productivity without you consciously being aware of it. Reducing stress in your everyday life is vital for maintaining your health, keeping your immune system strong, enhancing your mood, boosting your sense of humor, promoting longevity, and increasing creativity. It also allows you to be more productive while providing greater peace in life's experiences.

Increase Your Water Intake

A hydrated body is a healthy body, and most people are chronically dehydrated. How much fresh clean water should you be drinking? On average, a person needs eight 8-ounce glasses every day. That's about two quarts.

However, an overweight person needs one additional glass for every 25 pounds of excess weight. The amount you drink should also be increased if you exercise briskly or if the weather is hot and dry. When the body gets the water it needs to function optimally, its fluids are perfectly balanced. Once this happens:

- Endocrine-gland function improves.
- Fluid retention is alleviated as stored water is lost.
- More fat is used as fuel because the liver is free to metabolize stored fat.
- Natural thirst returns.

Chlorine in the water is an insidious poison that can harm health and is an inferior form of water treatment, so take steps to eliminate this from your water supply. Consider carrying tap water in your own reusable container. Buy a good granular activated carbon (GAC) filter or other suitable chemical-removing filter to get the chlorine and fluoride toxins out of your drinking water, too.

Enjoy Organic Foods and Superfoods

Our diets consist of far too many foods lacking in nutrients. These days it seems that too many individuals have major nutritional deficiencies in their bodies. An important thing we want to be doing is eating good food. Fresh food. Whole foods. Superfoods. And organic, if possible, because they aren't genetically modified or sprayed with pesticides and herbicides.

Superfoods, such as phytoplankton, cacao nibs, flax or chia seeds, blueberries, wild salmon, avocados, broccoli, etc., are foods that are more nutrient dense, lower in calories, and provide health benefits far beyond their recognized value in a healthy diet. They help us to embrace health rather than just fight disease. And the best thing is, superfoods make creating a healthy lifestyle fun while providing affordable, delicious ways to improve your health naturally.

Rest and Relax More Often

We've lost an ancient custom of rest and relaxation that would be a wise practice for us to reclaim. It is an important part of a healthy lifestyle for all ages,
and our self-care requires that we make relaxation a priority. It rejuvenates
our body, mind, and spirit, affects our mood, boosts our immune system, and
is an important aspect of learning and memory function. When our body is
deprived of sleep, we are unable to rebuild and recharge ourselves effectively.

Relaxation isn't just about resting your body; it's about resting your mind,
too. Far too often, our lives are too full, too hectic, and too out of balance.
Over time, this damages our quality of life, destroying the well-being of our
body, mind, and soul. We feel that we are working harder and running faster,
yet falling farther behind. Taking time to rest is especially important when
you are feeling stressed and overburdened. No matter how busy we are, we
need to take time for rest, peace, and relaxation. When you give your mind a
break during the day, even if it's a nature walk, you return with greater clarity
and peace of mind.

Adequate sleep is also vital for good physical health and emotional
well-being. Sleep deficiency leads to trouble solving problems and making
decisions. It makes it difficult to control your emotions and behaviors, which
can lead to problems getting along with others. One father I worked with
came to see me because of family issues at home. He wanted to send his son
off to a private boarding school. He felt his son's defiance and behaviors were
escalating and wanted someone to knock some sense into him. His wife was
adamantly against this idea, which led to nightly arguments. He was hoping
I could help him:

- Find the courage to see this through.
- Stand up more firmly to his wife and not have her anger affect him.
- Have the strength, reassurance, and peace-of-mind that sending his
  son off was the best thing to do.
- Relinquish responsibility for managing his son's community service
  requirements.

Working with his inner wisdom, we were not able to confirm that any
of this was in his highest wisdom and benefit to focus on. He was frustrated.
I asked him if there was anything else that was troubling him that we could

work on for that session. He said he wasn't sleeping well. It turned out this was the issue we could work with. Three weeks later, he reported that not only was he sleeping better, but he also no longer had a desire to send his son off to a military academy. His relationship with both his son and his wife had improved, and he felt a sense of relief. In this case, sleep played a huge role in how he got along with his family, and his inner wisdom honed into that which was most important for him to improve in his life.

Exercise and Play More

There are so many benefits to exercise that it is no wonder when it comes up as a message from inner wisdom that it may help us understand a health problem better. Just look at these possibilities:

- Boosts immune system
- Stimulates circulation
- Improves cardiovascular health
- Improves muscle tone
- Increases endorphins (the brain chemical that promotes a sense of well-being)
- Boosts energy
- Promotes better sleep
- Helps alleviate symptoms of depression and supports brain function
- Helps eliminate toxins from the body:
  ○ Perspiration helps remove metabolic waste.
  ○ Deep breathing releases toxic byproducts from the lungs.
  ○ Muscular activity moves waste material out through the lymphatic system.

The key to exercise is to do it regularly and to make it fun. Whether it is a sport you enjoy, walking, dancing, yoga, Qi-gong, hiking, gardening, or any physical activity, your body will benefit. If you enjoy yourself, it is easier for exercise to become a life-long, healthy habit. It can even be enjoyed with friends.

Play, laughter, and humor helps you to see the world with a sense of wonder, joy, and awe. It helps you to de-stress, lifts your mood, and is joyful to your soul. Play brings out the 'fun' with friends, acquaintances, and strangers. It stimulates your creativity and imagination. It enhances relationships and is as vital to your health and well-being as are food and sleep. The whole point of play is to enjoy life more. Take action to make it an essential part of your everyday life.

Fresh Air and Sunshine

Recirculated air, improper ventilation, exhaust, smog, and smoke causes the air we breathe to be de-vitalized and to lack the healthy oxygen we need to feel good. Lack of fresh air results in a lack of oxygen to the brain, which causes fatigue, drowsiness, irritability, and dulls the mind.

Fresh air has a different electrical charge than recirculated indoor air. Good quality fresh air can easily be found in natural outdoor environments. Research shows that this difference provides our body with tremendous benefits, such as:

- Improved sense of relaxation and well-being
- Improved function of the lung's cilia
- Decreased survival rate of bacteria and viruses in the air
- Revitalized mind and body
- Decreased stress hormones

Deep breathing has been scientifically proven to have beneficial effects on the heart, brain, immune system, digestion, blood pressure, and pH levels of the blood. It is a good practice to completely fill the lungs with fresh air several times during the day. Take a long deep breath in through your nose, hold it, and then exhale completely through your mouth. Repeat this a few times and notice how much better you feel.

Sunlight, with its abundant life-force energy in the sun's rays, is an essential element for maintaining good health, too. It is both a nutrient and a healing therapy that is readily available. It is not exposure to the sun but overexposure that can lead to skin damage. The beautiful thing is, your body naturally lets you know when you have had enough, and you are always in control of the amount you get. It is a great disservice to people to propagate misinformation and fear that the sun is the main reason for skin cancer and aging. Unfortunately, this deception is one of the main reasons most people don't get enough sun—that and having an overly hectic indoor lifestyle. Research has shown that most skin cancers occur among individuals who rarely spend time in the sun, and in those who use sunscreen that contains carcinogenic chemicals. In fact, it has been known for several decades that people who spend much of their time outdoors or live near the equator or at higher altitudes have the lowest incidence of skin cancers and are among the healthiest people on the planet. Sun exposure has the following positive attributes:

- Helps the skin produce vitamin D
- Prevents osteoporosis
- Strengthens the immune system
- Positively affects many types of cancer, including many types of illnesses
- Improves psychological health

Sunlight is the fundamental source of life on earth, and its life-force energy increases the effectiveness of other healing modalities. Plus, it feels good. Since ancient times, yogis have praised the virtues of sunbathing while concentrating on absorbing the life-force energy of the sun.

Meditation

For thousands of years, meditation has been a practice that enhances an individual's self-awareness, expands consciousness, and is highly recommended for anyone seeking high-level wellness. It increases greater peace of mind, greater focus and creativity, and supports rejuvenation and regeneration of your body-mind energy field. Now, scientists are finding evidence to support the claims that it is healing on many levels. Over 3,000 scientific studies show that meditation changes brain physiology, improving function and slowing down aging.

A natural benefit of a regular meditation practice is an increased flow of insights coming to your conscious level of awareness for the purpose of accelerating your personal growth. It naturally increases the vibrational frequency of your energetic field, creating a dynamic and ever-evolving equilibrium between life-force and self-awareness. This holds the keys to your vitality and wholeness, as well as your connection with your own inner Divinity. Meditation is a wonderful spiritual practice that encourages self-discovery on the journey toward finding your true essence.

Bodywork

There are times when bodywork may be just what you need to feel good once again. There are several options available, including the following:

- **Acupressure/Acupuncture:** An ancient form of traditional Chinese medicine in which meridians and pressure points are stimulated to increase the body's natural energy flows to aid healing.

- **Chiropractic Manipulation:** This practice focuses on disorders of the musculoskeletal and nervous systems and making adjustments where needed to restore proper functioning. Especially beneficial for subluxation (misalignment) of the spine.

- **Craniosacral Therapy:** The focus is on releasing restrictions in the soft tissue surrounding the central nervous system that can cause tension to form around the brain and spinal cord. Especially beneficial for migraines and headaches, brain and spinal cord injuries, TMJ syndrome, and scoliosis, to name just a few.

- **Energy Therapy:** An ancient practice of channeling life-force energy into the body to promote health and healing. It acts to upgrade the quality of information in the Field to energetically create the conditions for health, so the body can eliminate disease. Excellent for physical, mental, emotional, and spiritual health.

- **Feldenkrais Method:** In this method, the focus is on increasing neuromuscular awareness followed by movement re-education. The method is based upon the principles of physics, neurology, and physiology and the conditions in which the nervous system learns best. Especially beneficial to recognize habitual patterns of movement and discover how to move with more ease and flexibility.

- **Massage:** Manipulation of the soft tissues of the body for therapeutic purposes. Reduces tension and pain in muscles and joints. Especially beneficial for increasing relaxation, circulation, and well-being.

- **Physical Therapy:** The aim, here, is on restoring physical range of motion and increasing physical abilities. Especially beneficial after injury or surgery, or to increase sports performance.

This list is by no means complete. It is only meant to highlight some of the ways that a form of bodywork may play a role, and maybe hadn't been thought of, as part of the equation to resolve a particular problem.

A Case Study: Environmental Reactions and Allergies

One man who came to see me had an unexplained rash that was driving him crazy. He would find himself scratching at times until he bled. He said this rash came and went, but that ointments were not working. He felt he had some anger issues, stating he was often blowing-up at co-workers for little things that he shouldn't have gotten so worked up over. Since it appeared to be cyclical in nature, he was just sure that he had a 'Belief' that was behind his recurring problem.

We energy tested one thing after another, trying to pin down where the root cause of his rash was. It wasn't a belief, but it did have a message. It wasn't caused by an emotional wound or anything having to do with anger, outbursts, or stress. It wasn't energy testing as an allergy, nor did it have to do with anything in the past—it was, however, a current root cause. I was getting more curious as to where this would lead us as we brainstormed things that could be setting off this unexplained rash.

He hadn't changed his brand of laundry detergent, soap, or deodorant, but energy testing was leading us to something he was doing in his life that was producing his rash. Finally, I asked if he had his clothes dry-cleaned. Bingo! He was having a reaction to the chemicals in his dry-cleaning. Mystery finally solved! He stopped getting his clothes dry- cleaned, and his rash disappeared. His inner wisdom and subconscious knew the reason behind the rash, and it often takes careful detective work to get to the root of the problem. In this case, while there wasn't a subconscious interference pattern to change, the process helped us to answer that unresolved problem.

Seek Professional Services

Getting to the root of a problem may require another individual's insights, knowledge, and skills. It would be a grave disservice to yourself, or others, not to seek professional help when necessary and required. The beautiful thing is, that there are so many people with specialized knowledge and skill sets available to us in this day and age, who are willing to help on the journey toward health, healing, and well-being. These valuable resources cannot be overlooked, especially when a physical ailment or concern, such as the following, occurs:

- Setting a broken bone is not going to happen by just changing beliefs, healing emotional wounds, or exploring a past life.
- Addiction counseling, rehab, and treatment are vital support systems for reclaiming life after addiction.
- Dental care is necessary for a variety of dental problems.
- A Primary Care Physician, Naturopathic Physician, or Registered Nurse Practitioner has access to a wide variety of diagnostic tests, laboratories, medical treatment, and a network of referrals for a wealth of health concerns that make all the difference in our quality of life.

Cast Study: An Undiagnosed Ailment

At the end of one session while working with a man, the last energy test helped him to seek professional help. He had no idea why and said it didn't make sense to him—he said he felt fine, and it wasn't related to any of the work we had done during that session. He, however, did end up making an appointment to see his general health doctor. I don't know any of the details, but the outcome was that he discovered he had some sort of parasite.

I had no idea just how significant this unrecognized epidemic was until I was verifying research for this book and came across the fact that parasites have killed more humans than all the wars in history. It seems that every generation prior to our modern times made de-worming a regular part of their lives, but for whatever reason, our generation has lost touch or knowledge of this basic practice. Based on 20 years of experience with more than 20,000 patients, Dr. Ross Anderson, one of America's foremost parasitic infection specialists states, "I believe the single most undiagnosed health challenge in the history of the human race is parasites." And Dr. Frank Nova, Chief of the Laboratory for Parasite Diseases of the National Institute of Health, says, "In terms of numbers, there are more parasitic infections acquired in this country (the U.S.) than in Africa." I had no idea.

All these areas may require more investigation, but it gives you something to consider when looking for the cause and effect of a lifestyle choice. It is important to never overstep your scope-of-practice and to stay within the ethical boundaries of the service you provide. Energy testing and guidance from inner wisdom is not done for diagnostic purposes—those are always left to professionals—it is about guidance. Yet, it is good to know that you can work together as a team, finding ways of assisting wellness from different angles and skill sets.

"Take care of your body. It's the only place you have to live."
~ Jim Rohn

CHAPTER 14

Additional Beneficial Energetic Processes

---

*"In order to more fully understand this reality, we must
take into account other dimensions of a broader reality."*
~ *John A. Wheeler*

A couple more foundational pieces for the L.E.E.P. System that are of benefit at any time of the day and may come up during a session are:

- Scan and Delete
- Spirit Connection Ceremony

These show up when we need either a quick uplifting energetic shift that doesn't necessarily fall under a belief to change, an emotional wound to heal, or an influence from the distant past to take care of, but when we need to take a nurturing moment to reconnect with our self and spirit and remind ourselves that we are never alone.

Scan and Delete

This useful process utilizes an energetic frequency known as the violet light of transformation, which is a transmutation frequency. It not only converts chaos into greater peace and harmony, it also has the ability to transform dark, heavy energy and return it to a state of pure wholeness. You were attuned to this energy in Chapter 5 for channeling life-force energy for health and wellness, and Scan and Delete is another way of using this healing energy.

You can do this for yourself or another individual. I've even done this for a whole room full of people in movie theaters and on airplanes. It does take a little longer to clear the energy in a room with a large group of people in it— though it can have a profoundly beneficial effect on everyone without them even being aware of where it's coming from.

In the Infinite Energy Frequencies Attunement and Energy Healing Course I teach at the Heart and Soul Academy for Self-Empowerment and Conscious Evolution, there is an energetic control system, kind of like a 'universal mind' that runs in the background. It works with and combines all of the various frequencies, including the violet light of transformation, and acts like a perpetual buffering mechanism, which is called "Zufed," (as was handed down to me) and will come in handy for the process used here. Feel free to substitute and use any name you prefer that symbolizes a universal mind maintaining the internal energetic processes taking place within the Scan and Delete clearing.

Some envisioning is helpful here, but it is not absolutely necessary to make it effective.

- Envision or imagine, to the best of your abilities, three concentric rings of light around you, the individual, or the group.
- The colors of the rings will be: Violet—Orange—Violet—with you, or any others, in the center. [Note: Violet is a transformation energy, and orange is a clearing energy.]

For our purposes here, let's have you put yourself in the center of the circles. Imagine a violet circle of light around you, then an orange circle of light, then an outer circle of violet light.

- Then say, "Zufed, please scan and delete, until all is clear." It's that simple.

You may notice or feel a "pulling sensation" as the heavier, dense, negative energy is being cleared up. It usually only takes a few seconds or minutes.

- Be sure to thank Zufed afterwards.

Revitalization

Doing this helps clear out some of those stagnant energies you collect over time or find you've been carrying with you (some of the old sticky stuff that gets collected).

It may help with lifting some of those burned-out feelings as it transmutes the heavier energies. Just notice what you are sensing. You may feel a coolness, like a menthol feeling, or a light breeze sensation as your energy field clears. You may notice an uplifting feeling or not much of anything other than just feeling better.

Clearing a Myriad of Spaces

You can use this Scan and Delete Process for any place that the energy feels heavy, dark, or dismal, such as:

- An area of land, a park, movie theater, or even an airplane
- A house, building, or place of work
- An object, like a car, furniture, or clothing

Just imagine the three concentric rings of Violet—Orange—and Violet around the area of your focus.

- Say with intention, *"Zufed, scan and delete, and please continue scanning and deleting until all is clear. Thank you."*

Try it and see what you notice in the shift of energy. It makes a difference and is easy to do anytime, anywhere.

Spirit Connection Ceremony

The Spirit Connection Ceremony is a soul-filled prayer, an invocation to spirit, and a sacred ceremony all encompassed in one process. Although the Spirit Connection Ceremony will also appear in my forthcoming book about evolving human consciousness, I've included it here for several vital reasons:

- It can help you integrate the other energetic processes into your system.
- It helps you manifest your dreams, goals, and successful outcomes.

- It can easily be adapted to most any situation.

- It can be used on behalf of others when you don't know 'what' or 'how' else you can help them.

And, it builds a working relationship with greater connection to your expanded consciousness, so that you can take it to a deeper level, if you so choose, when you are ready.

My Experience in Action

During the 2011 Spring Equinox, that fell right on the tail of a full moon and was still under its influence, I was visiting Sedona, Arizona with one of my best friends, Darryl Gurney, when I received a download from spirit. It was the gift of a heart opening ceremony, which is meant to help us personally get into our sacredness and to more fully connect with the divine essence. I had been going through the Dark-Night-of-the-Soul when my entire life was in the midst of completely falling apart. I was experiencing many things: the end of a 28-year marriage along with all my hopes and dreams of our future together; the death of my mother, which was one of the hardest things I have ever gone through; followed a short time later by the death of my beloved grandfather. Then, my daughter's diagnosis with an aggressive form of cancer sent further waves of shock, disbelief, and helplessness through me; and finally, dealing with a dishonorable construction contractor who used the wrong materials, damaged our water tank, and walked off the job, refusing to correct the mistakes he'd made by not following the blueprints. The sheer sense of being overwhelmed by this constant barrage of crises, I have heard, would have left many individuals devastated.

At the time, this Spirit Connection Ceremony filled me with peace and gave me strength as I made my way through to the other end. I use it quite often as a touchstone for deepening my connection with life, for building synchronicity and flow, and for clearing away stress and lesser troubles, and I have found it to be very powerful in its simplicity. I most often do this ceremony in the early morning before I begin my day or later in the evening. I find that I like doing this ceremony either outdoors or near an open window where I can look outside at nature; it helps make this process feel more complete with a deeper connection to the world.

For You and the World

I have performed this ceremony on behalf of others in loving support of the trials they are going through or to assist them in the manifestation of something they hold dear. I stumbled upon this aspect of the Spirit Connection Ceremony when my mother was in the dying process, knowing there was nothing I could do to prevent or change the circumstances and needed the strength for myself. It then dawned on me I could perform it for her benefit, too, and just allow spirit to assist her in ways I could not. I felt the presence of spirit embracing me and found greater peace within as my heart opened and connected with spirit more fully. Since then, I have made use of this ceremony with my aging dog and my children. It's helped me to manifest the love of my life and the property of my dreams, and it has also helped create a new source of income that is in greater alignment with what I wish to accomplish in the world and in my life. When one has communion with spirit first, then synchronicity and flow shows up in innumerable ways, both subtle and material.

It is a heart-centered practice that adds to your resources for the evolution of your expanding conscious awareness, and it can be used as a heart coherent belief change process in addition to the one shared in Chapter 6, Unlocking Your Belief Potential.

Invoking the Spirit

"Source of all life, which flows through all things,
Bless my life.
Illuminate my path, so that I may see the way.
Open my heart, so that I may receive.
Ignite my passion, so that I may take appropriate action.
Thank you."

♡

Process:

- **Begin by standing within your power.** This can be done sitting, too. The main focus here is to gather your inner strength and be fully present. You are creating an empowered sacred moment.

- **Hold your hands out in front of you at chest-heart level, elbows bent comfortably, with your palms facing upwards.** This is an open and receptive posture for the flow of heart energy.

- Invoke spirit by speaking the following: *"Source of all life, which flows through all things."* Use any word or phrase you like that best represents the Divine for you and that you are also a part of at the same time. The Divine does not care by which name you call it, only that it has meaning for you.

- Continue by saying, *"Bless my life."* You can be either general or specific here by leaving the statement open-ended or adding words to it, such as:

  - *Bless my life with* . . . (a quality you would like to have: self-assuredness, peace, fulfillment, synchronicity, flow, abundance, etc.)

  - *Bless my life with* . . . (what you want to have: true love, radiant health, a home that lifts your spirit, meaningful work, etc.)

  - *Bless my life with* . . . (what you want to do: a vacation in Mallorca, a cruise to go swim with the stingrays in the Caymans, walking the sky bridge at the Grand Canyon, building an off-grid home, becoming a licensed pilot, etc.)

- Say, *"Illuminate my path . . . so that I may see the way."* This invokes spirit to guide you in having a new vision to see options that will move you closer to your desire.

- Give spirit permission to assist within the depths of your being to support in the manifestation of your blessing by saying, *"Open my heart . . . so that I may receive."* How would you be able to receive your gift if you still have your heart closed in some fashion that keeps you walled off and separated from your goal of living a more fulfilled life?

- Invite spirit to support you in manifesting what you desire by saying, *"Ignite my passion . . . so that I may take the appropriate action."* Oftentimes, we ask for assistance but lack the motivation or participation in taking our own necessary steps toward creating our dreams and goals in the co-creational aspect of working with spirit.

- Conclude with, *"Thank you."* Feel it when you say it. Gratitude is a powerful force all on its own in manifesting just about anything in your life—it helps open you to greater possibility.

- Bring your hands to your heart and take a moment to anchor the energies you have received.

- Finish by extending your arms upward and outward, and then bring them downward in a graceful motion where your fingertips meet, pointing toward the earth. In essence, your arm movement is tracing the outline of a big heart shape in the air. The intent is to take what you are manifesting on the inside and to manifest it as well in your expression in the outer world, then anchor it into the earth's energy grid.

"If we identify with the soul we awaken the authentic self,
inspire the spirit and fuel the fire of transformation."
~ Michael Teal

See Appendix II for instructions on how to download the Scan and Delete Process and Spirit Connection Ceremony at: www.theHeartAndSoulAcademy.org/resource-page/

CHAPTER 15

Put It All Together and Finally Discover What's Been Holding You Back

---

"If you are distressed by anything external, the pain is not due to the thing itself, but your estimate of it; and this you have the power to revoke at any moment."
~ Marcus Aurelius

Most of life's challenges are personal ones that have to do with our own unique set of interference patterns, which require a certain amount of energy to maintain and, when resolved, free up energy. The greatest challenges many self-help techniques or therapies deal with is being able to get to the actual root of the problem and, then, being able to resolve it in an effective and efficient manner. We need a protocol for being able to navigate through the subconscious, with help of higher guidance, to find the elusive source of the situation and the highest priority to focus on in order to resolve this interference pattern. From there, we need to determine which L.E.E.P. would be the most beneficial to use, which the subconscious mind will shift with, in order to get the job done in the easiest possible way.

In the first chapter, we discussed that the resolution of our problems requires at least three crucial elements.

1. Locating the source of the energetic influence to discover the message it has.

2. Learning the lesson the problem contains, so we won't have to repeat it.

3. Shifting the energy with a L.E.E.P. to resolve the interference pattern, freeing ourselves to 'let go' and move forward.

Access Inner Wisdom Communication System:

Using the protocol from Chapter 3, begin with the energy tests for accessing your inner wisdom, so that you know you are receiving reliable feedback.

Women	Men
"I am a woman."	"I am a man."
"I am a man."	"I am a woman."
Show me a YES.	Show me a YES.
Show me a NO.	Show me a NO.

- Once you have received a YES response to your gender and 'show me a YES,' and a NO response to the opposite gender and 'show me a NO,' then proceed to Summarize the Problem (below).

- If your energy tests responded with a YES to everything, then your body-mind energy system is over-energized. You will need to de-stress with a calming exercise from Chapter 3 then re-test.

- If you didn't receive clear energy test responses, then you are dehydrated to the point where your internal electrical impulses are too weak to respond to energy testing effectively. Drink enough water to boost your electrical conductivity for clear feedback from your energy tests, then proceed to the next step.

Overview:

Review the chart on the following page.

Summarize the Problem:

Describe the problem first. Then as briefly and to the point as possible, summarize the problem, so it can be energy tested. It can be anything related to health, wealth, happiness, or an area of your life you feel is being stifled in some way. It can be any situation where you feel challenged, can't seem to understand why you are stuck, or are disempowered and unable to move beyond the limitation.

Discover the Message with Energy Testing:

Once you've summarized the problem, you will energy test to discover the message.

- **Energy Test:** *"This (name the problem) has a message for me."*

If YES, then there is a message to be learned.

WHAT'S HOLDING YOU BACK?
Discover the Message with Energy Testing

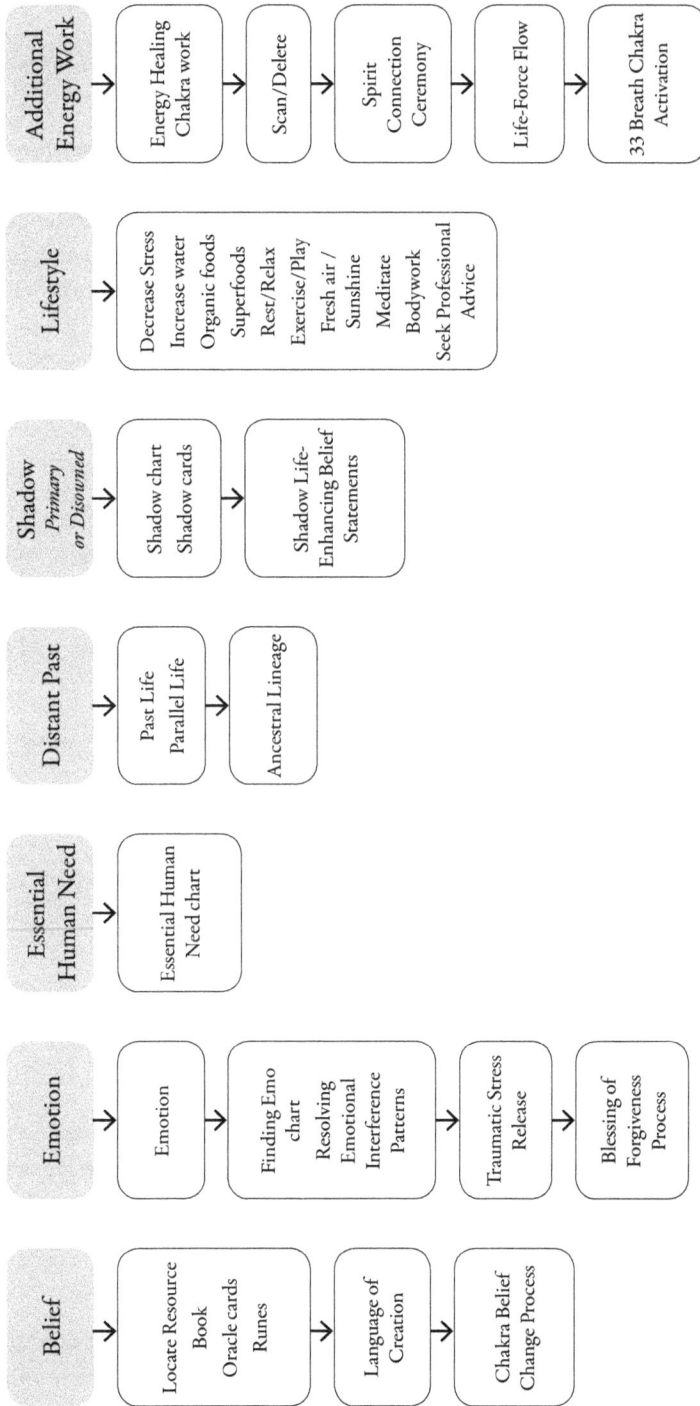

Belief
→ Locate Resource
Book
Oracle cards
Runes
→ Language of Creation
→ Chakra Belief Change Process

Emotion
→ Emotion
→ Finding Emo chart
Resolving Emotional Interference Patterns
→ Traumatic Stress Release
→ Blessing of Forgiveness Process

Essential Human Need
→ Essential Human Need chart

Distant Past
→ Past Life
Parallel Life
→ Ancestral Lineage

Shadow
Primary or Disowned
→ Shadow chart
Shadow cards
→ Shadow Life-Enhancing Belief Statements

Lifestyle
→ Decrease Stress
Increase water
Organic foods
Superfoods
Rest/Relax
Exercise/Play
Fresh air /
Sunshine
Meditate
Bodywork
Seek Professional Advice

Additional Energy Work
→ Energy Healing
Chakra work
→ Scan/Delete
→ Spirit Connection Ceremony
→ Life-Force Flow
→ 33 Breath Chakra Activation

- Next, energy test to discover if you can learn the lesson and resolve this problem:

  "It's in my highest wisdom and benefit to receive the message, learn the lesson, and resolve this problem."

If YES, then because it is in the highest wisdom and benefit for you, your L.E.E.P. will give you a life-enhancing improvement. If NO, then you have learned that some piece of this is not in your highest wisdom and benefit at this time. Change the wording to see if that will work, or you can energy test it another time or in another place, which may be more appropriate. Plan to come back to this at another time.

While you may or may not already have conscious knowledge of the message, it is a good idea to have your higher wisdom guide you to find it. It will *always* be located in a resource nearby. Your soul wants you to get the message and continue to move forward, grow, and evolve, so you can shine your light and live the life you were meant to have.

- **Energy Test:** *"This message can be discovered in one or more of the 7 Life-Enhancing Areas of Influence."*

If YES, narrow it down through energy testing by naming each of the areas until you come to the one where you get a YES response.

- **Energy Test:** *"The highest priority message can be found in (name the area of influence)."*
  - Beliefs
  - Emotions
  - Essential Human Needs
  - Distant Past
  - Disowned Selves
  - Lifestyle
  - Additional Energetic Process

Once you've found the area of influence you've been guided to, then you know that it holds the message for you as well as the life lesson that needs to be learned. You also know this is where you will begin with the L.E.E.P. for unraveling and resolving the problem at its source.

Learn the Lesson and Resolve the Problem

You learn the lesson and resolve the problem by going through the life-enhancing energy process you've been guided toward—this shifts your energy field. You are transforming and shifting your energy field from the interference pattern it has been accustomed to and reconfiguring it to greater freedom to better support the life you want to live.

When you have completed the L.E.E.P., energy test to find out if there is another process required in order to resolve the problem.

- **Energy Test:** *"There is another L.E.E.P. to complete in order to receive the message, learn the lesson, and resolve the problem."*

Sometimes, only one shift is needed in order to resolve the interference pattern, but there is often more than one. The beautiful thing is that energy testing and receiving guidance from your higher wisdom lets you know if there is more to unravel.

Depending upon the situation, an individual's system may only be able to handle so much at one time before it feels saturated. A lot of internal energies are being shifted with these life-enhancing energy processes; therefore, it is possible that you can receive all the messages for the problem on a given day and still have the situation persist. Your body-mind energy system needs time to readjust, stabilize, and establish harmony with the changes. Maybe this particular issue just requires more work to unravel. You can easily come back to it again on another day.

Moving Forward

Once the interference pattern has been released, it is a good idea to program the subconscious mind for where you would like to go. This sets its sights in the direction of something better. It is a conscious choice that is made and then confirmed if it is in the highest wisdom and benefit to do so.

I'll share three different real-life problems with you, plus my own, and walk you through this process, so you can get a feel for it.

Example: My Story

Describe and Summarize the Problem: I know what it's like to experience senseless acts of violence because I had my head whacked with a wooden baseball bat when I was young. I experienced a complete visual blackout and couldn't see a thing except bursts of stars inside my head. I remember trying to walk, feeling my way with this blinding pain, and ending up tangled in an abandoned playground swing set before someone found and helped me. Even after I had fully recovered, the experience left me with an underlying fear of strangers and being alone in public places. And, because of minor brain damage, I was always embarrassingly aware of my inability to distinguish left from right. I also struggle to find the right words to express myself, which made me self-conscious.

But that was just the beginning. A few other traumatic experiences during my early years caused me to become a shrinking violet for the majority of my life. I couldn't go to the grocery store without someone with me, wouldn't eat in a restaurant alone, and always kept my doors locked when I was home or in the car. Even though these experiences occurred years earlier, they were still having a huge impact upon the way I lived my life. It is easy to see how our fears and sufferings can take on a life of their own, leaving us on unsteady ground.

My summary of the problem: *"I don't feel safe in the world."*

> **What's Holding You Back?**
> Describe the Problem.
> *"I don't feel safe in the world."*

Discovering the Message:

- Energy Test: *"Not feeling safe in the world has a message for me."* YES; this means there is a message to be learned.

- Energy Test: *"It's in my highest wisdom and benefit to receive the message, learn the lesson, and resolve this problem."* YES.

- Energy Test: *"This message can be discovered in one or more of the 7 Life-Enhancing Areas of Influence."* YES.

- Energy Test: *"The highest priority message can be found in* (Beliefs)." YES.

For me, even though I could have easily and consciously thought to myself that I just needed to change my belief from being unsafe in the world to, *"I am safe in the world,"* or *"I feel safe in the world,"* it apparently was not the highest priority belief to begin with in order to unravel this particular interference pattern.

You can think of this like playing the game Jenga or Ta-Ka-Radi: Your interference pattern is like a tower of stacked blocks with only a few blocks in each row, but it is several layers tall. One layer of blocks lies lengthwise north and south, and the next layer will lie lengthwise east and west. You begin pulling out one block at a time for as long as the tower remains standing. The game ends when you pull out the block that finally causes the tower to come crashing down. By finding the highest priority piece to change, we are able to bring our 'interference pattern tower' crashing down in the least amount of moves. So, instead of doing 30 possible shifts to release an interference pattern, maybe we can get it down to six strategic shifts instead.

- Energy Test: *"This belief can be found in* (name of a local resource).*"*

(Book—Oracle Cards—Runes—Other Resource: You name the resource that you have on hand or easy access to. Refer to Chapter 8, The Elusive Belief, for a refresher.)

Narrow it down until you come to the right page and paragraph, or draw the card or rune. Read what is there and extrapolate a belief statement you can use to find out if that is the correct message.

My higher wisdom guided me to the highest priority of a belief: *"I want to live."*

I did the Chakra Belief Change Process, and, when finished, I celebrated my win with a fist-pump.

- I then energy tested: *"There is another L.E.E.P. to do in order to receive the message, learn the lesson, and resolve the problem."* YES.
- Energy Test: *"This message can be discovered in one or more of the 7 Life-Enhancing Areas of Influence."* YES.
- Energy Test: *"The highest priority message can be found in* (Beliefs).*"* NO.
- Energy Test: *"The highest priority message can be found in* (Emotions).*"* YES.

- Energy Test: "*The highest priority message can be found in* (the Finding Emo Chart)." NO.

- Energy Test: "*The highest priority message can be found in* (The Forgiveness Process)." NO.

- Energy Test: "*The highest priority message can be found in* (Traumatic Stress Release)." YES.

I was guided here to receive the message and learn the lesson by releasing the traumatic stress associated with the particular problem that had been stored within my subconscious all these years. This was the most effective and efficient way of doing this. When I completed the Traumatic Stress Release Process, I celebrated my win with a fist-pump.

- I then energy tested: "*There is another L.E.E.P. to do in order to receive the message, learn the lesson, and resolve the problem.*" YES.

- Energy Test: "*This message can be discovered in one or more of the 7 Life-Enhancing Areas of Influence.*" YES.

- Energy Test: "*The highest priority message can be found in* (Beliefs)." NO.

- Energy Test: "*The highest priority message can be found in* (Emotions)." YES.

- Energy Test: "*The highest priority message can be found in* (the Finding Emo Chart)." NO.

- Energy Test: "*The highest priority message can be found in* (The Forgiveness Process)." YES.

When I energy tested, "*It is in the highest wisdom and benefit to do the Blessing of Forgiveness Process now,*" I received a NO response. Yes, this was the next highest priority to do, but NO, now was not the right time. At this point, although there was more work to do to fully release this problem from my life, my higher guidance said it was not in my highest wisdom and benefit to continue. My body's energy system needed time to more fully integrate the energetic shifts, and I needed to come back to this L.E.E.P. at another time.

After a day or two I was ready to do the forgiveness piece, but not before then. When I came back to working through the problem of 'not being safe in the world,' I started with the initial energy tests of Accessing Inner Wisdom, then verified that it was in my highest wisdom and benefit to do the Blessing of Forgiveness Process at that time. I received a YES and went through that process. I simply picked up where I had left off for resolving this interference pattern.

- I then energy tested: *"There is another L.E.E.P. to do in order to receive the message, learn the lesson, and resolve the problem."* YES.

- Energy Test: *"This message can be discovered in one or more of the 7 Life-Enhancing Areas of Influence."* YES.

- Energy Test: *"The highest priority message can be found in* (Beliefs)." YES.

My gut feeling was that it was, *"I am safe, and I feel safe in the world,"* so I energy tested it and confirmed that this was the highest priority belief to shift using the Chakra Belief Change Process.

Afterwards, when I energy tested to see if there was another L.E.E.P. to receive the message, learn the lesson, and resolve the problem, I received a NO response—there was nothing further needed to resolve this problem in my life. I then opted to complete a few more life-enhancing beliefs to support my subconscious mind, feel self-assured and confident, and to reinforce that I was always in the right place at the right time for my highest well-being. This supported what I wanted to have instead of the fear that had been there and supported how I wanted to 'show up' and 'be' as I moved forward in the world.

Those shifts made a world of difference in my life. I am able to travel in confidence. Because I also had an underlying fear of 'those strangers who were attending my classes,' I did a belief change for, *"The people in my workshops are just friends I haven't met yet."* This helped me get through some of the uneasiness I felt at the beginning of those classes.

It no longer stresses me out if people observe that I don't know my left from my right—it might take me a couple seconds longer to figure it out, but I am totally comfortable with this. And, when there are times when I can't find the proper word to express what I want to say, I just say I can't find the right word at the moment and let it go. I am no longer embarrassed to the degree that had previously shut me down and kept me timid and self-conscious. I have a grace and peace with it now that I didn't have before; and therefore, my life is better because of this internal shift. I received the gift of inner strength by overcoming this problem, and I have great compassion and understanding for others who have suffered some form of trauma and live on unsteady ground.

Example: 16-Year-Old with Psychologically Induced Seizures

One young woman I worked with had recently begun experiencing epileptic-like seizures. She had been seen by a couple of different specialists who confirmed she had psychologically induced seizures; however, previous treatment efforts had proven unsuccessful. Her mother had attended one of my workshops and was hoping L.E.E.P.s could help her. It appeared that the girl's seizures had started shortly after she found out her father was soon to be released from prison (incarcerated on charges of incest and repeated rape). Her fear that he would seek her out once again, even with the restraining orders, was so strong that she was experiencing seizures as a way to block out her fear, her memories of him, and her feelings of being unsafe in the world if he was free.

Guidance of her inner wisdom with energy testing using the outline above led us to Traumatic Stress Release. From there, we completed a couple of life-enhancing beliefs before resolving some past-life influences, and then completing the Blessing of Forgiveness. This took place over the course of three sessions. In that time, we not only resolved the energetic interference patterns causing the seizures, but we were also able to establish supportive subconscious beliefs that helped her to lead an empowered life. She began sleeping better and also lost some excess weight.

Example: A Young Man with Financial Blocks

A young man came to me to find out if he could resolve some of his financial blocks. He worked hard but felt that there was never enough money to go around and that something was holding him back from achieving his financial goals. Lack of money was his problem. We began the session with him holding a $100 bill and looking at it while we did an energy test—his whole energy system went weak. That was a pretty good message right there! He had an interference pattern with an aversion to money. It was no wonder he never had enough of it to go around.

His higher wisdom led us to a past-life influence that needed resolution, as well as an ancestral lineage influence on his mother's side. His distant past was having a tremendous impact upon his financial freedom in this lifetime. It is very likely he would have never found these energetic ties with conventional methods of transformation or with conscious awareness practices.

By resolving his financial interference pattern and programming his subconscious with new life-enhancing beliefs, he was able to earn a six-figure income that year and went on to acquire a healthy investment portfolio over the next three years.

Example: An Allergy to Strawberries

I worked with a woman who had been allergic to strawberries for most of her life. She remembered being able to eat them when she was younger, but during her teenage years, she began to experience a tingling on her tongue. Later, there was an onset of itching with hives and a tightness of her throat, making it difficult to swallow. She loved strawberries and wanted to enjoy them once again.

Over the years, I have learned that many allergies only appear to be caused by food, animals, or some kind of substance (such as dust, smoke, pollen, etc.), but in actuality are due to a person. It seems that at a time where they had just eaten something, had some substance in their system, or were sitting with a pet, they experienced an emotional interaction with someone where they felt disempowered. Their body's chemistry reacted adversely to the situation to the point of being 'stuck-in-time' while being associated with that element; in this case, strawberries.

With an apparent allergy, you can begin with an energy test:

- *"This apparent allergy is, in fact, an allergy to a person."*

If YES, you can figure out who it is by energy testing. It will usually be someone close. Ask the person you are working with who first comes to mind. Start with close family members (mother, father, siblings, husband, wife, son, daughter, uncle, aunt, etc.). If it is not a close family member, then it may be a roommate or co-worker if the allergy started later in life. Confirm by energy testing who the person is:

- *"This (name of food, animal, substance) allergy is actually an allergy to (name of person and their relationship)."* For example, Kevin's father Tom.

If YES, then work to reconcile that relationship. Forgiveness is usually a good place to start. It could be as simple as a belief, *"I forgive my father for his shortcomings,"* using the Chakra Belief Change Process. Simply continue to find and shift the pieces that come up until you energy test, *"There is another L.E.E.P. to do in order to resolve the allergy,"* and you get a NO response. In many cases, the apparent allergy subsides within a few days or weeks as the body's chemistry adjusts to a pre-allergy state of being.

Easily Navigate Each Unique Situation

What I love best about the L.E.E.P. System is the ability to navigate through each unique set of circumstances. No two sets of problems will unfold in the same way because each individual came to his or her particular problem by way of a different path. You can let go of the 'need to know' how to handle the situation and just let it unfold naturally under the direction of inner wisdom and guidance. I never have a set agenda when working with myself or anyone else. I simply energy test to discover where we should go and trust that it is in the highest wisdom and benefit to do so. You can observe the gap collapsing from where the problem originated as the interference pattern gets resolved and witness the reality that supports greater empowerment and better living.

When Life Hands You Lemons, Make Lemonade

This system is not about changing the other person if you experience a problem with him or her as it may be beyond your scope of influence, authority, or ability to change. And it's not about being able to change things you don't have control over. It's about how you are *responding* to the situation and how you want to *feel* with respect to the living situation. For example, if it gets on your nerves and pushes your buttons when:

- He walks through the kitchen and opens cupboards and drawers but doesn't close them when he leaves.
- She insists on having house plants, but they all look half dead.
- You live in the flight path of a large municipal airport and can't stand the noise.
- The traffic along your work route stresses you out.
- Shoppers in the grocery store leave their carts in the middle of the aisle, blocking your path.
- Your neighbor's music bothers you.
- Your co-worker's voice gets on your nerves.
- (Your own unique situation)

If you can't change them, only the way you feel and respond, then how would you like to be in that situation? This situation is teaching you something about yourself, so when you make a decision to learn about it and change it, it helps you reclaim your lost power.

Reframing Your Response

When you resolve an interference pattern, you let the abundance of life come through. You just need the tools and the 'know how.' If you reframe the situation with compassion for yourself and program positivity into your subconscious, you will find you are at greater ease, contentment, and freedom than ever before.

- In life's big picture, someone leaving the cupboard doors and drawers open isn't really that big of a deal. There are far worse things to suffer through. Look for a way of reframing that helps you feel better about the situation. Possibly, *"There are so many wonderful things to love about this man that his little quirks put a smile on my face."* Or, *"I am content and easily accept that he leaves doors open because I share my life with someone I love."*

- Look for ways to be supportive and create a win/win environment while feeling at ease with half dead houseplants. *"It is easy for me to support her joy of houseplants, and I'll even help water them."* Or another perception could be, *"I willingly support her endeavors as she discovers her strengths and weaknesses. I have patience as she learns what works for her."* Or even, *"I love and appreciate my wife as she explores her green thumb and trust she will discover her talents."*

- Search for how you *want to feel* instead of being annoyed with the sound of airplanes. What would your inner child say? Maybe, *"I love the thrill of planes taking off and landing. The sound fills me with excitement."* Or, *"I feel a thrill inside that puts a smile on my face every time I hear the roar of a plane take off or land."* Or another possibility, *"The roar of planes fades into the background until I hardly notice them at all."*

- How can you reframe your response so that you are at peace around people who are oblivious or inconsiderate? *"I am content and filled with peace even when others are rude."* Or, *"I accept others are not always thoughtful, and I am content and at ease with that."*

- Your neighbors have their music at a respectful volume, but it annoys you to no end. How do you find peace without resorting to wearing noise-blocking headphones? *"I easily tune my neighbors out and find peace with my surroundings."* Or perhaps, *"I enjoy hearing others when they're happy and am content with the sounds of daily life."*

- You can't do anything about your co-worker's voice, so how do you shift your reaction so that it doesn't get on your nerves? *"Each voice is a unique expression of another person, and I delight in my co-worker's individuality."* Or, *"I am calm and filled with peace when (name of other person) speaks."* Maybe even, *"I appreciate and accept others just the way they are."*

You Have the Power

If something is not working for you, annoying you, or pushing your buttons, ask yourself how you would like to feel instead. Other individuals are just being themselves, doing their own thing, and living in their own little world.

If you are stressed, then it is important to know that *you have the power* and the option to change how you let others affect you.

In one workshop I was teaching, a woman who was upset with her stretch marks said she didn't like how her body looked. Another woman reacted to her vanity with visible anger and grief over her inability to have a child, rather than being compassionate and understanding about the first woman's feelings. They both realized they had their own buttons being pushed for different reasons. The first woman ended up embracing and appreciating her stretch marks as a sign of life and the gratitude she had for her child. The second woman realized that she could respect others and accept them for the way they are without comparing them to her own set of circumstances.

Each time we face a challenge in our life, it gives us the opportunity to reclaim our power, vitality, and freedom to live better.

In Summary

- Access inner wisdom.
- Summarize the problem.
- Discover the message.
- Learn the lesson and resolve the interference pattern with a L.E.E.P.
- Higher wisdom will always guide you to resources that are within the local vicinity.
- Only make changes that are in the highest benefit and wisdom to do.
- It is possible that not all of the energetic shifts necessary to resolve the interference pattern may be able to be done in a single session.
- A lot of internal energies are being shifted with these life-enhancing energy processes, and an individual's system may only be able to handle so much at one time.
- An apparent allergy may in fact be an allergy to a person.
- Let go of the 'need-to-know' how to handle the situation and let it unfold naturally under the direction of inner wisdom and guidance.
- Sometimes, it is not so much about changing the other person, situation, or circumstance, as much as it may be about changing how you are responding to a given situation.

- It is a good idea to instruct and align your subconscious and energy field for moving forward in life.

- You have the power within to create a better life.

There are things in life that we don't fully understand, yet they affect us just the same. I have seen how these processes of transformation have touched the lives of individuals in beautiful, healing ways. This system is simple, direct, and verifiable. L.E.E.P.s can change long-standing interference patterns within a matter of minutes.

"To be yourself in a world that is constantly trying to make you something else is the greatest accomplishment."
~ Ralph Waldo Emerson

See Appendix II for Downloadable *Resource: L.E.E.P. System Discovery Process*

CHAPTER 16

You Risk Everything
by Not Being Yourself

"And the day came when the risk to remain tight in a bud
was more painful than the risk it took to blossom."
~ *Elizabeth Appell*

People have a tendency to make things more difficult or more complicated than necessary. It seems to be ingrained into our culture, but it doesn't have to be that way. And maybe we just haven't been exposed to the information we've needed in order to create what it is we truly desire.

Our banks, corporations, government, military, and top one percent of the wealthiest people on earth cannot solve the world's problems, but we can. Our consciousness is different because it is focused upon higher ideals, and, therefore, we are the ones who make a positive difference in the world. We are the ones who bring about the paradigm shift we have been yearning for.

The time has come for humanity to step into its empowerment. People don't need to be saved or rescued. People need to be aware of their power and how to use it. At our core, each of us knows this is our birthright. Deepak Chopra said, "There are no spare parts in the universe," which means that *each and every one of us* represents a vital contribution to the whole of humankind. Your unique contribution lies deep within, waiting to blossom. The only things that have been holding you back are your interference patterns. They hold the keys to personal transformation, fulfillment, and possibilities in life. They contain the wisdom we need to transcend our limitations and discover our true essence. When we become whole and integrated individuals, it opens us up to a world beyond that which we had previously known.

Our Journey's Authentic Purpose

We all come here with a life purpose to contribute our unique gifts, talents, and skills to the world in a way that only we as individuals can. When we are flowing from our purpose, doors open, synchronicities happen, and life brings us new meaning. In every moment, life is about living fully in the moment; it's about love, and it's about the journey. It's about connection with our essential nature and living from a greater expression of our own authenticity. This not only enriches our life, but also enriches the lives of others.

People wish to be happy, yet most never make the effort to adopt a course of action that leads to happiness. No matter what one considers the goal to be in life, meeting the right person, getting a better job, losing those last ten pounds, making more money, or living in a different city, happens because of the choices you're making right now. Life is happening right here in this very moment... and it's within our control. When we resolve our interference patterns, we connect with our genuine dreams, aspirations, and empowerment. It accelerates our personal evolution.

From Challenge to Champion

Despite our best efforts, we cannot control what the universe sends our way. Difficult circumstances will still arise as we come up against the walls of our own limitations, compelling us to learn and grow. Consider for a moment that every person, event, and incident in life offers an opportunity for you to awaken to your own inner wisdom and has been training you to discover your own strength, so you can bring your special gift to the world. It can feel a bit threatening at first, though, if we remember we have access to wisdom within and a life-enhancing system to help free ourselves from our restraints, we can change our experiences and expand into greater freedom. It takes courage to stand and face our problems, to heal the past, and to step into greater self-empowerment because every time we do we are expanding into our soul's uncharted territory.

In order to feel safe enough to share our gifts with others and the world, we need to heal the things within that diminish our light, for we know that our soul should not be confined by false boundaries. At some point, you'll become so comfortable about exploring and doing your inner work that you will find you look forward to discovering anything that has been holding you back. You'll come to the conclusion that things really can keep getting better and better, and life becomes a greater adventure.

The Maturation of Wisdom

Whenever we feel limited, fearful of the future, and are not living up to our potential, we risk not being and living the fullest expression of who we are. When you suppress your hopes, dreams, ideas, and creativity, you suppress your unique individuality and authenticity. Being authentically you is when you are in alignment with the deeper aspect of yourself. It is the part of you that yearns to be expressed, to shine your light, adding value and the spice of life to living. It means being completely honest with how you feel, knowing what you truly want, and what you deeply value in life.

Life itself, everyday life, can be our most valued teacher. It has a tremendous capacity to show us truth and to wake us up. We gain wisdom every time we receive a message and learn a lesson. I know I have. I go into the discovery process, navigate my way through a problem or setback, and when I have completed the L.E.E.P., I discover somewhere along the way that I have gained clarity, a new perspective, and a deeper understanding for doing the work. I become wiser than when I began.

Each experience leads to greater wisdom and compassion. Part of how we learn is to resolve the things that are limiting and restricting us. We receive the message, learn the lesson, and rise to a higher level of awareness. This is all a part of how our soul grows. I made it through my Dark-Night-of-the-Soul and am far better off now than I ever was. I learned that whenever we give in to our fears or insecurity, or conform to social pressures, it always causes internal conflicts. This is part of the reason why too many individuals live lives of frustration, mediocrity, and desperation. When we are true to ourselves and act in accordance with our fundamental nature, we live with greater passion, joy, fulfillment, and self-respect. When you respect yourself, others respect you, too. When we share more of our true selves with others, we create a greater sense of kinship, which helps to heal the separation between us.

"Imagination is more important than knowledge.
For knowledge is limited, whereas imagination embraces the entire world,
stimulating progress, giving birth to evolution."
~ *Albert Einstein*

Imagine = I—M—A—Gin—E [pronounced: I am a genie.]

Imagine instead of waking up to gloom and despair on a daily basis, you woke up with a smile on your face, knowing you are able to express your most genuine passion and joy in life, excited about whatever it is you are doing. A life where you are sharing your natural passion, skills, and talents with others, living where you want, and how you want.

Imagine if each of us embarked upon a mission of greater personal expression, freedom, and empowerment in our lives. What would that look like? Magic?

Our imagination is part of what we use to create magic within our lives. Magic is not an act of faith—it is an understanding. It means having the ability to use unseen forces to bring about a desired outcome. Those forces are: information and energy, belief and emotion patterns within the subconscious, heart coherency, and the living essence of the Field. In essence, everything you take in, believe in, and embrace is a bridge between the invisible and visible world.

In the end, I've not only found the secret to self-empowerment, I also discovered that by utilizing life-enhancing energetic processes I had become very much like the genie I had wished to be when I was little. I've created what others would deem impossible. Personal magic.

When We Heal Ourselves, We Collectively Heal Humanity

We gain beautiful insights, ah-ha moments, inspiration, and solutions every time we make a L.E.E.P. in our life. And with every shift, a nice chemistry change takes place within our body that supports our health and well-being. We could naïvely perceive this as enlightenment, though, the highs that come with enlightenment are not enlightenment itself. Those highs are only the blissful, flowery feelings of chemistry as we commune with our soul. While nice, these residual feelings of spiritual connection are fleeting, and they will pass. Enlightenment takes place afterwards in the way we choose to participate in life. One has to live the sacredness of what has been inspired and awakened within. The highs will come and go, but that enlightenment must be lived.

Personal growth and enlightenment must not be measured simply by a change in consciousness, but also by the application of it in one's life. Higher consciousness changes you for the better whenever you come into contact with it. It not only enriches you personally, but, because of its influence upon you, it also enriches humanity. When you shine your light, you inspire others to shine as well, giving them the opportunity to step more fully into a higher aspect by following your lead. Their actions will naturally unfold to a higher expression when given the opportunity. Enlightenment is only the beginning. As spiritual beings, we must use enlightenment for the benefit of all.

Looking at the Big Picture

When you reclaim the energy that has been drained from your personal life, you can start making a positive difference in the world at large. When we are living in our power, we are striving to positively change the world with a purpose that is aligned with our heart and soul. We disconnect from the drama and withdraw our energies from the political parties with hidden agendas and corporations that profit without integrity. The media and advertising that leaves us feeling empty and inadequate are replaced by an ability to make a difference in levels of homelessness, poor living conditions, and environment. Passion for agriculture, science, healthcare, arts, culture, education, and entertainment that were lost become found. We remember what is real, what is necessary, and what is in harmony with the planet and all her inhabitants. Our consciousness is raised to a higher level than before. People get back in touch with their authenticity, which further supports each one of us being true to our individual selves. We experience greater connection, less separation, and take a greater stand for respectful, sustainable living.

The world belongs to all of its inhabitants—not just a privileged few— but all who are born here. The land, water, plants, seeds, forests, and minerals belong to everyone. We are the caretakers, custodians, and keepers of the earth and must reclaim it through our healing, consciousness, and actions, and we must look for solutions to worldly problems. The paradigm shift starts within us. We are the ones who express the divine principles, gifts, talents, and abundance through our beings. The blueprint for a new social structure, in which everyone is free to express their natural gifts and talents with the world by living as they are, is within our control.

A Utopian World—The Natural Order of Life

We've been led to believe we live on a planet of scarcity, and this is part of what keeps us in our stingy petty-mindedness, when in fact we live on a planet of incredible abundance. For instance, every apple tree produces many apples, and they contain the seeds for future trees and an exponential supply of fruit that keeps the cycle going. Our world is mostly water, and there will never be a shortage. There is an endless supply of free energy in the form of solar power, ocean currents, and wind, with better designs invented every day. We have eyes to see abundance everywhere, and we need not buy into the lies of a scarcity mind-set.

We have all the necessary resources to create heaven on earth, and now it is time for us to truly live up to our potential. The technology and knowledge—the skills and talents—are within our grasp. Creating a utopian world simply requires willingness, compassion, and inspiration as well as dedication, cooperation, and the drive to create unity. Again, that begins within us. When we know what we want and what the next step is, we contribute by making a positive difference in the world. We resonate with other like-minded individuals and, together, make the world a living paradise.

We are on the brink of free energy and have enough food to feed the world. Now, imagine this new consciousness being lived worldwide. Plenty of food, water, shelter, clothing, and free energy to go around. Everyone being equally valued and respected for the gifts, talents, and skills they bring to the world. Imagine all your needs being met and living your life's passion. What would that passion be? Choose now to live a portion of your day doing what you love. Whether for 20 minutes, one hour, or 2–3 hours, do what you love, whatever feeds your soul, and also makes a positive difference in the world.

With more and more individuals opening up to new levels of freedom, empowerment, and passion, we shift the consciousness of the planet and co-create heaven on earth. Every social or political system we've ever had has failed us. Therefore, if global economic collapse continues on its projected path, you've helped to avert the disaster by creating a new world paradigm by living and breathing your passion and joy while making the world a better place. As more and more of us do this, we shift out of the old way of living and back into the natural harmony of evolution. This improved level of consciousness takes away the stress, changing humanity and the planet.

Philosophy, Insights, and Pillars in Living

My basic philosophy in life comes from my revelations and awakenings and can be summed up as 1 Path, 6 Insights, and 4 Pillars of Transformation, Self-Empowerment, and Conscious Evolution.

1 Path

There is only one path, and that is *yours*—there is no other path. This is the one you have been on since the moment you were born. You can be inspired by another's path but cannot walk theirs—only your own. You do not need to compare or measure your path against anyone else's either. Your path has always been leading back to your original goal, which is, back to the wholeness of your own self and finding your connection with spirit. Once you've found your connection, then your purpose is easy to discover because it is what makes your heart and soul sing with the true expression of your essential nature. Your purpose is to make a positive difference by shining your light out into the world. It is what the world needs, what humanity needs, and it is what you were meant to do.

6 Insights

Separation is an illusion. This is the only dis-ease on the planet. When we separate our brain from our heart, and our everyday life from our spirituality, we lose connection. Be wary of any belief, leader, religion, or ideology that advocates division between you and other people. You came from the stars—your bones are made from the same dust. You are spirit made manifest, love, light, and consciousness embodied in the here and now. Do your best to see everyone as equal, or as an extension of some version of yourself. There is no such thing as real separation; it is only an illusion. Remember that.

Challenges are opportunities to step into our power. We have interference patterns within us that are the root cause of every issue, problem, or challenge in our life. When we experience anything as a challenge, it's actually a chance to free ourselves of limitations and live beyond past boundaries. These opportunities help us heal old wounds, clarify misperceptions, and raise our consciousness to a higher level. Continue to look for solutions to problems because there is hidden truth everywhere and in everyone. Strive for progress, not perfection. When we resolve and heal our distorted perceptions, our outer lives better reflect who we truly are.

In every moment, life is about love. In the beginning, in the end, and now, life is about love. Every action in life is either 'an expression of love' or 'a request for love.' Be the being who sees from your heart. Awaken the hearts of others with your heart and compassion, for we are all meant to evolve and grow.

You have a gift. You just have to love yourself and share your gift. We all come here with a life purpose. Go within and get in touch with the vision you have of yourself. When you are flowing from your purpose, doors open and life brings new meaning. It is time to step more fully into who you are and who you are becoming by taking action. Let your heart and vision guide your actions and share the gift of who you are with the world.

Live authentically. Live life as an expression aligned with your own heart. Let truth, life, and love emanate from your being once you have awakened it. Live from your own unique perspective, values, and integrity by being true to yourself. Believe it or not, you are the center of your own life, just as each person is the center of his or hers. When we all are living from our authentic selves, it is easy to celebrate and appreciate our differences. Have the courage to live from this special place. The more you stand up and be who you are, the more opportunities will find you.

Honor yourself. Lack of self-worth, self-appreciation, and self-love is an epidemic on our planet. You are a radiant spirit, a spark of the Divine, walking around and living in an amazing body composed of the substance of our beautiful Mother Earth. Get into your sacredness—present yourself as spirit within. Walk proud. Love yourself. It is one of the greatest things you can do. Honor your journey and experiences—this will help others get into their sacredness as well.

4 Pillars of Transformation, Self-Empowerment, and Conscious Evolution

1. **Into the Silence:** People need to let go of their stress and enter into the silence of solitude. Practice some form of meditation, mindfulness, prayer, or even journaling. This is a two-fold practice of going within and radiating out. Going within is a form of silent wisdom, which looks like meditation or mindfulness, where you focus on and connect with the peace within and deeply listen to the Divine guiding and inspiring you. Radiating outward is like your silent blessing to the world, where you are ready to share your life, light, and consciousness simply by being who you are.

2. **Channeling Energy:** Learn some form of energy healing (see Appendix III). You have the power to activate the life-force energy moving through you to aid, accelerate, and nurture your body's self-healing abilities for health and well-being. It plays a beneficial role in transforming interference patterns, as well as raising vibrational frequencies for personal and spiritual growth.

3. **Communicate with Your Subconscious Mind:** This helps you unlock your potential in every area of your life and to better live the life you want. It gives you greater freedom to explore the world and make a positive difference and allows you greater empowerment to step into a life of your design rather than living as a reaction to circumstances. It is important to regularly and actively nourish your subconscious with truth: life-enhancing beliefs, thoughts, emotions, ideas, creativity, health, and possibility.

4. **Resolve Interference Patterns.** Commit to a regular practice of resolving interference patterns in your life. It will free your energy up, allowing you greater expression of who you are and who you are becoming. You will live with greater synchronicity and flow. It expands your conscious awareness and allows greater ease for the universe to work through you.

This Is Your Time

This life is yours. It is just waiting for you. You alone have the power to choose how you want to experience it. Choosing to live a happy life is up to you; no one else can do that for you. It is time for you to transform and resolve whatever has been holding you back. I may not know your gifts, talents, and skills—these are yours to discover—but I do know what a difference you make in the world. It's a better place because you exist, so take your power and decide what your life would look, feel, and be like if you were living authentically, empowered, and from your heart and soul. This is what living life fully is all about. We all have this magic inside us.

Let the adventure begin . . .

"Change and growth take place when a person has risked himself and dares to become involved with experimenting with his own life."
~ Herbert Otto

Some Parting Thoughts

The Heart and Soul Academy

"If we cultivate our own inner treasures, they will reward us
with bliss, joy, and happiness beyond our fondest imaginings."
~ *Tarthang Tulku*

I have shared all the expertise possible within the pages of this book about the L.E.E.P. System and how to use the Life-Enhancing Energetic Processes for the transformation of subconsciously held interference patterns. I've invested my heart and soul in these pages and given you my very best. While you have within your grasp everything I can think of to help you resolve limitations, problems, and obstacles that hold you back in life, obviously, books by their very nature are general; therefore, you may wish to know more about some of the things you've discovered here. So, if you're wondering where to go from here, the next step is up to you.

If you're ready to delve deeper and explore additional training, The Heart and Soul Academy offers online courses to further your skills, confidence, competence, and understanding of the processes presented in this book.

The Heart and Soul Academy

Online Courses

These on-demand courses may be enjoyed in the comfort of your own home, on your own time schedule, and for very reasonable rates.

Infinite Energy Frequencies Attunement and Energy Healing Course

Imagine being able to not only expand your energy healing abilities, but also being able to significantly increase the energy healing frequencies you can channel. This energy healing course features the world's most advanced energetic attunement—The Infinite Energy Frequencies—that includes a unique set of energy tools that *very few* individuals will ever have the opportunity to work with and experience.

An attunement is like an initiation, an energetic procedure that amplifies the vibratory rate of an individual's energy field, which includes his or her etheric and physical body. With the attunement, there is a tremendous amount of life-force moving through your energy field, through your energy centers (chakras), and through your body. It loosens up and sloughs off the dense, heavier, lower vibrations—cleansing the energetic debris—and raises your personal energy vibration with each pulse of the 74 specific energy signatures in a step-by-step fashion. This is part of what makes this attunement the world's most advanced. It goes far beyond any other known process of this nature and is unique unto itself.

This course is for either a true beginner, who has never had an energy healing course before but would like to know more, or for someone with an extensive background and experience in energy healing, who would love to greatly increase the capacity and capabilities of his or her energy healing skills. In this course, you will learn:

- The rich history and science of energy healing and receive more detailed information about the Infinite Energy Frequencies
- How to attune to the Infinite Energy Frequencies

- The importance of multi-dimensional grounding and how to do it
- How to energize things, from the food you eat, to the water you drink, to objects, gifts, your car, home, jewelry, and more
- The Scan and Delete process
- How to energize and encode a goal to help it manifest faster
- The step-by-step process of self-energy healing
- How to facilitate hands-on energy healing with someone else
- Surrogate skills for distance energy healing
- A little known 5,000-year-old practice of how to gather, collect, and store energy
- The step-by-step chakra process for health and how to share it with someone at a distance
- Life-enhancing beliefs to support the energy healer within you
- Life-enhancing beliefs to increase your psychic abilities
- Guided healing meditation techniques for rejuvenation and stress release
- The opportunity to participate in an online Energy Healing Circle

"Years ago, Dhebi helped me through an illness, and I am so very grateful to her and her work. I was excited to take this course, and it did not disappoint in the least. My energy and self-awareness of the energy around me has increased. I work with patients that have so much trauma in their lives, and I have already started helping others with the learnings. The information is fascinating as well as effective. I found all the segments so wonderful. I could not pick one over the other. Dhebi has a true gift, and she shares so much knowledge throughout the course. I am in awe of this information and how it helps fine tune your energy awareness. I can't wait for more classes. Thank you so much!"
~ *Tami Tanninen*

"I am so glad I attended the Energy Frequencies Attunement, not only because I waited for it to finally be offered, but also because I knew it would change my own frequency level. The classes certainly exceeded my expectations by far! The process of attunement was a profound and touching experience that I could not have expected in the way it happened. That part alone made me feel and realize with every cell of my body that we are connected, and I would not want to have missed it! What we learned in the following classes was very helpful for my daily life. The 74 frequencies brighten up everything! Wow, wow, wow, love, love, love it!!!"
~ *Sandra Kaya*

"I did not exactly know what the course would hold and was most pleasantly surprised by the chance to get attuned to 74 different energy frequencies. I remember the energetic shift I had felt years ago when I was attuned to the energy of Reiki. I could not imagine how powerful it would be to be attuned to 74 energies. Wow! I felt an amazing elevation of energy awareness, which I thoroughly enjoy. I am an Energy Healer, and I now use the Infinite Energy Frequencies often during treatments with my clients but also for myself. This has so beautifully brought the concept of the work I do together and brought it to a whole different level."
~ *Claudia Tressel*

Unlocking Your Potential

Introductory video training course and *Special Gift Offer.*

My mission in life is to make a positive difference in the world with the skills I have to help individuals step into their self-empowerment. With this ideal in mind, I set an audacious goal for myself: to help over one million individuals with self-empowerment, for I believe that when one is empowered we all win. The only way I can help touch the lives of as many enlightened individuals as possible is if I don't let money stand in the way of helping others. So, instead of this online video course being taught for hundreds of dollars, it is being offered at the special rate of $33 (to help cover production costs and service fees) and may even be shared with a friend. I give you my personal guarantee that I will do everything within my power to make this worth your time and energy. The course includes the following:

- The science and philosophy of how manifesting works
- Instruction about how and why heart coherency is vital for creating the life of your dreams
- Step-by-step instruction in:
    - the secret **Language of Creation Process** to communicate with your subconscious mind and the living energy field
    - accessing your inner wisdom with the valuable skill of **energy self-testing**
    - the **Chakra Belief Change Process,** a heart coherent energetic process to align your body-mind energy field with your dreams, goals, and destiny
    - another energetic process for making belief changes by tapping into an alternate dimensional reality with the Vortex Infinity Alignment
- Receive an **Energy Attunement** to the violet light of transformation and the golden light of expanded consciousness to accelerate transformation
- Receive lists of life-enhancing beliefs that support you stepping into your strengths and your empowerment within many aspects of life
- Advice on creating your own life-enhancing beliefs
- Invite a friend to share the course with you (Note: You both need to register online at the same time). Feel free to share this special gift offering with others and help me spread the word.

"Thank you, Dhebi, for a tremendous program. I believe you are on to a core, transformative, powerful, growth and healing process. I also appreciate your science, technique, and follow through. You are loving and professional."
~ In grateful love and light, Jim Gregory, Glass Chemist and Artist

Resolve Emotional Interference Patterns and Free Up Life-Force Energy

Emotional interference patterns (EIPs) consist of well-defined waveform energies that move in pulse-like waves and can exert a powerful influence upon us. They are created by repressed, denied, and/or unresolved emotions. EIPs block us from our natural tendency to love and from fulfilling our deeper potential in every aspect of our lives.

- Discover how to find the hidden EIPs that have been holding you back
- Enjoy step-by-step guidance through three effective processes (Emotional Interference Patterns Resolution, Blessing of Forgiveness, and the Traumatic Stress Release) to release these destructive forces and return to vitality
- Receive step-by-step guidance for accessing your inner wisdom with the skill of energy self-testing
- Dissolve the outdated energetic heart shield that is no longer worthy of who you are or who you are becoming (85–90 percent of all individuals have one but don't know it.)
- Receive a simple heart-centered breathing practice for emotional release
- Receive charts: Finding Unresolved Emotions and Healthy, Helpful Emotions

"My experience with Resolving Emotional Interference Patterns has been phenomenal, so far as both a practitioner and a client. I have seen miracles happen! This is the easiest technique I have ever used, and the results cannot even be explained. What I like most is that it is not necessary to go through emotional pain or trauma to release it; the body and subconscious mind let go of it easily using this process. I am really enjoying it."
~ *Annick J. Burke, CHT, Oakheart Intuitive Therapies*

The New Wealth Consciousness

Wealth consciousness is about unleashing who *YOU really are* inside. Deep inside, you know that wealth is about so much more than money, which is only a tool we use to create potential for ourselves and others. True wealth consciousness has certain *unique qualities* about it; it's a mind-set with successful actions and is in perfect harmony with spiritual truths. **Shift out of survival mode and into thrival mode and:**

- Discover the interference patterns that have kept you from wealth and abundance
- Re-pattern your subconscious and energy field around money, wealth, and prosperity
- Learn how to make money work for you
- Clarify your personal values to support wealth consciousness
- Change your internal programs and patterns around money
- Receive 100+ Life-Enhancing Belief Statements for the New Wealth Consciousness

"I had a session with Dhebi and took her first class of the year. Immediately after the sessions with Dhebi I saw incredible changes in my life. I started getting job offers, and my business started getting more clients. After taking the class, it only got better from my relationship, to my energy level, to my financial state. Everything in life is only getting better from incorporating her practices into my life. I have recommended her to several other people and will be taking all of her classes from here on out."
~ Jeffrey Jensen

Radiant Health

The greatest obstacles to your health may very well lie hidden within, defeating you instead of supporting you in living the very best life you can.

- Learn the 8-Steps for Self-Healing

- Re-pattern your subconscious mind and energy field for optimal health and well-being
- Receive life-enhancing statements for Health, Weight, Youthful Vitality, Agelessness, Chakra Healing, and more
- Participate in a guided sacred heart journey within to your Sanctuary of Health and Wellness
- Learn the basic foundation for a healthy lifestyle
- Learn simple energy practices, plus other things that you can easily incorporate into your daily lifestyle that make a world of difference in how you look and feel
- Plus, I'll share my superfood breakfast and lunch recipes with you.

Shadow Energetics

This advanced course is designed to move you in the direction of wholeness and unconditional self-love by finding the parts of yourself that you have disowned.

- Discover the immense value shadow personalities have and how they can enrich your life
- Explore the shadow personalities and understand how disowned selves operate inside you, as well as the effect they play in your life, health, behaviors, and relationships
- Learn the Shadow Integration Process (that can't fully and effectively be taught in a book)
- Learn strategies that simply and effectively allow you to energetically reconcile your relationships with your disowned selves in order to embrace them back into wholeness
- Separate from your inner critic and gain greater confidence and self-esteem
- Deepen your connection with your inner self and gain greater access to your magic, wonder, playfulness, and imagination

Facilitator Training

This advanced training is designed for those who want to take their skills to the next level and successfully facilitate all of the L.E.E.P. System processes presented in *The Messenger Within* with others in private practice.

- Highly interactive, practical, hands-on facilitation experience
- Exploration and discovery of how to effectively navigate private sessions from start to finish
- Participate in shifts that support your own personal growth while learning to facilitate it with others
- Discover messages behind problems, challenges, or issues
- Facilitate effective sessions via Skype or phone
- Small nurturing group environment

Heart and Soul Personal Retreats

Join me and a group of dedicated individuals on a journey to beautiful, spiritually nurturing places in the world. Participate with others in advanced life-enhancing practices tailored to achieve powerful transformations. Connect, enjoy life, and have fun.

"The whole of life is but a moment in time.
It is our duty, therefore to use it, not to misuse it."
~ Plutarch

APPENDIX I

Life-Enhancing Belief Statements

Life-enhancing beliefs are essentially statements of agreements, empowering ideas, concepts, or choices we consciously choose to become part of our subconscious mind's operating system, and, therefore, part of our destiny. They are not only the foundation, but also the autopilot that supports and powers our life's goals, potential, opportunities, and future.

Feel free to use these life-enhancing belief statements as they are or modify them to better suit your needs. Use them as inspiration and as examples of positive, life-affirming subconscious programming statements. They also work well to condition your conscious mind for positive thinking. Life-enhancing belief statements support an individual in unleashing new potential and new possibilities in living life to its fullest. Skip over any that don't resonate with you—these are only examples offered to support or expand your thought processes to help you look at life from another perspective.

If we do not possess these qualities already, then we need to intentionally create them in our subconscious with a L.E.E.P., so that it becomes second nature to us. Equipped with this new quality, we succeed in our life's undertakings, whether spiritual or material.

Let's Play

Look over the lists below. Choose life-enhancing beliefs you'd like to integrate into your subconscious patterns and programs, then use the Chakra Belief Change Process found in Chapter 6 to practice this skill and program your subconscious mind.

Essential Qualities of Human Potential and Life-Enhancing Beliefs

 1. **Abundance**
    - Abundance is the generosity and flow of the universe. I am abundant.
    - The universe is a friendly place full of infinite possibilities and willingly provides whatever I need.
    - Abundance is natural, and there will always be enough.
    - What I have to offer is of value to others.
    - I create abundance to fulfill my material and non-material desires.
    - Golden opportunities are presented to me now.
    - I create my own value and worth.
    - Money is a symbol of appreciation for the value I offer the world.
    - Money is a solidified form of love and appreciation.
    - Money is a system for creating possibility for myself and others.

 2. **Acceptance**
    - I accept the things I cannot change and change the things I can.
    - I am at peace while I do what this moment requires me to do.
    - I accept myself for who I am. I accept others for who they are.
    - While I recognize and accept the self-imposed limitations of others, I look beyond that to what I know they are capable of doing and accomplishing and see the beauty of their being.
    - My self-acceptance leads me to new possibilities, personal growth, and a fulfilling reality.
    - I value the difference in myself and others.
    - I recognize and respect that others think differently and have different opinions.
    - I am flexible, allowing others the freedom to be themselves.

 3. **Charity**
    - I choose the path of charity, compassion, generosity, and kindness.
    - I give of myself to help others learn and grow.

- I willingly support others and make a positive difference in the world.
- I lend my support to help others reach their goals.
- By helping others, I am part of a bigger mission and the resolution to lingering problems.
- Satisfaction fills my heart when I lend a helping hand.

4. Choice

- I have the freedom to choose.
- My life is filled with choices and possibilities.
- I am confident, and I trust the choices I make.
- I trust that I always have options in any given moment.
- I decide what is right for me.
- I am a natural decision maker.

5. Communication

- I express myself openly and honestly.
- I trust in my ability to say the right thing at the right time.
- I trust in my ability to communicate confidently and effectively.
- I listen with genuine interest to what others have to say.
- I am comfortable and confident when I express my ideas to others.
- I speak my personal truths with love, compassion, and commitment.
- I have the courage to speak up for myself or others when I know it is the right thing to do.

6. Compassion

- I am able to feel deeply or to give generously for another, if I so choose, while remaining free from expectations.
- I live, walk, and breathe compassion for the world and all its inhabitants.
- I am able to have compassion for another's situation while remaining true to my own reality.

- I hold sacred space for other beings to be who and what they are in every moment.
- I am compassionate toward others in distress and am able to remain in my own power and strength as well.
- I am able to sit with either my own or another's grief, suffering, or pain and remain relaxed and calm.

7. **Competence**

- I am capable and competent.
- I am able to accomplish anything I choose.
- I have the power, strength, and knowledge to handle everything in my life.
- I trust myself and my inner guidance.
- I am assertive in meeting my own needs even while respecting the needs of others.
- I deeply respect and appreciate who I am.

8. **Confidence**

- I am confident and self-assured.
- I believe and trust in myself.
- I know I am a capable person.
- With each experience, I gain greater confidence in myself and my understanding of life.
- I feel content and confident with myself even when in new situations or with unfamiliar people.

9. **Connection**

- I easily attract friends and colleagues who are supportive and caring.
- When I open and soften my heart, I connect more fully with others.
- I create win/win situations.
- I communicate with love, clarity, and openness.
- I am included. I feel included.

- I connect with others in harmony, synchronicity, and flow.

10. Coping with Grief, Tragedy, and Loss

- I honor and respect the grieving process.
- I am able to sit with my own or another's grief, suffering, or pain and be at ease.
- Allowing myself to grieve is part of my healing process and way of embracing reality. I take all the time I need.
- I allow my feelings and emotions to move through me and release them in healthy ways.
- My grief resolves itself in its own time, and I move forward in peace.
- I accept the things I cannot change and change the ones I can.

11. Courage

- I am assertive in meeting my own needs.
- I have the courage and strength to face obstacles when they appear.
- I believe and trust in myself.
- I have the courage to speak up for myself or others when I know it is the right thing to do.
- It is easy for me to do what is right even when there is pressure from others to do otherwise.
- I have the courage and confidence to face unrealistic fears, so that I may experience, explore, and participate in life more fully.

12. Creativity

- I am inspired from within.
- I use my imagination and have a continuous flow of new and interesting ideas.
- My mind produces creative and artistic ideas.
- I have an adventurous mind and seek new outlooks on life.
- I have rich, creative talents.
- I treat each new challenge I encounter as an opportunity to be creative.

- I have an unusual ability to reach creative decisions and to find creative solutions for problems.

13. Discernment

- I use good judgment when I make decisions and take action.
- I choose the best outcome for me.
- I take time to evaluate circumstances and situations fairly when I make a decision.
- I evaluate my choices based upon real options.
- I use good judgment to consistently produce optimal results.
- I evaluate and use my knowledge and perceptions for the best results.

14. Dissolve and Release Fear from the Body

- I am safe.
- I am in charge of my life.
- I am self-assured and filled with peace.
- I have confidence in myself and the courage to meet obstacles directly and straightforwardly.
- I am nurtured and supported through my connection with the Divine.

15. Faith

- I trust in my heart's perception to know the truth and value of a person, idea, or situation.
- I am able to have faith while at the same time using discernment, reason, and common sense.
- I have faith in myself to experience and express my highest good with ease and grace.
- My faith in myself gives me inner strength.
- I have faith and patience that the truth will reveal itself to me.

16. Fitness and Sports

- I strive to do my personal best.

- I have fun as I accomplish my fitness goals.
- My endurance improves every day and in every way.
- I celebrate my achievements.
- I quickly learn from errors, integrate necessary adjustments, and focus on successful results.
- I enjoy my current level of performance, and I look forward to getting even better.
- I give my body the time it needs to heal and rejuvenate.

17. Forgiveness

- I forgive as an act of self-love.
- I forgive and release all those who have caused me pain or grief.
- I forgive myself for taking things too deeply, to the depths that shut me down or that keep me in my smallness.
- I forgive myself for judging or diminishing myself in any and all ways.
- I forgive myself for any harm I have done to others.
- I bless and release all for the highest wisdom and benefit of all, including myself.
- I take responsibility for my own life.

18. Health

- My body regenerates and rejuvenates itself easily and effortlessly.
- My body knows how to heal itself and does.
- My immune system is strong, maintains health, and protects me from disease.
- I relax into the healing process. I allow spirit to do what it does.
- My body aligns to the natural order of health, harmony, and vitality within.
- My body restores and maintains my blueprint for radiant health.
- I am healthy. I want to live.
- I nurture my body in healthy and loving ways.

19. Healthy Sense of Humor

- A healthy sense of humor comes naturally to me.
- I use jokes and jests to spice up life.
- I deserve to be playful and enjoy humor.
- I appreciate the sense of humor in others.
- My sense of humor keeps me youthful.
- I relax, have fun, and easily express my playfulness.

20. Improve Energy Testing Skills

- I remain relaxed, calm, and curious when performing an energy test.
- I receive clear energy testing results.
- I receive accurate feedback that I can trust.
- I trust my Higher Wisdom and the energy testing results I receive.
- It is easy for me to energy test.
- I am confident and competent with energy testing.

21. Integrity

- My integrity is the real power behind my achievements.
- I am honest and trustworthy in my thoughts, actions, and behaviors.
- I take the right actions and create win/win situations and solutions in all areas of my life.
- I respect myself and am respectful of others.
- I take 100 percent responsibility for my choices and actions.
- I allow others to take 100 percent responsibility for their choices and actions.
- I make decisions based on what I know to be true in my heart, not necessarily by popular vote.

22. Joy

- I naturally and openly express joy in my life.
- I recognize and take time for pleasure and play in my life.

- Joy fills every cell of my body, mind, and spirit and infuses my life.
- I have fun and am a fun person.
- I deeply appreciate and enjoy the beauty of my life.

23. Leadership

- I consistently look for and expect the best from myself and others.
- I naturally take action and organize my life around my priorities.
- I build on the strengths of myself and others.
- I appreciate and support the contribution of all members on my team.
- I develop and sustain effective working relationships with others.
- I am confident in my leadership abilities.
- I easily move from insight to action.

24. Living Your Unlived Life

- I am willing to sacrifice society's approval in order to be true to myself.
- I am willing to disappoint another in order to be true to myself.
- This is my life to shine and live to the fullest extent of my abilities.
- I am ready, willing, and able to live my authentic self with an open heart.
- I am willing to rise above my fears and move toward my true desires now.
- Boldness propels my authentic self out into the world of adventure and possibility.
- I live in the moment being true to myself and in integrity with others.

25. Love

- I recognize and accept love as my true nature.
- My life is filled with love, meaning, and purpose.
- I am worthy of the best that love has to offer.
- I love myself. I love my life. I am loved.
- Within my heart is all the love I will ever need.

- I accept love, add to it, and pass it on.
- I am lovable because love is the true essence of who I am.
- Love is an action I practice moment-to-moment.

26. Motivation

- I am motivated and making the necessary changes in order to accomplish my goals.
- I have the drive, incentive, and inspiration to go beyond the limits I had.
- I am being creatively motivated to make my goals a reality.
- I have the energy, drive, and initiative to complete whatever I start.
- I have the power, desire, and drive to accomplish my goals efficiently and effectively.
- I am able to make my work easy and fun.

27. Playful, Carefree Social Butterfly

- I deserve to take time for pleasure and play in my life.
- I allow my inner child to come out and play.
- I flirt to bring out the fun with friends, acquaintances, and strangers.
- My flirting is carefree and brings out the best in others.
- I live a magical life filled with love, vitality, and joy.
- I thoroughly enjoy living in the moment and being myself.
- It is natural for me to express love by singing, dancing, exploring, and creating for fun.

28. Relationship

- I genuinely seek mutual benefit in all my relationships, both personal and professional.
- I develop and sustain effective healthy relationships with others.
- I find meaning and purpose in my relationships.
- It's okay for me to set boundaries in relationships, and I do.
- I allow myself to learn from others as they learn from me.

- I am responsible for my actions in any of my relationships; others are responsible for their actions.
- My relationships are loving, supportive, and inspiring.

29. Responsibility

- I am 100 percent responsible for the results and circumstances I create in my life.
- I acknowledge my ability and responsibility to make a positive difference in the world.
- I allow others to take 100 percent responsibility for the results and circumstances in their own lives.
- My healthy level of responsibility brings me greater joy and freedom in life.
- I take responsibility for my life, health, wealth, and happiness.

30. Security

- I *am* safe. I *feel* safe.
- I relax and know that I am safe and secure in all situations.
- I trust I am in the right place at the right time.
- I trust my life experiences to work out for my highest good and benefit.
- I am nurtured and supported in my life's experiences.

31. Self-Worth

- What I do and who I am makes a positive difference in the world.
- I deeply respect and appreciate myself for who I am.
- I take responsibility for my own happiness and well-being.
- I am the best me I can be in each moment.
- I trust myself and my inner guidance.
- I am worthy of the best that life has to offer.
- I am a good person.
- I express who I am with natural style and grace.
- I am content and satisfied to be me.

32. Serenity

- I relax, do my best, and am nurtured in my life's experiences.
- I experience inner peace, harmony, and serenity.
- I am filled with peace even in the midst of chaos or conflict.
- I am relaxed and calm even when surrounded by adversity.
- I am serene even in the middle of commotion or pandemonium.

33. Sexuality

- Sexual energy radiates in and through me, bringing a sense of joy, passion, and playfulness to my life.
- I love my body, even with its imperfections, and I enjoy being pleasured.
- I let my lover know what I like, both in and out of bed.
- I deserve a sex life that enhances my capacity for deep connection in the present.
- I make sexual choices that are consistent with my desires, seeking neither to comply with nor rebel against social or relationship pressures.
- I am comfortable, confident, and enjoy expressing my sexuality in a relationship.
- I treasure my sexuality with a sense of sweaty, playful, liberating pride.

34. Spirituality, Enlightenment, and Soul Connection

- Love allows my heart consciousness to expand, enhancing my connection with the Divine.
- My DNA and nervous system are evolving to allow more spiritual information and light to come into my conscious awareness.
- I am ready to accept responsibility for, and connect more fully with, my Divine knowing.
- I am an open channel for the highest wisdom and truth for myself and others.
- I am nurtured and supported through my connection with the Divine source.

- When I follow my higher wisdom, the universe nurtures and supports me.

- My life is sacred. It is for being lived.

- I am one with Source. I am one with Divinity. I am one with Divine Love.

- My body is a temple for the Sacred and Divine within me. I live in sacredness.

- I recognize and celebrate the perfection in all beings and in all things.

- Enlightenment needs to be lived. I apply the insights of enlightenment in my life to the best of my abilities.

- We are all one, unified in love, light, and consciousness.

- I co-create health, wealth, peace, and wisdom with higher consciousness.

35. Success

- I choose to be successful.

- I take advantage of my ideas and talents and put them to good use.

- I look for ways to delegate work in order to empower others while I honor my goals and responsibilities.

- When considering taking on a project, I check in with myself to be sure I can complete the project without suffering or sacrificing my self-care.

- My success is the result of intelligent planning, focused intent, and clear goals.

- My success is a joy that allows me to grow spiritually.

- I re-evaluate my priorities as necessary and focus on what really matters.

- I attract supportive people and an environment that contributes to my success.

36. Understanding

- I seek first to understand then to be understood.

- I do my best to understand another's point of view.

- I focus and listen while other people speak, absorbing what they have said.
- I consider what a person has said before speaking my own truth.
- I honor and respect another person's perspective.
- I listen with open respect for another person's point of view.

37. Wisdom

- I trust wisdom to unfold within me and within the moment.
- I am able to see the gift in each problem and the opportunity in every situation.
- My conscious awareness flows between love and wisdom.
- I am able to distinguish truth from fiction.
- I strive to use knowledge, reason, and common sense to guide my actions in all areas of my life.
- When I follow my higher wisdom, the universe nurtures and supports me.
- I strive to create greater balance in my life between common sense, beneficial knowledge, understanding, and compassion.

APPENDIX II

Downloadable Resources

If you would like to create a binder of the processes and charts presented within this book for your personal use (or for working with others), here is a list of downloadable resources from the Heart and Soul Academy as discussed in *The Messenger Within*. Please go to: www.theHeartAndSoulAcademy.org/resource-page/

1. L.E.E.P.s 7 Areas of Influence Chart
2. Access Inner Wisdom
3. Chakra Diagram—Blocked Energy Flows
4. Wisdom of the Chakras Chart
5. Life-Force Flow Meditation
6. 33-Breath Chakra Activation Practice
7. Light Infusion Breathing Practice
8. Violet Golden Light Attunement—listen to audio
9. Sacred Heart Alignment
10. 2 Minds 1 Brain Chart
11. Language of Creation Form
12. Chakra Belief Change Process
13. Calming an Over-Energized State of Being
14. Energize the Pattern
15. Belief Change Flow Chart

16. Emotional Interference Pattern Resolution Process

17. Finding Emo Chart

18. Healthy, Helpful Emotions List

19. Traumatic Stress Release

20. Blessings of Forgiveness Guided Process

21. Essential Human Needs Chart

22. Past Lives Discovery Process

23. L.E.E.P. for Healing Ancestral Lineage Guided Process

24. Shadow Discovery Process

25. Scan and Delete Process

26. Spirit Connection Ceremony

27. L.E.E.P. Discovery Process

28. 1 Path, 6 Insights, 4 Pillars

29. Life-Enhancing Belief Statements (from Appendix I)

30. Compiled Inspirational Quotes Used Throughout *The Messenger Within*

APPENDIX III

Energy Healing Course Recommendations

This is by no means a complete list of resources; it is only meant as a place to start your research and discover what resonates with you for further exploration.

The Heart and Soul Academy's Infinite Energy Frequencies Attunement and Energy Healing Course: see description under the Heart and Soul Academy Online Course offerings.

Reiki: a form of energy medicine developed in 1922 by Japanese Buddhist monk Mikao Usui. Reiki is a simple, natural, and safe method of spiritual healing and self-improvement that everyone can use. It is taught by many Reiki Masters all over the world and is easy to learn.

Alberto Villoldo: Shaman energy medicine at The Four Winds' Light Body School. You learn how to directly connect with the energy of life to work with grace, power, and beauty, whether on an individual basis or in your growing practice.

Donna Eden: Eden Energy Medicine is a systematic and comprehensive program about self-healing and ways to work with the body's natural healing energy for optimal health and vitality.

Barbara Brennan: School of Healing is a global healing institute for a hands-on healing system that works with an individual's energy consciousness system to create physical, emotional, mental, and spiritual health. BBSH is dedicated to the evolution of the human spirit.

Dr. Richard Bartlett, DC, ND, founder of Matrix Energetics: a complete system of healing, self-care, and transformation that produces observable and verifiable changes that can be taught to anyone.

Glossary

Alchemy: A science and philosophy of power and process for changing one thing into another. A seemingly magical process of transformation, taking something from an ordinary or lesser state of being and turning it into something of greater value, sometimes in a way that cannot easily be explained.

Amygdala: A nodal point deep within the center of the brain that directly routes incoming sensory information in all forms to the higher centers of reasoning in the frontal cortex. The amygdala can either send messages on to other parts of the brain—for intelligence—or it can shut down the information right there, so a person never consciously receives it.

Appreciation: An emotion with an expansive energy frequency that has the power to attract, increase value, and amplify the fullness of life experiences.

Apprenticeship: A kind of training that involves learning and guidance from someone who is highly skilled and knowledgeable in his or her craft, trade, or area of expertise.

Atlantis: One of the names used for a legendary, formerly worldwide advanced civilization, based on archaeological evidence, which is said to have existed at least 12,500 years ago.

Attunement: This is like an initiation, an energetic procedure that amplifies the vibratory rate of an individual's energy field, which includes his or her etheric and physical bodies. With the attunement, there is a tremendous amount of life-force moving through the energy field, through the chakra energy centers, and through the body. It loosens up and sloughs off the dense heavier, lower vibrations—cleansing the energetic debris—and raises a person's energy vibration.

Belief System Battle: A clash between older, ingrained subconsciously held belief patterns that differ from newly introduced ideas, thoughts, and beliefs. The subconscious mind's defense mechanisms activate to distract or divert conscious energy into other things, taking your attention away in an attempt to defend its programmed beliefs.

Biophotons (meaning "life" and "light"): These are photons of non-thermal origin in the visible and ultraviolet spectrum emitted from a biological system. All living cells of plants, animals, and human beings emit biophotons. Biophoton light is stored in the DNA molecules within the cells of the body, creating a dynamic web of light constantly being released and absorbed by the DNA and may serve as the organism's main communication network and as the principal regulating instance for all life processes. This light emission is an expression of the functional state of the living organism, and its measurement, therefore, can be used to assess its state of health.

Chakra: The energetic processing centers of the body that are associated with different types and levels of consciousness flowing through the body-mind energy field. They are powerful focal points of energy that have a spinning motion to them, which open and close, increasing or decreasing life-force energy flows in the body, affecting how the energy of our body-mind energy field functions depending upon various circumstances.

Conscious Evolution: This has both personal and collective components and is a process of expansion. It takes place when we intend to grow or develop our conscious and spiritual levels of awareness and use our increasing awareness to guide our actions and achieve a positive future. It is an awakening process by which we can individually and collectively take responsibility for our future through purposeful action. Evolution is an inherently creative principle in matter or in life, and, according to modern cosmology, the entire universe is an evolutionary system.

Consciousness: A subjective state of awareness of internal and external events. Individual awareness of your unique thoughts, memories, feelings, sensations, and environment. A stream of shifting perceptions and a constantly changing continuum of experience from one moment to the next. The quality of consciousness is represented by the level of integration of information.

DNA: Deoxyribonucleic acid, a molecule consisting of a large number of chemical units called nucleotides attached together in single file to form a long strand. Usually two such stands are linked together parallel to each other and coiled into a helix. DNA is the material of genetic inheritance, but, in higher organisms, only a small portion of the DNA appears to be in the genes. DNA strands pass on their structure to copies of themselves in the process of replication.

Energy Channeling: This is also known as energy healing, energy therapy, or energy medicine, and is an umbrella term for any therapy that manipulates the energy fields or structures in our physical or subtle bodies to produce an effect, regain balance and harmony, and facilitate our body's innate healing abilities. Energy medicine is about upgrading the quality of information in the Field to energetically create conditions for health, so the body can heal itself.

Energy Testing: A form of bio-feedback, also known as bio-kinesiology, applied kinesiology, or muscle testing. Energy testing is a fairly reliable feedback system for communicating with the subconscious as well as Higher Wisdom. It is a useful process for obtaining current information about how the internal energy signals are flowing through the body.

Enlightenment: A greater awareness that brings about a higher expression of consciousness. Enlightenment is not simply measured by a change in consciousness. It is what takes place after the inspiration and insights and how we choose to apply those insights and participate in life.

Emotion: A state where moods or feelings cause motivation toward or away from something. A complex set of physiological sensations combined with other thought processes (e.g. internal images and thoughts) to which meaning is attached.

Epigenetics: This term means "above genetics" and is an area of science that studies the epigenetic changes and expression of gene function that are caused by non-genetic factors, causing genes to be expressed differently without a change in the actual genes themselves. Such changes can be passed on through cell divisions and from one generation to another. Non-genetic factors can include the influence of perceptions, environment, toxins, and trauma that affect bio-chemistry and the environment the cells reside in.

Feedback: The continuous automatic return of data from a system for the purpose of making corrections.

Heart: A highly complex, self-organized information processing center with its own functional "brain" that communicates with and influences the cranial brain via nervous system, hormonal system, and other pathways. These influences profoundly affect brain function and most of the body's major organs and ultimately determine the quality of life. (See HeartMath Research

Center, Science of the Heart: Exploring the Role of the Heart in Human Performance pdf.)

Heart Coherent Energy: A rhythmic beating pattern generated by the heart that creates a harmonious, coherent energy field and is more than 5,000 times greater in strength than the energy field generated by the brain. Feelings of love, compassion, appreciation, joy, and enthusiasm create smooth and ordered coherent energy rhythms. The body's nervous system, organs, and gland systems all come into harmony with the heart's coherency, and this leads to increased heart-brain synchronization, which supports us in attaining our goals.

Higher Wisdom: That part of us which is beyond our rational, logical, and conscious mind, usually associated with our super-conscious or higher conscious mind that we are connected with and that knows what is in our highest wisdom and benefit. I've used higher wisdom and inner wisdom interchangeably while knowing there are slight variations and interpretations associated with these two terms and also recognize that there is a preference between left-brain processors and right-brain processors of information.

Information: This term literally means to put into form or shape. Information is now generally taken to be the source of form or order in the world.

Inner Wisdom: Intuition, insight, guidance: the little voice inside you that represents the real you and is connected with your highest wisdom and benefit. I've used higher wisdom and inner wisdom interchangeably while knowing there are slight variations and interpretations associated with these two terms and also recognize that there is a preference between left-brain processors and right-brain processors of information.

Interference Patterns: These consist of well-defined detrimental energies that move in pulse-like waves and influence us in a powerful way. They are created by repressed, denied, or unresolved emotions that can distort and close off the natural life-force energy of the body. They can also be created by limiting, judgmental, and disharmonious beliefs that don't support who we are or who we are becoming. This damaging vibration is carried into the energetic networks of our body-mind energy field, obstructing proper functioning.

Imaginal Cells: These cells lie dormant inside us as little seeds of future potential. They are activated and nurtured by heart coherent energy, then begin to resonate at the same frequency, passing information back and forth, releasing internal chemistry, until they hit a tipping point. They coalesce with the vision held, opening a person up to transformation and beautiful worlds of possibilities.

Kinesthetic: This relates to a physical sense, or learning through a physical sense, that detects bodily position, weight, or movement of the muscles, tendons, and joints. A type of learning style (one of three different learning styles popularized by Neil D. Fleming in his VAK model of learning) that relates to learning by actively feeling and doing physical activity while learning.

Living Essence of the Field: The Source of all life that moves through all things. The living, pulsating luminous Field of intelligent energy that surrounds us.

Magic: This is sometimes called manifestation, alchemy, or co-creating with spirit. The making of magic is in alignment with the heart, imagination, joy, and laws of the universe. It is working with unseen forces to bring about a desired change. It is a bridge between the visible and invisible worlds. Magic involves wondrous happenings that are beyond the bounds of human reasoning, giving a sense of enchantment to life, and uniting you with what you want.

Manifestation: This takes place when a strong energetic pattern has been established and has become dense enough to form a visible, tangible substance of matter in our three-dimensional reality.

Matter: The substance and basis of all reality in the philosophy of materialism. According to relative theory, mass and energy are naturally transformable, and material systems are now regarded as both forms of energy.

Medicine Woman/Man: This person is usually referred to as a traditional healer and spiritual leader among indigenous people of the world. The primary function of "medicine people" is to secure the help of the spirit world for the benefit of the entire community. To be recognized as one who performs the function of bridging the natural world and spiritual world for the benefit of the community, an individual must be of high integrity, worthy, and validated by that community.

Meditation: The art of connecting with and receiving Source energy. It is a spiritual practice of communing with the Divine that enhances an individual's self-awareness, expands consciousness, and is highly recommended for anyone seeking high-level wellness.

Memory: The totality and capacity of all past experiences that can be remembered, recalled, recollected, or recognized. Memory in its various forms, both conscious and subconscious, is due to morphic resonance.

Microtubule: A hollow cylindrical structure in the cytoplasm of most cells, involved in intracellular shape and transport, which now appears to fill communication and information processing roles. According to Hameroff and Watt (1982; Rasumssen et al, 1990; Hameroff et al, 1992), tubulins within microtubule lattices interact with neighboring tubulins to represent, propagate, and process information at the molecular level. In another paper, Hameroff and Penrose present a model linking microtubules to consciousness using quantum theory. In their model, quantum coherence emerges and is isolated in brain microtubules until a threshold related to quantum gravity is reached. The result creates a "now" event. Sequences of such events create a flow of time and consciousness. The information processed through the microtubules show that the existence of internal photons—inner light—is very real and is the basis of virtually all human cellular and systemic function. This is exceptionally important work that has far-reaching implications.

Morphic Fields: These are the energetic structures within and around a substance, organism, or "unit" that organize systems at all levels of complexity and are the basis for wholeness that we observe in nature, which is more than the sum of its parts. Morphic fields underlie the form and behavior of a unit at all levels of complexity. They are shaped and stabilized by morphic resonance and contain a cumulative memory.

Multi-Dimensional: Relating to, or having several different dimensions, levels, or aspects. Involving more than one level of density of consciousness at a time.

Neuroscience: Any or all of the sciences, such as neurochemistry and experimental psychology, which deal with the structure or function of the nervous system and brain.

NLP (Neuro-Linguistic Programming): This encompasses the three most influential components involved in producing the human experience: neurology, language, and programming. The neurological system regulates how our bodies function; language determines how we interface and communicate with other people, and our programming determines the kinds of models of the world we create. Neuro-Linguistic Programming describes the fundamental dynamics between the mind and language and how their interplay affects our body and behavior.

Oracle Cards: A special type of card deck designed for exploring oneself, divining inspirational truths, and seeking inner wisdom.

Process: A series of actions or steps taken in order to achieve a particular end.

Reality: All of the stimuli available for experience at a certain moment in time and point in space. The part of the universe that is not fantasized. That which is perceived by the physical senses.

Reincarnation: The rebirth of a soul in a new body. The belief that the soul, upon death of the body, comes back in a new incarnation or embodiment of a person.

Religious Dogma: The doctrine of belief or set of beliefs that is accepted by the members of a religion without being questioned or doubted.

Self-Empowerment: Taking charge of one's own life, relationships, health, success, happiness, and well-being. Being self-empowered enables people to envision and create what they really want in life. It means realizing their self-worth and the power to be in charge of their own life, determining their own choices, and accessing opportunities residing within them, and having the ability to influence and change the environment and circumstances in which they live.

Self-Realization Fellowship: A worldwide spiritual organization founded in 1920 by Paramahansa Yogananda to teach scientific methods of meditation and principles of spiritual living that lead to self-realization and direct personal experience of the Divine.

Sensory Neurites: These are neurons that detect hormones, neurochemicals, heart rate, and pressure information, then translate it into neurological impulses that are sent through nerve pathways flowing from the heart to the brain. It is also through these nerve pathways that pain signals and other feeling sensations are sent to the brain, entering into the area called the medulla, located in the brain stem. The signals have a regulatory role over many of the autonomic nervous system signals that flow from the brain to the heart, blood vessels, and other glands and organs. These signals also cascade up into the higher centers of the brain where they may influence perception, decision making, and other cognitive processes.

Spirituality: The definition is different for everyone, though there are common themes associated with spirituality, such as: the idea of a process or journey of self-discovery and the learning of not only who you are, but also who you want to be. The challenge of reaching beyond your current beliefs or trying to better understand yourself and others. Belief, understanding, or knowing there is a higher power, whether rooted in religion, nature, or some kind of unknown essence. Spirituality comes from one's soul and is a personal relationship with the Divine. Spirituality fosters unity and allows for self-growth through loving acceptance of our self and others. It speaks of unity, compassion, acceptance, and loving kindness.

Subconscious: The part of the mind that is below the normal level of conscious awareness, is most often inaccessible, but affects behavior and emotions. It is often referred to as the unconscious, though the author prefers to differentiate the subconscious from the unconscious.

Transformation: An act, process, or instance of being transformed. The induced or spontaneous change from one way of being into another way of being.

Unconscious: The interruption of awareness of oneself or surroundings or the lack of ability to notice or respond to stimuli in the environment. Not conscious. A person may become unconscious due to oxygen deprivation, shock, or central nervous system depressants, such as alcohol, drugs, or injury.

Vagus Nerve: The tenth cranial nerve that originates in the medulla oblongata. Researchers discovered that the heart and brain are hard-wired together via the vagus nerve and that the heart sends more information to the brain than the brain sends down to the heart. Eighty to ninety percent of the nerve fibers of the vagus nerve are dedicated to communication.

Vortex: A rapid whirling or circular motion that draws objects into its powerful current. Any activity, situation, or way of life regarded as irresistibly engulfing.

Vril: A word alleged to have its origin in the ancient language of Atlantis and expresses the idea of the principle of vital life-force energy.

"Change within the health care field comes most readily from its professionals who identify new trends and see the need for establishing credible practice in a new direction. This time has arrived for the growing field of Energy Psychology."
~ *Gregory Nicosia, PhD*

Recommended Reading

Rather than provide a bibliography, I would instead like to share a short list of highly recommended books on the major subjects I refer to in the book. All of these, which may not have been direct resources for the book, had an influence on my own education.

Braden, Gregg. *Walking Between The Worlds: The Science of Compassion*. Bellevue, Radio Bookstore Press, 1997

Chopra, Deepak. *Quantum Healing: Exploring the Frontiers of Mind/Body Medicine*. New York: Bantam, 1989

Dennison, Paul. *Brain Gym Teacher's Edition Revised*. California: Edu-Kinesthetics, 1994

Diamond, John. *Your Body Doesn't Lie*. Warner Books, New York, NY, 1979

Fraser, Peter, and Massey, Harry. *Decoding the Human Body-Field: the new science of information as medicine*. Vermont, Healing Arts Press, 2008

Holub, Alexander and Budd-Michaels, Evelyn. *Psychokinesiology: Doorway to the Unconscious Mind*. Bridger House Publishers, Inc., Carson City, NV 1999

James, John. *The Great Field: Soul at Play in a Conscious Universe*. Elite Books. Printed in USA, 2007

Laskow, Leonard. *Healing With Love: A Breakthrough Mind Body Program for Healing Yourself and Others*. HarperCollins Publishers, New York, NY 1992

McTaggart, Lynne. *The Field: The Quest for the Secret Force of the Universe*. New York: HarperCollins, 2002

Pert, Candace. *Molecules of Emotion: The Science Behind Mind-Body Medicine*. New York: Scribner, 1997

Rein, Glen. *The Effects of Conscious Intention on Human DNA*. Published in: Proceeds of the International Forum on New Science. Denver, CO. October, 1996

Ruiz, Don Miguel. *The Four Agreements: A Toltec Wisdom Book*. California. Amber—Allen, 1997

Stone, Hal and Sidra. *Partnering: A New Kind of Relationship*. Nataraj Publishing, a division of New World Library, Novato, California, 2000

Volume six of The Arcane Teaching. *Vril or Vital Magnetism: The Secret Doctrine of Ancient Atlantis, Egypt, Chaldea, and Greece*. Chicago: A.C. McClurg & Co., 1911

Williams, John. *The Wisdom of Your Subconscious Mind*. Prentice-Hall, Inc., Englewood Cliffs, New Jersey, 1964

Index

About the Author

Dhebi DeWitz is an international personal empowerment coach and founder of the online Heart and Soul Academy for self-empowerment and conscious evolution. She has spent a lifetime exploring ancient mysteries, expanded states of consciousness, energy healing, and how we create our reality. For over 25 years, she has taught individuals across the globe how to work with their subconscious, to step more fully into their empowerment, and to create the life they want to live.

Dhebi is called 'Isumataq,' an Inuit word meaning 'Keeper of sacred space: one who creates the atmosphere where wisdom may reveal itself.' She believes that when one person is empowered, we all win.

Her uncommon background and training began at the tender age of 6; she began meditation at age 11, and by 21 she received her certification in hypnosis. Part of her lifelong training has included medicine woman/shamanic apprenticeships and initiations, energy healing attunements and certifications, mystery school teachings, DNA activations, and Shadow Energetics training. Her greatest interest is exploring the nature of consciousness, and she has developed a system of life-enhancing energetic processes that are making a positive difference in the lives of many.

When she is not writing or teaching, she can be found 'Dhebi'ing About,' tending her indoor garden, feeding chickens with her dog companions, shooting pool, dancing with her husband, traveling to far off places, and reading with her grandchildren.

Dhebi lives in Ashland, OR.

www.ingramcontent.com/pod-product-compliance
Lightning Source LLC
Chambersburg PA
CBHW022005080426

42733CB00007B/481